W9-ASZ-216

Praise for

Quest 52

"Well, Mark Moore has done it again! *Quest 52* gives us another year's worth of insight into a better walk with Jesus. Mark asks and answers the most insightful and important questions about Jesus's life, his teaching, and why he is so passionate about all of us. If you want to start a quest to know more about how much Jesus Christ wants a deeper relationship with you, then I highly recommend this study for you."

—AL ROBERTSON, pastor, author, star of A&E's *Duck Dynasty*, and cohost of the *Unashamed* podcast

"For the last forty years, Mark Moore has been a compelling teacher of Jesus. When it comes to the life and times, conversations and miracles, precepts and cares of our Messiah, Mark knows the gospel truth. In *Quest 52* you will go on a trek with Mark, discovering the power and passions of the Savior. By spending just fifteen minutes a day, you will gain insight and inspiration to pursue Jesus like never before. Take the quest and be encouraged."

—KYLE IDLEMAN, bestselling author of *Not a Fan* and *One at a Time*

"I can't think of anything more life-changing or rewarding than pursuing Jesus, but do you ever struggle to know how to move deeper in your journey? In this wonderful book, Mark has provided a detailed map to the greatest adventure in life: knowing Christ."

—SHEILA WALSH, author of *Holding On When You Want to Let Go*

"Spending daily time with Jesus doesn't have to be as hard as we sometimes think, and *Quest 52* proves it. In this book, Mark Moore gives us everything we need to spend a year of daily moments learning to know and love Jesus more. It's accessible and energizing."

—MARK BATTERSON, *New York Times* bestselling author of *The Circle Maker* and lead pastor of National Community Church

"Do you aspire to know and love Jesus more deeply? *Quest 52* is a remarkable and practical tool for either individuals or groups. I urge you to engage with these daily exercises as a pathway to follow the most important figure in human history."

—NANCY BEACH, leadership coach with Slingshot Group
and author of *Gifted to Lead*

"Mark has done it: *Quest 52* is a plug-and-play curriculum of exactly what your whole church needs to learn. When parents and kids are having the same faith conversations, you will experience growth in unity like never before. *Quest 52* will help your church take a quantum leap forward in biblical literacy! Don't wait a year! Give your church the road map to understanding Jesus better with *Quest 52*."

—JOHNNY SCOTT, lead pastor of Generations Christian Church

"Of all my friends and mentors, Mark Moore has taught me the most about Jesus. Not only does Mark love Jesus deeply, but he also walks with him daily. *Quest 52* is an invaluable resource that will help you do the same."

—CALEB KALTENBACH, pastor and bestselling author of
Messy Grace and *Messy Truth*

"Jesus Christ has made the greatest difference in my life, so I really want you to know him. *Quest 52* is a yearlong, fifteen-minute-a-day tool that can help you get there. Pastor Mark teaches at one of my favorite places—Christ's Church of the Valley. It is a place where common people can go to encounter the uncommon Christ. This book can help you see how."

—MICHAEL JR., comedic thought leader, actor, and author of
Funny How Life Works

"*Quest 52* is the kind of devotional that people have been asking for. It will help you answer some of faith's toughest questions while you discover Jesus in a brand-new way."

—CAREY NIEUWHOF, podcaster and author of *At Your Best:
How to Get Time, Energy, and Priorities Working in Your Favor*

QUEST
52

QUEST
52

A FIFTEEN-MINUTE-A-DAY YEARLONG
PURSUIT OF JESUS

MARK E. MOORE

WATERBROOK

QUEST 52

All Scripture quotations are taken from the ESV® Bible (The Holy Bible, English Standard Version®), copyright © 2001 by Crossway, a publishing ministry of Good News Publishers. Used by permission. All rights reserved.

Italics in Scripture quotations reflect the author's added emphasis.

Details in some anecdotes and stories have been changed to protect the identities of the persons involved.

Copyright © 2021 by Mark E. Moore

All rights reserved.

Published in the United States by WaterBrook, an imprint of Random House, a division of Penguin Random House LLC.

WATERBROOK® and its deer colophon are registered trademarks of Penguin Random House LLC.

LIBRARY OF CONGRESS CATALOGING-IN-PUBLICATION DATA

Names: Moore, Mark E. (Mark Edward), author.
Title: Quest 52 : a fifteen-minute-a-day yearlong pursuit of Jesus / Mark E. Moore, Ph.D.
Other titles: Quest fifty two
Description: First edition. | Colorado Springs: WaterBrook, [2021] | Includes index.
Identifiers: LCCN 2021005319 | ISBN 9780593193723 (acid-free paper) | ISBN 9780593193730 (ebook)
Subjects: LCSH: Jesus Christ—Person and offices—Biblical teaching— Textbooks. Jesus Christ—Example—Biblical teaching—Textbooks.
Classification: LCC BT207 .M66 2021 | DDC 232—dc23
LC record available at https://lccn.loc.gov/2021005319

Printed in the United States of America on acid-free paper

waterbrookmultnomah.com

2 4 6 8 9 7 5 3 1

First Edition

Interior book design by Virginia Norey

SPECIAL SALES Most WaterBrook books are available at special quantity discounts when purchased in bulk by corporations, organizations, and special-interest groups. Custom imprinting or excerpting can also be done to fit special needs. For information, please email specialmarketscms@penguinrandomhouse.com.

To my grandchildren, who will journey beyond me on the quest for Christ but who make my own journey toward sunset more delightful than the sunrise:

Jackson Howerton
Nya Moore
Dominic Moore
Duke Howerton
Rosalie Moore
Lennon Howerton
Bear Moore
Dean Howerton

Contents

Introduction

Chasing after Jesus is the journey of a lifetime. In Jesus's own words, "The kingdom of heaven is like a merchant in search of fine pearls, who, on finding one pearl of great value, went and sold all that he had and bought it" (Matthew 13:45–46). Jesus is that pearl of great price. He is worth every effort to obtain him and every sacrifice required along the way. *This is the quest—to chase after him, the pearl of great price.*

This is *my* quest. Even after teaching the life of Christ for twenty years at the college level, I am surprised with breathtaking regularity when I get a glimpse of him I haven't seen before. I am still mystified by his majesty. The deeper I dig, the higher I realize he is. He is always beyond my grasp, even when he walks beside me. The more I see of him, the less I think I really know him.

I am reminded of an incident in the middle of Jesus's ministry. His closest disciples had been with him for more than a year. Now they were alone with him in a boat (Mark 4:35–41). A storm threatened to swallow them while Jesus was sound asleep in the stern. The men woke him. They needed all hands on deck, probably to help bail out the boat. They had no clue what Jesus could actually do. He stood up in the boat and rebuked the wind and waves, which obeyed. Instantly.

Just as quickly, the disciples' terror shifted from outside the boat to inside. They had been afraid of drowning in a storm; now they were afraid of standing in his presence. They huddled in the bow of the boat and asked, "Who is this man?" That is the question. *This is the quest— to discover the authentic Jesus.* Not the cartoon-figure Jesus or a haloed icon in stained glass. The real Jesus—the Jesus who wants to be known.

The Importance of the Quest

Perhaps you're not a religious person; many on the quest are not. That's okay. Jesus is worth the pursuit regardless of our past. After all, no other individual has had as great an impact on our world as Jesus of Nazareth. He challenged us to love our enemies, thus reordering the rules for social engagement. He prioritized the outcast, renovating social justice. He introduced servant leadership, transforming politics. He demanded that we examine our hearts and not just our behavior, revolutionizing ethics. He introduced God to the world as *Father,* thus changing the very nature of prayer. There is no quarter of our modern lives that has not been affected by Jesus of Nazareth—not education, science, religion, society, law, ethics, art, or entertainment. Therefore, he is worth pursuing. He is worth devoting a year to discovering what those first disciples discovered in the boat: he is beyond our expectations and beside us all the way.

Do you want to know him, the real Jesus? Do you want to absorb his influence so you can influence others? If so, *welcome to the quest.*

This is not a journey across the flatlands. It can, at times, be a torturous trek. But the greatest challenge we face on this quest is not the terrain out there. Rather, it is our own presuppositions, thinking that we have already reached our destination. We *think* we know who Jesus is. That is the greatest impediment to our quest.

The Challenge of the Quest

In the beginning, God made humans in his own image (Genesis 1:27). We have been returning the favor ever since, trying to make God look like us. It was obvious when ancient priests fashioned idols to reflect their highest ideals of war, sex, riches, and beauty. Their images revealed what they really worshipped. We may imagine ourselves to be more sophisticated, but we have done virtually the same thing when we portray Jesus as supporting our cultural values, ethical sensibilities, and economic aspirations.

It is most obvious with our artistic renderings of Jesus. International images of Christ look like their creators' countrymen. He has darker skin in Africa, lighter hair in Europe, and distinct eyes in Asia. In one sense, that's fine. After all, Jesus came to earth in a recognizable physical form so we could relate to him. We all need to see Jesus in a way we can access. The problem comes when we assume that if he *looks* like we do, he must also *think* and *act* like we do.

Our portrayals of Jesus don't end with paintings; they extend to our preaching. We speak into existence a Jesus that reflects our own image. Virtually every nationality and ethnicity have co-opted Jesus for their own political and social agendas. We assume that he agrees with our cultures and lifestyles. This quest is too long to carry our presuppositions with us, so let's shed them now. Can we admit our biases and begin the quest with humility, honesty, and submission, determined to follow the path wherever it leads and whatever it costs?

The goal of this book is to help you do just that. Think of it as a field guide to your quest for Christ. All it can do is point you in the right direction. The quest is your own. No one can take this journey for you, although some may take it with you.

The Strategy of the Quest

The first four books of the New Testament—Matthew, Mark, Luke, and John—describe the events of Jesus's incomparable life. *Quest 52* will highlight fifty-two incidents from Jesus's life. These will include people Jesus met, miracles he performed, things he taught, and qualities he modeled. After you read about these incidents in the Bible, *Quest 52* will guide you through some thoughts and exercises to help you see Jesus authentically. Think of these fifty-two incidents as mile markers along the way.

Between each mile marker are five days of exercises. It is here that Jesus will meet you face to face.

- **Day 1:** Read the passage(s) from the Bible. You must not short-circuit this step. Begin in the Bible; then move to the essay. Each essay focuses on one biblical concept from one gospel passage and answers one key question relevant to your life.

- **Day 2:** Look back to the wisdom of the Old Testament to gain perspective on this mile marker.

- **Day 3:** Look forward to the letters in the New Testament, where fellow pilgrims expressed their own take on this mile marker.

- **Day 4:** Discuss with fellow pilgrims what you are learning on this leg of the journey.

- **Day 5:** Take your next step in following the path of Jesus.

The book you hold in your hand is the primary resource for this quest for Christ. However, as a bonus, we have provided other tools to add value to this book, especially if you are going through the material with a group:

A video from the author introducing each essay to help make the material in the book more personal. This is a great way to kick off the group for visual learners.

A topical study for overachievers who want to dig deeper into some historical or theological topics. This may help individuals oriented toward biblical research.

An audio lecture from one of my college classes on the life of Christ. This will benefit auditory learners.

These optional resources are housed at www.Quest52.org.

This quest will likely demand more than we expect, but the pearl of great price is more valuable than we could ever imagine. So let's pursue Jesus relentlessly; he wants to be found. He may even join us along the journey. Let's begin.

Section I

The Person of Jesus

We begin our journey by looking to the person of Jesus. We are trying to discover where he came from and what drove him to his destiny of death. The first series of essays is all about the **beginning** of Jesus's life—his birth and the striking events surrounding his arrival. The section on his **purpose** looks at his primary motivations from the time he was twelve through his three-year ministry. The third series of essays looks at his **relationships** with particular attention to how he treated people: disciples, family, opponents, and sinners.

Beginning: chapters 1–4
Purpose: chapters 5–8
Relationships: chapters 9–13

1

Is God Jesus?

Biblical Concept: Incarnation
Read: John 1:1–18

Who is God? It's a foundational question. I thought I had an answer when I was baptized on my ninth birthday. Three years later, that answer morphed with my parents' divorce. It altered again when I got married and changed even more when my son was born. One wonders whether the question can ever be answered. Are we just making God in our own image? Is God a projection of our own needs and experiences? Is he good? Is he all powerful? Is he one or many? Is he "he" or "she"? Everyone— whether a theologian, convict, atheist, or philosopher—seems to have an opinion. Who actually has the authority or experience to give an answer?

According to John 1, there is one—Jesus—who can definitively answer the question. Whether or not you believe the Bible to be authoritative, I suspect we can agree that if someone met God *face to face* in heaven and then came to earth to tell us about him, that person's description would trump our personal opinions. This is precisely what John claimed: "No one has ever seen God; the only God, who is at the Father's side, he has made him known" (verse 18). If Jesus is whom he claimed to be (God), if he did what the Bible says he did, then he is the perfect place to begin our quest to know our Creator. I believe Jesus is God. Nevertheless, beyond bias or opinion, anyone would have to admit that Jesus of Nazareth has had more impact on humanity than any other person in history. So people searching for God would do well to start their quest with the person of Jesus. He may be the answer to this foundational question: Who is God?

Jesus Is Creator

Let's begin at the beginning: "In the beginning was the Word, and the Word was with God, and the Word was God" (verse 1). If this sounds familiar, it should. It echoes Genesis 1:1: "In the beginning, God created the heavens and the earth." John connected Jesus, the Word, with the God who created the world with a word. What an audacious claim. What if it's true? To be fair, John was not the only Jew to claim Jesus created the world. Paul said it like this: "By him all things were created, in heaven and on earth, visible and invisible, whether thrones or dominions or rulers or authorities—all things were created through him and for him. And he is before all things, and in him all things hold together" (Colossians 1:16–17). The New Testament claims that the Creator, God, inhabited human flesh in the person of Jesus.

Is there evidence for this? Well, one could point to the prophecies he fulfilled (Luke 24:44; John 5:39), his divine birth (Luke 1:30–35), his sinless life (Hebrews 4:15), or a plethora of miracles. However, the most remarkable (and historically verifiable) evidence is his resurrection from the dead (see chapter 49). It was this singular event that transformed Paul from persecutor to preacher, replaced Peter's cowardice with courage, and changed James from antagonist to advocate. The Resurrection moved worship from Saturday to Sunday, introduced baptism and the Lord's Supper to a fledgling church, and opened the door to all ethnicities. The Resurrection is not merely an intellectual historical question; it is the genesis of the church as we know it.

Ultimately, you need to make up your own mind about who Jesus is.

However, you would be in good company if you declared him Lord. After all, *Jesus claimed* to have all authority (Matthew 28:18), even to forgive sins (Mark 2:10) and judge the world (John 5:24–30). He said he grants eternal life (John 14:6) and raises the dead (John 11:25) and declared himself to be the Son of God (Mark 14:61–62), one with the Father (John 10:30), and the only one who fully knows God (Matthew 11:27).

Furthermore, his *disciples affirmed* he was God's Son (Matthew 14:33), even God himself (John 20:28). His followers worshipped him (Matthew 28:9; Luke 7:36–50), and the crowds proclaimed him as savior (Luke 19:35–40). Even his *enemies admitted* he was the Son of God (Matthew 27:54; Mark 15:39; Luke 23:39–43), and no demon doubted his identity (Luke 4:41). Throughout the New Testament, we have clear declarations of the divinity of Jesus (John 1:18; 12:41; Romans 9:5; 2 Thessalonians 1:12; Titus 2:13; Hebrews 1:8; 2 Peter 1:1; 1 John 5:20). However, he is a different kind of deity—one who is accessible precisely because he is near.

Jesus Is Here

"The Word became flesh and dwelt among us, and we have seen his glory, glory as of the only Son from the Father, full of grace and truth" (John 1:14). This idea that God became flesh is called the Incarnation. Of course, it sparks all kinds of questions: How can God be one and three at the same time? If Jesus is God, did he pray to himself? Is there a hierarchy in the Godhead? Perhaps you have heard such questions. Without being dismissive (because these are interesting questions), can we just admit that the answers are above our pay grade? How could humans describe the essence of the unseen? This is actually more comforting than disconcerting. After all, I don't want to worship a God I can fit in my own intellectual box. He is above and beyond. However frustrating that may be, it is comforting to know that the God I worship is beyond my capacity to comprehend.

The more important question, by far, is this: How could we ever know the unknowable God if he didn't make himself known? We can't take a

shuttle to heaven. We can't use human language to describe what is beyond our limitations. So, if God wanted us to know him, does it not make
sense that he would come to us in a form we could recognize? We all
know how this works. If you want to play with a child, what do you do?
You get on the floor, look at her eye to eye, and use age-appropriate vo-
cabulary. That's what God did in Jesus. Call it the Incarnation if you like.
I just call it considerate. He met us where we are.

Now here is where the conversation gets really interesting. If you
made a list of all the things you know about God, then eliminated all the
things you know about him only because you have seen Jesus, what kind
of God would you be left with? My guess is this God would still be powerful but not personal. He would be just but perhaps lacking in mercy. He
would be creative and beautiful but not relational.

We believe the best things we believe about God because we have seen
them in Jesus. Three of these things are unique to Christianity:

1. **God is near.** Many religions have deities, such as gods of water,
    wind, and fire, that are present but not personal. However, when
    a deity is personal—Yahweh or Allah, for example—that deity is
    viewed as distanced from humanity. He is in heaven, exalted,
    untouchable, and, hence, unknowable. Christianity is the only
    global religion where God is both personal and knowable. We
    are invited into a relationship with him. To this point, John 1:12
    says, "To all who did receive him, who believed in his name, he
    gave the right to become children of God." This was a brand-
    new idea in the Bible, that through Jesus we can pray to God as
    Father, even calling him Abba (Romans 8:15; Galatians 4:6).
2. **God is love.** Oh sure, some deities may have affection for their
    own adherents, but they hate the pagan and the infidel. Jesus,
    however, said, "Love your enemies and pray for those who perse-
    cute you" (Matthew 5:44). And he modeled that from the cross,
    saying, "Father, forgive them, for they know not what they do"
    (Luke 23:34). Only through Jesus do we know the full extent of

God's love: "God shows his love for us in that while we were still sinners, Christ died for us" (Romans 5:8).

3. **God suffers.** Now, there is a crazy idea! How could the divine suffer? Scour the Old Testament, and you will find only scant suggestions of a suffering God (Isaiah 53; Zechariah 12:10). This is actually an offensive idea in many religions. Yet in Jesus we see a God who suffers for those he loves even while they are un-lovely. That is a God worth worshipping. It is a God we never could have imagined without the incarnation of Jesus.

Jesus Is Clear

This brings us full circle to John 1:18: "No one has ever seen God; the only God, who is at the Father's side, he has made him known." Without Jesus, no one would have painted God with these particular brushstrokes. Imagine how much poorer our world would be without the compassion modeled by Jesus. Showing generosity to strangers, loving enemies, and elevating women and children are all concepts tied to the Incarnation.

Even if I didn't believe in the Incarnation, I would still teach it as an indispensable foundation of human decency, social justice, and human rights. This image of God as near, loving, and suffering is not merely a theological idea; it is a practical model of being human. These qualities are what make for the best CEOs, coaches, parents, and pastors. Jesus shows us the most important attributes of God. For this reason, rather than asking, "Is Jesus God?" we ask, "Is God Jesus?"

Key Points

- The entire New Testament claims that Jesus is God.
- The Incarnation is necessary if we are going to know God.
- The Incarnation is not merely a theological truth; it is the best model of being human.

This Week

❏ **Day 1 (Eyes):** After reading the essay, consider this question: What is the most important thing you know about God because of Jesus?

❏ **Day 2 (Ears):** Where do you see Jesus in Psalm 2 and Psalm 110?

❏ **Day 3 (Heart):** Meditate on Romans 9:5; Titus 2:13; Hebrews 1:8. Using these three verses, write a brief prayer, telling God what you believe about Jesus.

❏ **Day 4 (Voice):** Discussion:

- What would it take to convince you that your brother (or coworker) is God's Son?
- Other than Jesus, what resources do we have to know who God is?
- What might you believe about God if you knew nothing of Jesus?
- What do you believe about God because you have seen Jesus?

❏ **Day 5 (Hands):** Practice one aspect of the Incarnation—presence. Schedule an evening with your family when you will shut off all screens (phones, computers, TVs, etc.).

Further Resources: Quest52.org/1

2

Is Life Random?

Biblical Concept: Genealogy
Read: Matthew 1:1–17 with Luke 3:23–38

Have you ever been bored reading the Bible? You can admit it; you won't get struck by lightning. The genealogies are the worst. Every time I come to the genealogies, I practice speed-reading. Does that make me a bad person? I know I'm not alone. So, why did God begin the New Testament with a genealogy? The good news of the gospel starts with a real downer.

That's what I thought until my friends Ron and Linda Hayward returned from Papua New Guinea. They were Bible translators who had just come back to the States after translating the New Testament into a native dialect. They spent over a decade learning the language and culture. They toiled over every sentence to make sure it communicated the truth of the gospel. They went through all the stories of Jesus—his miracles, sermons, death, and resurrection. The last thing they translated in Matthew was the genealogy. They didn't think the tribal people would be interested in a list of Jewish names. Boy, were they wrong. When Ron and Linda showed them Matthew's genealogy, the natives were stunned. "You mean to tell us these are real stories?" they asked.

"What do you mean?" replied Ron and Linda.

"Jesus had a family history," they said. "That means he is a real person!"

The importance of this seemingly boring list of names struck Ron and Linda (and me). The gospel doesn't begin "Once upon a time." It is about real people with real problems, just like you and me.

Genealogies were particularly important to Jews. The story of their salvation was summarized in a list of names. It begins in Genesis with the genealogies of Adam, Noah, and Abraham. Through these families, we trace the history of salvation. *When God saves the world, he does it through imperfect people.* Adam and Eve introduced sin. Noah got drunk right out of the ark. Abraham denied being married to his wife. You get the picture. The genealogies may be full of foreign names, but the biographies of those people are familiar. This is incredibly encouraging because we, too, have the potential to play a role in God's work in our world despite our failings.

Genealogy in Matthew

Matthew did something both subtle and brilliant. He broke down the genealogy of Jesus into three sections, each with fourteen names: "All the generations from Abraham to David were fourteen generations, and from David to the deportation to Babylon fourteen generations, and from the deportation to Babylon to the Christ fourteen generations" (Matthew 1:17). Have you ever stopped to count them? I did (which tells you something about my social life). The first and third sections do, in fact, have fourteen names. But the middle section has only thirteen names. Stop and fact-check me if you'd like, but I recounted this a dozen times because I couldn't believe my eyes![1] (Bear with me for just three short paragraphs while I get into the weeds. I promise it is worth it.)

I thought perhaps that's all Matthew had to work with and he was just rounding up. Nope. If you go back to 1 Chronicles 3, that pesky section has *seventeen names*. What? Why would Matthew leave out four names, then say there were fourteen? It makes no sense . . . unless you are Jewish.

Now, there is no problem with Matthew leaving out names. Jewish genealogies didn't demand an exact list. So it's not a cultural problem; it's a math problem. Matthew said there were fourteen names when he was one short. Did he miscount? Maybe, but remember, he was a tax collector, and they were not prone to being negligent with numbers.

The solution is in how Matthew counted. He did something very Jewish: he gave one person a double portion (counting that person twice). Who? David. David is the last name in the first section *and* the first name in the second section. Thus, David is the symbolic firstborn in Jesus's genealogy. In fact, the entire book of Matthew is a treatise on how Jesus is the new King David. Moreover, Matthew telegraphed this move in the very first verse. Read it again, noticing that it is out of chronological order: "The book of the genealogy of Jesus Christ, the son of David, the son of Abraham" (1:1). Since Abraham is older, he should have received pride of place. But Matthew's story is about a king, not a patriarch. David is in the privileged position.

Here it gets even more interesting. The Hebrew language didn't have numbers, so the alphabet was also used for counting. A = 1, B = 2, and so on. In Hebrew, the name *David* is spelled *DVD*. *D* is the fourth letter and *V* is the sixth. You do the math: 4 + 6 + 4. How about that? Matthew opened the story with a numerological puzzle; when you solve it, you discover that Jesus is the Son of David, the Messiah of Israel. While this is not a common way of reading the Bible in the West, it would be familiar to Jewish rabbis. Once we see with their eyes, our own eyes widen in wonder.

Inclusion of Women

Matthew's use of numbers is quite Jewish. His inclusion of women was *not*! Women were seen as second class in first-century culture. For a woman to be included in a genealogy, she would have had to be extraordinarily noble. The women in this genealogy, however, were anything but. *Tamar* pretended to be a prostitute and seduced her father-in-law in order to have a child as an heir (Genesis 38:13–30). That's messed up! *Rahab* was a pagan prostitute who hid the spies when Joshua led the invasion of Jericho (Joshua 2). Not exactly the poster child of morality. *Ruth* was a Moabite, the traditional enemy of Israel (Ruth 1:4). *Bathsheba* married a Hittite and had an affair with King David (2 Samuel 11:3–4). All of them were noted for some kind of scandal.

Mary fits right in, at least in public opinion. She was an unwed teen mother in a small village. She felt the heated glare of her peers. She knew the sting of gossip. The pain felt by Tamar, Rahab, Ruth, and Bathsheba was native to her soul as well. Like the others, she kept the faith for future generations.

Lessons from the Genealogy

God uses people to accomplish his purposes. God doesn't typically intervene with miracles; he invests in relationships. He walks with each of us to develop us into difference makers. God uses our gifts and successes, but he can also turn our failures into faith. Regardless of your past, God has a plan for your life. And though the jumbled mess of circumstances seems arbitrary, we see the tapestry only from the underside. When we rise to God's perspective, we see his intricate, extraordinary design in the details—*all* the details—of our lives.

The people God uses are fallible. The women in this genealogy offer a ray of hope for everyone. Tamar and Bathsheba survived the trauma of sexual sin caused by the abuse of powerful men. We don't know Rahab's background, but it is unlikely prostitution was her chosen profession. She was probably a victim of poverty or culturally sanctioned human trafficking. As is so often the case, their sin was not just what they did but what was done to them. And Ruth was a victim of the tragic death of her husband, compounded by racism. Yet God redeemed the pain of these women by including them in his plan. He will do the same with you. You can play a part in sacred history! Your name will not be included in Scripture, but there is a book of life in heaven being inscribed right this moment. Your name could be included there as part of the lineage of Jesus. You have a verse to contribute, and it has eternity written all over it. You have a role to play, regardless of the pain of your past.

Jesus is God's Son. Humanly, Jesus was Mary's son. Legally, he was Joseph's son by adoption. Fundamentally, he was God's Son. "Like Father, like Son" has never been truer than in the case of Jesus. Though he stepped into human history through a very real genealogy, he came from the Father's side, from heaven to earth. The story of Jesus is both eternal and historical. He is the bridge that spans the divide between our physical realities and the eternity we sense in our souls. Through him, we rise beyond our own genealogies to a forever future with God.

Life is not random. It may feel as if our relationships are disconnected and our choices make no difference. As if all is chance. But this "boring" genealogy betrays the truth that God has a plan *and* that you are part of it. Matthew meticulously catalogued this list of names, but it was God who wove it together over two thousand years. Generation by generation, God has been orchestrating a plan to restore the beauty of Eden. Wonder of all wonders, you are part of that plan.

Key Points

- Genealogies tell the story of salvation.
- In Matthew's genealogy, we see God's meticulous plan of salvation.
- The inclusion of the women in the genealogy reminds us that all are invited to play a role in God's drama of salvation.

This Week

❏ **Day 1 (Eyes):** After reading the essay, consider this question: How would you like God to describe your contribution to the story of salvation?

❏ **Day 2 (Ears):** Read the story of Rahab in Joshua 2 and 6. What are the similarities between her life and yours? Her faith and yours?

❏ **Day 3 (Heart):** What was it about Rahab that made her such a model of faith according to Hebrews 11:31 and James 2:25? Relate that to Galatians 4:4.

❏ **Day 4 (Voice):** Discussion:

- Share a bit of your family history. Where did your family come from? Was there anyone famous or infamous in your extended family?
- What strengths and weaknesses did you inherit from your father and mother?
- What verse would you like God to write about your contribution to the story of salvation?
- What barriers might keep you from fulfilling your verse? What resources or skills will you need to acquire or develop to fulfill your verse?

❏ **Day 5 (Hands):** Do one thing this week to acquire a resource or develop a skill you listed in the previous question.

Further Resources: Quest52.org/2

3

Can God Use Me for Big Things?

Biblical Concept: Annunciation
Read: Luke 1:26–45

It matters whether our lives matter. The desire to leave a mark on the world is a universal human longing. This is not arrogance. It is spiritual genetics. This impulse for significance comes from the Creator himself. He wove it into our spiritual DNA. It drives the majority of decisions we make: what teams we root for, what occupations we choose, what relationships we build. It matters that we matter.

The difficulty, however, is that our goals are typically loftier than our character. We want to be better than we actually are. This is certainly true for me. If you scratch just beneath the surface, you'll expose my insecurity. I want to make a difference, but I doubt my ability to do much that matters. That's why the story of Mary is so inspiring. She shows us the way to do big things for God. By examining her example, we can follow a path toward significance.

God's Call, Not Our Character

Mary is venerated all over the world for her faith. Yet there is a huge gap
between her biography and her legacy. What God intended for her was far
beyond her provincial circumstances. We see this contrast in the very first
sentence of this passage: Gabriel was an archangel; Mary lived in Nazareth, a backwater village disdained by the locals (John 1:46). She was a
peasant girl, and her fiancé was a day laborer. Yet God chose her to bear
his own Son.

No wonder she was confused when Gabriel greeted her: "Greetings,
O favored one, the Lord is with you!" (Luke 1:28). She couldn't figure out
why such an important messenger had been sent to her. She was not just
confused; she was concerned. Gabriel had to put her at ease to even have
the conversation: "Do not be afraid, Mary, for you have found favor with
God" (verse 30).

There is an important lesson here: *the impact of your life is determined
not by your ability or your history but by God's call.* You may doubt your
ability and question your character, but God has a plan for you that is
based on his goodness, not yours. Mary was willing to submit her life to
God's plan. That is the single qualification any of us needs to be used by
God for big things.

God's Power; Our Willingness

Gabriel made a wonderful and horrible announcement. Mary was going
to have a child. That's wonderful. Not just any child—an extraordinary
child. Gabriel had to stretch superlatives to adequately describe the Christ
child. He began with a simple statement that this child would be great.
How great? Well, he would be Mary's son by birth but God's Son by vocation. That means he would sit on David's throne as the greatest king of
Hebrew history. More than that, he would reign over the house of Jacob,
the father of all Israel. Hence, he would be the greatest patriarch of God's
people as well as the greatest monarch in the nation's history. In fact, his

kingdom would extend into eternity, having no boundaries in space and time.

Mary asked, "How will this be?" (verse 34). After all, virgins don't give birth. That's obvious enough. She may have been an ancient peasant, but she knew how babies were made. Nonetheless, the God who spoke life into existence could certainly populate a single womb with a word. The Spirit that hovered over the chaotic waters (Genesis 1:2) could generate life in the womb of a virgin. As the angel Gabriel said, "The Holy Spirit will come upon you, and the power of the Most High will overshadow you; therefore the child to be born will be called holy—the Son of God" (Luke 1:35). Just so we are clear, this was asexual. It was not God cohabitating with a human as was common in Greek mythology. This was creation, not cohabitation. It was the power of God coming upon Mary, creating life in her womb as he had done with his word in Genesis 1.

Was this unprecedented? Well, it had never happened before. So yes, it was unprecedented, but it was not unpredicted. The ancient prophet had promised that God would invade our space (Isaiah 7:14; 9:6–7). He would come to us in a way that was knowable, relatable, and accessible. It was the only way for humans to truly connect with the divine. We cannot get to him; he must come to us. And we see it in the baby's name, *Jesus.* This is the Greek translation of the Hebrew name *Joshua,* which means "Yahweh saves." In the ancient days, Joshua was the Hebrew hero that led Israel into the promised land. Jesus does globally what Joshua did nationally. Joshua led a single people into the promised land; Jesus leads the whole world to the new earth. Joshua saved his people by destroying their enemies; Jesus saved his enemies by sacrificing himself. Joshua fought with a sword; Jesus won with a cross. By his death, he saved our souls; by his resurrection, he overpowered the grave. Gabriel's promise is phenomenal!

Yet Gabriel's promise also has a horrible element because Mary was betrothed. In Jewish culture, betrothal was a legally binding agreement. If this teenage bride-to-be wound up pregnant, the contract would be nullified. In fact, her very life could be jeopardized. According to the Mosaic law, Mary could be stoned for adultery if she were unfaithful to her fiancé (Leviticus 20:10). Best-case scenario, her reputation would be trashed. She would be judged a tramp, which was devastating in a village like Nazareth. Nonetheless, she did not protest or barter. Without hesitation, she replied, "Let it be to me according to your word" (Luke 1:38). Read that carefully. She was *wishing* that God's will would prevail regardless of the cost. She was willing to risk her life to carry out God's will. Is this not the very nature of the son she would bear? Perhaps that is why God chose her of all maidens.

That is the secret of God using any of us for big things. It's not about our ability but about our willingness to submit to God's will. He can use you if you're willing to sacrifice. Would you risk your relationships to do something big for God? It may take that. Would you sacrifice your comfort to leave a legacy? It will demand that. Would you risk your reputation to make a difference for God? There is no other path into God's purpose than an unqualified "Let it be to me."

God's Provision

All this was overwhelming for Mary. In the days ahead, she would wrestle with doubt and difficulties. She would face ridicule and rejection from family and friends. God knew what she was up against. That is why he gave Mary two things he will *always* give you when you accept the challenge of his call: *a reason to believe God* and *a relationship to sustain you.*

Elizabeth was a relative of Mary. She was old and barren. Yet by the miraculous hand of God, she was pregnant with John the Baptist. The young virgin Mary took a sixty-mile hike to visit her. Twice the text specifies that it was the sixth month. Sixth month of what? Elizabeth's pregnancy. At the beginning of Elizabeth's third trimester, Mary arrived at her door. Mary was so barely pregnant that she might not have even missed her first period. Yet the moment they met, the fetus in Elizabeth recognized Jesus in Mary's womb and leaped for joy (verse 41). Notice how specific Elizabeth was: "Why is this granted to me that the mother of my

Lord should come to me?" (verse 43). That is a lot of freight to put on a zygote. Truly Elizabeth spoke truth: "Blessed is she who believed that there would be a fulfillment of what was spoken to her from the Lord" (verse 45).

Mary would stay with Elizabeth for the next three months, likely until John was born. She was a witness to the faithfulness of God. Mary was sustained by Elizabeth's mentoring. God provided clear evidence of his sovereign hand. He provided the loving touch of an understanding elder. Those three months gave Mary the strength she needed to return home, to face Joseph, and to endure a difficult pregnancy. Let this be a lesson to us. If God calls you to a task, he will provide what you need to accomplish it. He will always give you enough evidence to believe and the mentor you need to fulfill your call.

There will be days of doubt when you question your call. In those days, look back to the promises of God, look around at his faithful provision, and look forward to the rewards of being used by God for big things. The people God has put in our lives and the reminders of his sovereign plan are all around if we just lift our eyes from our present pain to absorb the eternal goodness of God. You can do anything he calls you to if you will only say, "Let it be to me."

Key Points

- The impact of your life is determined not by your ability or your history but by God's call.

- To do great things for God, we must relinquish our wills and be willing to say, "Let it be to me."

- When God calls you to a task, he will provide both a reason to believe and a relationship to sustain you.

This Week

❏ **Day 1 (Eyes):** As you read the essay, what similarities did you see between your situation and Mary's?

❏ **Day 2 (Ears):** Read Isaiah 9:1–7. What descriptions of Jesus are found in this prophecy?

❏ **Day 3 (Heart):** Meditate on Colossians 1:15–17; Hebrews 1:3; Revelation 1:8. What do these verses say about the eternal Christ?

❏ **Day 4 (Voice):** Discussion:

- Who are the heroes in your life that led you to a place where you could believe? These could be family members, mentors, or peers.
- If you were Mary, what would be your greatest concerns about accepting God's call? What are your greatest concerns about your own calling?
- What is God calling you to do with your life to bring him glory?
- What are the obstacles keeping you from your next step in fulfilling God's plan for you?

❏ **Day 5 (Hands):** Write a brief description (three sentences) of what you perceive God wants to do with your life over the next three to five years. Now list three action steps you need to take this year to move toward that goal.

Further Resources: Quest52.org/3

4

Does God Play Favorites?

Biblical Concept: Nativity
Read: Luke 2:1–20

I am the middle of three children. I know what it means to be over-looked. When I was about five, I remember listening to my older brother talk so freely with my father and thinking, *Dad loves him more.* It turns out my father just felt more comfortable having more mature conversations than I was capable of at the time. Nonetheless, the feeling was very real to me. Then there was my younger brother, who always seemed to have the attention and protection of my mother. I thought, *She loves him more.* Trust me when I say this question sits close to home: Does God play favorites? Even now I look at others who seem to be closer to God, who pray more easily, who receive more public praise, and I wonder whether I could ever have that close connection.

Yes, God Plays Favorites

It's hard to deny that God seems to play favorites. After all, the world is filled with inequality. Even in this passage, Caesar Augustus reigned su-preme on the throne in Rome. God allowed him to have immense power.

Quirinius was governor of Syria (an unfriendly neighbor of Israel). He had wealth and fame. Joseph and Mary, on the other hand, had neither wealth nor power. There is virtually nothing fair in this story:

- Joseph was a day laborer who had to escort his pregnant fiancée seventy miles on foot back to Bethlehem, his ancestral home, to pay their taxes. Both their dress and their accent betrayed their social status.

- Israel was under the brutal subjugation of Rome. Though the historical records of this census have been lost, there is no doubt that Rome exacted tribute from peasants in places like Palestine.

- There was not enough space for Mary and Joseph once they got to Bethlehem. Side note: The common Christmas play has Mary and Joseph turned away from a hotel to give birth in a barn. The problem with this picture, however, is that Bethlehem didn't have a hotel. It was too small and too Jewish. Inns were a Roman industry. Jews relied on hospitality from their extended family. The good folks in Bethlehem would never have allowed one of their own to be turned out during childbirth. The word Luke used for "inn" is elsewhere correctly translated "guest room," as in the Last Supper (Luke 22:11). A more realistic historical reconstruction would have the couple housed downstairs because the upstairs was already packed with pilgrims. The new parents stayed in the family living quarters, along with the household animals (yes, that was a thing). Animals were valuable commodities kept in the home at night and fed from a trough (aka manger) right next to the front door.

But God's Favorites Are Not Who You Think

Of all the people who might have first witnessed the birth of God's Son, no one would have predicted shepherds. Mediterranean culture was as stratified back then as the caste system of Hinduism today. At the bottom were "expendables" who would die early and miserably: miners, beggars, lepers, and prostitutes. Just above them were certain groups stuck in disparaged occupations for generations. Shepherds were one of those, just above bottom-feeders. They were denigrated because their work rendered them ritually unclean. Moreover, these particular shepherds were stuck on the night watch. They were marginalized even among their peers.

Yet it was these lowly shepherds, the underdogs of society, that God chose to be the first witnesses of the Good Shepherd, born in the City of David. Don't miss the irony here. David was the shepherd-king whose royal heir was birthed in his hometown. History came full circle when the prophecies came to fruition. The moment was marked with nothing less than an angelic announcement: "Fear not, for behold, I bring you good news of great joy that will be for all the people. For unto you is born this day in the city of David a Savior, who is Christ the Lord" (Luke 2:10–11).

As if that were not enough, an entire angelic army arrived, not with a battle cry but with a proclamation of peace. The only time an army announces peace is after the battle has been won. How is it that here, at the beginning of the story, the battle is already won? We see something similar in movies when a bully takes on a humble martial arts master. We say something like "He's done." The birth of Jesus set in motion his certain victory over sin and death. It also revealed God's favorites—the lowly.

Throughout the Bible, we see this prescription: God exalts the humble and humbles the exalted (2 Samuel 22:28; Proverbs 29:23; Ezekiel 21:26; Matthew 23:12; Luke 14:11; 18:14; James 4:6, 10; 1 Peter 5:5–6). The idea is everywhere but nowhere more pronounced than with shepherds. While literal shepherds were marginalized, metaphorical shepherds were revered:

• David, the shepherd-king (1 Samuel 16:1–13)

- elders of Israel (Jeremiah 23:1–4)

- Jesus (John 10:1–18; Hebrews 13:20; 1 Peter 2:25; Psalm 23)

- elders of the church (1 Peter 5:1–2)

There's a lesson in this for us. The way our culture values people is contrary to God's metrics. Our culture values possessions; God values generosity. Our culture values youth and beauty; God values wisdom and fidelity. Our culture values entertainment; God values sacrifice. Often people who think the least of themselves are honored most by God (Luke 18:9–14). This explains why Jesus prioritized children, honored widows, and called fishermen. You may think you are nothing, while God thinks you are really something. The world may despise you, while the Lord esteems you. Perhaps you work the night shift like the shepherds. Perhaps you are not wealthy or respected. Perhaps you have no power, fame, or social status. You may have been bullied, neglected, or rejected, or you may be a forgotten middle child. Well, congratulations—you may just be one of God's favorites!

What does this mean for you? Two things. First, the way for you to determine your real value is not through social media, median income, or an organizational chart. Without a clear view of God's value system, you may severely underestimate (or overestimate) the priority God places on you. Far too many of us walk around with a sense of self-worth shaped by elementary school politics or high school sports. If you are like me, you were not the first picked for kickball. Perhaps you lost the election for school council. You were never accused of being the teacher's pet or voted the most likely to succeed. Nonetheless, if you were the first to share with the less fortunate, you are a favorite of God. If you trusted Jesus in spite of broken trust with family or friends, God may have a particular preference for you. If you carry the stigma of a disability or injury yet you shower love indiscriminately, God may give you priority.

Second (and this is important), being a favorite of God gives you not more privilege but more responsibility. Perhaps you have been reading this chapter thinking, *God can't play favorites; that's not fair.* Well, you're right. God isn't fair and that's fairly obvious. Not everyone has access to clean drinking water, the good news of the gospel, opportunities, or health care. If you find that offensive (or find yourself defending God), perhaps you've missed a key attribute of God. God isn't fair; he is gracious. When he gives more to one than he does to another, he creates an opportunity for grace. In other words, God's gifts are never for the one who receives them. God's gifts are to be given away. It is this inequity of distribution that creates mutual dependence, which leads to unity in a world otherwise divided by position and power.

If you have an ability, you are to use it to bless someone else. If you have resources, you have the opportunity to show generosity. If you know the gospel, you are to share it with another. Every injustice in this world is due not to a resource problem but to a distribution problem. In God's economy, we don't receive in order to possess. We are funnels of God's grace, not buckets of his blessings. If every Christ follower would follow this simple principle, there would be no children dying of starvation. There would be no one drinking contaminated water. And most importantly, there would be no pockets on the planet where Jesus's name has yet to be proclaimed.

One last look at the shepherds in Luke 2 makes this principle transparent. As soon as they saw the Shepherd-King lying in a manger, they broadcast this news everyone needed to hear: "When they saw it, they made known the saying that had been told them concerning this child. And all who heard it wondered at what the shepherds told them" (verses 17–18).

If you're reading this, you are favored by God. You have been blessed by him and given a significant charge: Take care of the sheep. Let them know the Good Shepherd has come to live with them, die for them, and raise them to eternal life. You are both blessed by God and responsible to be a blessing to others. This proves you are one of his favorites.

Key Points

- It does seem that God plays favorites, since there is inequity in our world.

- God's favorites are the lowly, not those exalted in the world's economy.

- God favors us so we can show favor on his behalf.

This Week

❑ **Day 1 (Eyes):** How did this essay change your perspective on God's favoritism toward *you*?

❑ **Day 2 (Ears):** Read Psalm 23 and John 10:1–18. What do God and Jesus do as shepherds that you could do for those you lead?

❑ **Day 3 (Heart):** Meditate on Matthew 23:12; James 4:10; 1 Peter 5:5–6. How have you seen this principle of reversal play out in your life?

❑ **Day 4 (Voice):** Discussion:

- What kinds of inequity in this world bother you the most?
- Growing up, were you ever anyone's favorite (a parent, coach, teacher, employer)? How did that feel?
- Do you perceive yourself as favored by God? In what way?
- What gifts has God given you? How will you use those to share God's grace this week?

❑ **Day 5 (Hands):** With whom do you need to share the good news of Jesus? If you have seen him, you share him. Invite someone to coffee and share what you know, or invite someone to church so he can hear what you hear.

Further Resources: Quest52.org/4

5

Did Jesus Know He Was God When He Was a Boy?

Biblical Concept: Maturity
Read: Luke 2:41–52

Puberty was not kind to me. One time I went swimming with Larry, a neighborhood buddy. We were both about twelve. We were playing dodgeball in the pool. He raised his arms to catch the ball, and I noticed something I'd never noticed before. He had hair in his armpits! Mine were as bald as Mr. Clean. It made me so self-conscious that I quit the game, got out of the pool, and made some lame excuse about having to go home early. It would be two years before my pits caught up to Larry's, and by then he was shaving. This experience was replicated in different ways for me pretty much for the next decade!

It makes me wonder what Jesus was like in those awkward years. Did his voice ever crack while he was reading Scripture in the synagogue? Did he begin to notice pretty kosher girls? Did he eat Mary out of house and home? Did he ever sleep until noon? If you're curious about Jesus as a kid, you are not alone. Between the second and fifth centuries, there arose numerous fictitious stories about Jesus's upbringing (such as in *The Infancy Gospel of Thomas* and *The Protevangelion of James,* both readily available online). These are interesting fables about Jesus striking a kid down for bumping into him or outdoing his peers on playdates by miraculously making his clay sparrows fly away. But Scripture barely touches on Jesus's youth. In fact, we have only one account of a single incident.

Why Tell *This* Story?

The lone account of Jesus's childhood is recorded in the gospel of Luke (2:41–52). Not only is the story fascinating; so is its source—Luke. He is the only non-Jewish writer in the entire Bible. Why would he be the only one to record a story of Jesus at age twelve? Well, because he was Greek. Greco-Roman biographies told tales about their heroes becoming men. While we in the West relish rags-to-riches stories, in the ancient Middle East, fate held sway over your future. If a man were a king, he would have a regal birth. If he were a conqueror, his childhood would show celestial signs. This was true of Cyrus the Liberator, Alexander the Great, and Julius Caesar. Boyhood tales predicted what kind of man each would become. These stories were crafted with a specific question in mind: *Was the boy like the man?* If he was, he was fated to lead his nation. If not, he was an impostor who must be ousted.

Luke, writing to a Greco-Roman audience, met their expectation with a kosher tale of Jesus visiting the temple. Remember, the purpose of the story is to answer this question: *Was the boy like the man?* Verses 40 and 52 bracket the story, anticipating how the reader would answer: "The child grew and became strong, filled with wisdom. And the favor of God was upon him" (verse 40). "Jesus increased in wisdom and in stature and in favor with God and man" (verse 52).

The story doesn't just tell what kind of man he would become; the details predict what he would ultimately accomplish. It was *Passover,* when the sacrificial lamb was slain for the release of the people from bondage. It was in the capital city of *Jerusalem,* the seat of his people's political and spiritual power. It featured the *temple,* a shadow of Jesus's own body, where people came to meet God. Finally, he was missing for *three days,* a reference to his resurrection. All these details paint a picture of his ultimate act of redemption.

The Jewish Background

Boys Jesus's age would go through the rites of manhood (today called bar mitzvah), including going for the first time through the court of the Gentiles, through the court of the women, and into the sacred space of the temple proper. Jesus would enter Jerusalem as a boy but leave as a man. This was a man-making, boundary-marking moment.

Passover was an annual Jewish pilgrimage. It was a seven-day celebration, and most of the important sacrifices were completed in the first three days. Most people would return home after the main sacrifices to get back to work. The end of Passover was reserved for rabbinic discussions that would primarily engage the elite. Though we can't prove this, it appears that Jesus stuck around for the teaching, while Mary and Joseph started the journey back to Galilee.

Who leaves their kid in a major city without noticing he's gone? Actually, as a parent, I can tell you it's easier than one might think and even easier for Jewish couples like Mary and Joseph. You see, when they went from Nazareth to Jerusalem, Jesus was a boy. Therefore, he would have traveled with the caravan of women. When they returned, however, Mary would expect him to travel with the men. After the first full day of travel, Mary and Joseph found each other as they set up camp for the night. It was then they discovered Jesus was with neither of them. Mary was a remarkable woman, but I can still imagine her saying some unedifying things to Joseph in the heat of that moment. I can also sympathize with Joseph. He wasn't used to caring for a child, and in his first big moment, he dropped the ball.

They couldn't really travel at night, so as the sun rose the next morning, they returned to Jerusalem, hearts racing as fast as their feet. When they arrived, they retraced their steps, asking each stranger whether he or she had seen a precocious preteen. At last, they found him in the temple, sitting with the scholars, participating in their theological debates: "After three days they found him in the temple, sitting among the teachers, listening to them and asking them questions. And all who heard him were amazed at his understanding and his answers" (Luke 2:46–47).

One wonders what kinds of questions Jesus would have asked: "Right now we have to keep sacrificing, but what would happen if we had a perfect sacrifice?" Or "God asked Abraham to sacrifice his own son. What was the purpose of that passage?" Or "Isaiah talked about someone sacrificed like a lamb to take away our sins. Who provides that sacrifice?"

The Big Reveal

Mary was livid. Any mother would be. She lit into him: "Son, why have you treated us so? Behold, your father and I have been searching for you in great distress" (verse 48). I can relate, having lost my son in a public market in San Antonio. I think I know precisely what she was feeling—only my son was missing for three minutes, not three days!

Jesus was dumbfounded (he was a preteen after all): "Why were you looking for me? Did you not know that I must be in my Father's house?" (verse 49). He couldn't imagine what all the hubbub was about. Was it not logical that the Son of God would be in his native environment? The phrase "in my Father's house" could also be rendered "about my Father's business." It is a nebulous phrase that basically means "in my Dad's stuff." Is it any wonder that "they did not understand the saying that he spoke to them" (verse 50)? How could they? They saw him as their little boy, yet he was speaking to them as God's Son. Even so, he continued to obey his heavenly Father by submitting to his earthly parents: "He went down with them and came to Nazareth and was submissive to them. And his mother treasured up all these things in her heart" (verse 51).

Lessons to Be Learned

The story is about Jesus. He was the same person at age twelve as he would be at age thirty. He was God's Son, devoted to God's business. Nonetheless, if you hold this story up as a mirror, it asks a question of you: Are you, at your own age, at your own spiritual stage, living your potential? Are you carrying out your created purpose?

If not, there may be a reason. This, too, is embedded in the story. Jesus, fully aware that he was God's Son, submitted to the authorities God had placed over him. If there is a gap between your current life and your created purpose, that gap may be due to your lack of submission to earthly authorities. You cannot be God's man or woman without submitting to the authorities he has placed over you.

If you are living under your parents' roof, they are God's authorities over you (even if they don't give God allegiance). When you go to school, the teachers, too, are God's authorities over you. Coaches, pastors, political leaders, and employers are all divine tools to shape your destiny and align you with your purpose. We're tempted to think, *But they aren't godly.* That may be true, but a person does not have to be godly to be a divinely appointed authority. We submit to God by submitting to the authorities he has placed in our lives.

Key Points

- This story is designed to answer the question *Was the boy like the man?*

- At age twelve, Jesus was like the adult Jesus—about his Father's business.

- Jesus was God's Son at every stage of his life. The lesson for us is to act on what we know at each stage of our spiritual journeys, to carry out the mission God has for each of us.

This Week

❏ **Day 1 (Eyes):** After reading the essay, how clear are you about God's purpose for your life?

❏ **Day 2 (Ears):** The life of David includes a fascinating tale about submitting to God's earthly authorities. Read 1 Samuel 24. What leader do you need to show more appropriate honor to?

❏ **Day 3 (Heart):** Meditate on Romans 13:3–7; Ephesians 6:2–3; 1 Timothy 5:17. How does our honor of others increase our spiritual capacity?

❏ **Day 4 (Voice):** Discussion:
- What did you struggle with while going through puberty? Do you have a funny story you would be willing to share?
- What advice would you give to your younger self about the man or woman you wanted to become?
- From your childhood (or parenting), why is submission to authority so important for spiritual growth and mental health?
- Share one area where your actions are below what your level of maturity should be at your age.

❏ **Day 5 (Hands):** "Jesus increased in wisdom and in stature and in favor with God and man" (Luke 2:52). Ask a friend to help you identify one act or discipline you have been putting off that would honor God and increase your favor with others.

Further Resources: Quest52.org/5

6

If Jesus Was Perfect,
Why Was He Baptized?

Biblical Concept: Baptism
Read: Mark 1:1–13 with Matthew 3:1–4:11; Luke 3:1–4:13

We celebrate birthdays, graduations, and weddings because they are important markers of new seasons of life. They represent our forward progress. Baptism is one of those markers. We are putting away the old life and moving into a new mode of being under the lordship of Jesus. That makes sense. But why was Jesus baptized? Was he transitioning from an old mode of being to a new life? Was he leaving a life of sin? No. So, why was he baptized? Let's start at the beginning.

The Beginning

Mark began his book with the word *beginning*. He was likely the first to write a gospel and, as far as we can tell, the first to use the word *gospel* in any religious sense. *Gospel* literally means "good news." The word was originally used for political announcements, generally about a general or the emperor, such as "Our general won the war" or "Our emperor has an heir."

In the Old Testament, the word refers to news about the defeat of

Yahweh's enemies (2 Samuel 18:26). "Good news" thus became theological shorthand for God's deliverance, as in Isaiah 52:7:

> How beautiful upon the mountains
>> are the feet of him who brings good news,
> who publishes peace, who brings good news of happiness,
>> who publishes salvation,
>> who says to Zion, "Your God reigns."

Mark, writing in Rome, opened his book with an announcement of good news. His original readers would have heard it against the backdrop of political success and military victory. Mark bolstered our expectations with a couple of political titles: *Christ* (a Jewish term for "king") and *Son of God* (a reference to the emperor). In other words, he couched his introduction to Jesus in multicultural political terms. Both Roman and Jewish Christians would have heard this introduction as a political challenge to the rulers of their day. Talk about setting high expectations! Jesus is the new emperor, the new king of Israel. Yet what follows forces us to reconfigure our expectations—or at least our definitions of leadership.

Baptism

Jesus is the supreme ruler of God's advancing kingdom. He was "inaugurated," though, by John the Baptist, a ragtag prophet in the desert. Why would Jesus go to him? He dressed like a hermit and ate bugs. Nonetheless, John was fulfilling prophecy. He was preparing the way for the Messiah (Isaiah 40:1–3; Malachi 3:1) and turning the hearts of Israel back to their ancestral fathers (Malachi 4:5–6). Even so, shouldn't John have been baptized by Jesus rather than vice versa? Doesn't the king trump the prophet?

What makes this question even more poignant is the fact that John's baptism was "for the forgiveness of sins" (Mark 1:4). That is the exact phrase Peter would later use on the day of Pentecost to describe Christian baptism (Acts 2:38). So it bears asking again, Why was Jesus baptized?

John himself was shocked by Jesus's request. He tried to deter him: "I need to be baptized by you, and do you come to me?" (Matthew 3:14). Jesus simply replied, "Let it be so now, for thus it is fitting for us to fulfill all righteousness" (verse 15).

There's the answer: "to fulfill all righteousness." That's why Jesus was baptized, but how does that work? Jesus was sinless yet was baptized for the forgiveness of sins. Some will say, "Jesus was setting an example for us." Okay, but how does setting a positive example "fulfill all righteousness"? My guess is that Jesus's baptism is a bigger deal than we have imagined. He was actually baptized vicariously for our sins, just as he would later be crucified for our sins. Not only did his baptism give us a model to follow; he also foreshadowed his own death, burial, and resurrection. In this way, Jesus's baptism pointed forward to the Cross, just as our baptism points backward to the Cross. That's *huge*.

There are, in fact, three markers of the magnitude of this event. First, as Jesus came up out of the water, the heavens were torn open. Mark used a specific word, *schizō*, which means "to tear." It is a rare word for Mark. The only other time he used it was in Mark 15:38. As Jesus was crucified, the curtain of the temple was torn in two from top to bottom. As an interesting aside, according to the historian Josephus, embroidered on this thick curtain were the stars of the heavens.[1] Hence, this heavenly schism bookended Jesus's earthly ministry.

The second thing that happened was the Spirit of God descended in the form of a dove. This was a rare moment when the Spirit took physical form (or at least visual form). Third, God audibly spoke, saying, "You are my beloved Son; with you I am well pleased" (Mark 1:11). Again, this is rare; God spoke only three times during Jesus's ministry (Mark 9:7; John 12:28). For the first time in human history, the entire Trinity appeared in one place: Father, Son, and Spirit met in the river when Jesus was baptized. That's how big a deal that moment was. The plan of God was unfolding in front of them. God's Son, led by the Spirit, would die for our sins and be raised again for our eternal life.

Temptation

As soon as he came up from the water, Jesus was thrust into the wilderness. *Thrust* is the right word. This Greek word (*ekballō*) paints a picture of the Spirit putting his foot in the small of Jesus's back and impelling him into the wilderness. Mark wasted no time getting Jesus into the wilderness and spent little time with him there. He simply said that Jesus was with the wild animals (indicating that he was in danger and all alone) but the angels watched over him (indicating God's protection, even when the odds were against him). Unlike Matthew and Luke, Mark didn't describe the three temptations in considerable detail. He shared only that Jesus was tempted for forty days.

Forty, in biblical literature, tends to signal God's work among humanity. It rained for forty days and forty nights while Noah was in the ark. Moses was on Mount Sinai for forty days and forty nights. Israel was in the wilderness for forty years. Elijah traveled for forty days without eating. There were forty days between Jesus's resurrection and ascension. Forty is found more than a hundred times in the Bible and is a key element in a number of narratives. In this story, Jesus was reenacting the wilderness wandering of Israel. You might be thinking, *Wait a minute. Israel was in the desert for forty years, not forty days.* Right. But how long *should* they have been in the wilderness? Answer: forty days!

You might recall the twelve spies who went into the promised land to check it out (Numbers 13). Two of them said, "The land is awesome. It is beautiful and bountiful." Ten of the spies took a different tack. They said, "The walls are too high; the people are too strong. We will never succeed." The majority followed the advice of the ten skeptical spies. Because of their unbelief, the nation wandered in the wilderness for forty years rather than forty days. In a sense, then, Jesus embodied the entire nation of Israel (as he did when he was baptized for their sins). He circled back to this pivotal moment, leading through faith rather than fear. Jesus accomplished in his wilderness temptation what the nation should have done so many years earlier. History repeats itself, and this time, Jesus turned the tide in the right direction.

Lessons to Be Learned

In both the baptism and the wilderness stories, Jesus took on the sin of Israel. In some way, which we may never fully understand, Jesus stood for all Israel and reversed their mistakes. This is precisely what is offered to us when we follow him in baptism. Just as Jesus represented all Israel and set their history right, we now can be absorbed into him and he will set our histories right. In a sense, that is what our baptism is all about. The portrait the Bible paints of baptism is of us being immersed in Jesus, being buried as he was buried and raised as he was raised. Likewise, following baptism, when we are tempted, we can lean into his life and find a way through the wilderness wandering. He can turn our forty years into forty days, often providing an expedited experience of temptation and suffering. Oh, we still must face temptation. We still must resist. Nonetheless, he has already defeated our Enemy and provided a model of how we can resist our unbelief and receive the promises of God.

In his baptism, Jesus looked forward to his sacrifice on the cross, while in ours we look backward to his sacrifice and resurrection. Our very lives are incorporated into his impeccable life, his substitutionary death, and his victorious resurrection. As Colossians 3:3–4 says, "You have died, and your life is hidden with Christ in God. When Christ who is your life appears, then you also will appear with him in glory." *That* is why Jesus was baptized.

Key Points

- *Gospel* literally means "good news." Originally it was used in connection with earthly kings, but Jesus is the king over every kingdom.

- Jesus's baptism was for the forgiveness of sins—not his but ours. This foreshadowed what would happen on the cross and is reflected in our own baptism.

- Jesus's temptation in the wilderness reversed the failure of Israel. If you walk with Jesus through your temptation, through your own past failure, he can turn your history around.

This Week

❑ **Day 1 (Eyes):** Did reading the essay change how you see baptism?

❑ **Day 2 (Ears):** Read Numbers 13–14. Where do you see yourself in the story? Are you like the ten spies who feared? Like the two who believed? Or like the crowd who refused to obey?

❑ **Day 3 (Heart):** Meditate on Romans 6:1–7 and 1 Corinthians 10:1–5. How do these two descriptions of baptism relate to Jesus's baptism?

❑ **Day 4 (Voice):** Discussion:

- Share a story of someone in your life who paved the way for you. It could be a sibling, parent, mentor, or coach.
- Have you ever willingly taken the blame or punishment for someone else or paid the price someone else owed? How did that feel?
- What does it mean to have your life absorbed in Jesus (Colossians 3:3–4)?
- If you have not been baptized, what is hindering you from taking that step?

❑ **Day 5 (Hands):** Share with an accountability partner what you discovered about yourself in the day 2 exercise. Ask that person what she thinks you would have to do to be more committed to fully obeying God.

Further Resources: Quest52.org/6

7

Did Jesus Have a
Life Purpose? Part I

Biblical Concept: Life Purpose
Read: Luke 19:1–10

I often conclude my sermons by saying, "Let's go out and make Jesus famous." It's not merely a catchy slogan; it's a deeply theological statement of my life purpose. (If you're interested, I explain exactly what that means in chapter 45 of my book *Core 52.*) To be more specific, my life purpose is to make Jesus famous by using the gifts he gave me to teach others about him. I've thought through this carefully and for a very long time. So should you. Life doesn't happen by accident. Or perhaps I should say, the life you want doesn't happen by accident. It requires you to direct your energy and ability toward a desired outcome. Jesus was quite clear about that. Three times he declared his life purpose. That's worth looking into.

Jesus stated his life purpose in John 10:10: "I came that they may have life and have it abundantly." That's as clear as it gets. His entire life was about giving life, especially to those living on the edges of life. The word John chose for "life" is significant. The Greek language had three words for "life." The first is *bios,* from which we get the word *biology.* It is the life we experience in the physical body and implies "physical health" (Luke

8:14). That is not the word John used. The second word is *psychē*, from which we get the word *psychology*. It speaks of one's soul or mind and implies "spiritual health" or "mental health" (Matthew 16:25). That is not the word John used. The word he used is *zōē*, from which we get the word *zoology*. It refers to the life force derived directly from our Creator (John 1:4). He does not just give us this quality of eternal life; he gives it abundantly. When Jesus comes into your life, his life overflows from you.

How does Jesus give us this quality of life? Let's let him explain himself by leaning into his other two purpose statements. Both have full-throttle meanings, so we will tackle them one at a time. We will begin with Luke 19:10 in this chapter, and we will give full attention to Mark 10:45 in the next.

The Son of Man Came to Seek and Save the Lost

In the final week of Jesus's life, he made his way to Jerusalem. He took the major trade route that passed right through Jericho. In Jesus's day it was a cosmopolitan commercial city, which explains why a chief tax collector like Zacchaeus made his home there.

As Jesus passed through, expectations were flying high. Some were ready to make him king by force. Others were prepared to force his death. His reputation for extraordinary miracles marshaled great crowds. Since it was the Friday before Passover, pilgrims were streaming by the thousands down the same well-worn path as Jesus's entourage. Is it any wonder that scores of eager locals lined the street? Some did not get a front-row seat, including some of the rich and powerful like Zacchaeus.

Zacchaeus was not a mere tax collector. He was in upper management of the financial system in this major commercial center. In other words, this "wee little man" was a really big deal. Even so, he could not weasel his way to the front of the crowd. While Zacchaeus could dictate legal affairs in the IRS of his day, he was sorely disliked by his neighbors—and for good reason. He extorted their hard-earned money and gave a cut to their Roman overlords! Little wonder he was despised, which explains why he was up in a tree. Since he was vertically challenged, he could not see over the shoulders of others who lined the path of the parade. Yet he was insatiably curious about this rabbi. So he climbed a tree! He literally went out on a limb to see Jesus.

The crowd went wild. "Hey, Jesus, we love you!" "Hey, Jesus, hold my baby!" "Hey, Jesus, can you heal my gout?" In the midst of the ticker-tape parade, Jesus suddenly stopped. He looked up into the sycamore fig tree harboring our protagonist. The broad, low limbs made the tree easy to climb, and the broad, thick leaves made it easy to hide. Zacchaeus desperately wanted to see Jesus, but it is not likely he wanted Jesus to see him. Often those up-and-comers like Zacchaeus were quite tentative with public spiritual leaders who could expose their secret lives. At best, Jesus could humiliate him. At worst, he could convert him, changing the course of his career.

Yet Jesus called Zacchaeus by name, and his invitation was irresistible: "Zacchaeus, hurry and come down, for I must stay at your house today" (Luke 19:5). The crowd was appalled. Everyone was vying for Jesus's attention, and all were more deserving than Zacchaeus. Jesus, however, accepted the one everyone else rejected. It is actually more than that. Jesus did not just accept him; Jesus needed him. The Greek word translated "must" refers to a need or necessity. Jesus called Zacchaeus, loved Zacchaeus, and fully intended to use Zacchaeus. Why in the world did Jesus need Zacchaeus? As the story unfolds, we will watch Zacchaeus preach without words to those who would never come to "church."

What happened next none could have predicted. We are not talking about the party in Zacchaeus's house. We saw that coming. We could even have foreseen the unsavory friends on Zacchaeus's invitation list. Who else would come to his house but those who were in his inner circle? (Peter and Simon the Zealot must have been quivering with discomfort!) The shocking event no one saw coming was Zacchaeus's sudden liberality and total transformation. Zacchaeus stood and said to Jesus, "Behold, Lord, the half of my goods I give to the poor. And if I have defrauded anyone of anything, I restore it fourfold" (verse 8). Giving fourfold was what the law of Moses mandated (Exodus 22:1). Zacchaeus, however, started with "the law of Christ" (Galatians 6:2; James 2:8) by giving half his possessions to the poor. He was living up to the name Jesus gave him: "son of Abraham" (Luke 19:9). Jesus treated the outsider like an insider, and Zacchaeus immediately acted like one. This all led to the statement of Jesus's life purpose: "The Son of Man came to seek and to save the lost" (verse 10). This is a consistent pattern for Jesus (Luke 15:4, 6, 9, 24, 32). Though he cares about the ninety-nine in the fold, that one lost lamb gets his attention *every time*! This is important. It's a model of how to do church.

How to Adopt Jesus's Purpose

Many churches give outsiders the impression that if they behave, then they can believe. Once they believe, then they can belong. The progression is behave, believe, belong. Jesus, on the other hand, said, "You belong," and people responded, "I believe." *Then* they began to behave. Clearly, Jesus had the progression correct: belong, believe, behave.

It's natural to look at people's behavior and assume their intentions. If they make a lot of money, we assume they are driven by greed. If they are sleeping around, we assume they are driven by lust. If they are focused on sports, we assume they are driven by adrenaline. We see their habits, their jobs, or their relationships and assume we know what they are looking for. Not necessarily true.

Jesus has an uncanny ability to see beyond people's behavior. He looks beyond our performance and sees our past. Often our actions are indicative of our previous pain, not our future dreams. Those driven by money may have father issues. Those driven by sex may have abandonment issues. Those driven by adventure may be looking for the divine in his creation. Both the up-and-comers and the down-and-outers are responding to their experiences (we all do, of course). The way we're living now isn't necessarily what we want; it may be all we know. Given the chance to meet Jesus, many would go out on a limb just to get a glimpse of what you now have.

Given the chance to have Jesus in their homes, they would sell half their possessions. Given the opportunity to experience freedom, they would give up their careers and follow him to the cross.

What often keeps people from Jesus is not Jesus's opinion of them but Christians' assumptions about them. Perhaps it's time to prioritize those Jesus prioritized—the one lost sheep, not the ninety-nine. Is there someone at work, at school, in the neighborhood, or on your team that you have shied away from but that Jesus would run to? Find your one. Invite him first to your home, then to your church. You may get rejected; Jesus certainly was from time to time. If we call Jesus our Lord, should we not call friends those he prioritized?

Key Points

- Jesus came for all people but seems to take a special interest in the marginalized.

- Jesus knows you and *still* loves you. In fact, he really, really likes you!

- Jesus doesn't just know you; he needs you. He has a purpose for your life, and it likely involves introducing someone in your circle to him.

This Week

❑ **Day 1 (Eyes):** As you read the essay, did anyone specific come to mind who in some way is like Zacchaeus in your life?

❑ **Day 2 (Ears):** Read Ecclesiastes 5:8–6:12 through the eyes of Zacchaeus. How would he have interpreted this passage?

❑ **Day 3 (Heart):** Meditate on Romans 1:16; 2 Timothy 1:7–8; 1 Peter 3:15–16. While reading each passage, ask the Holy Spirit three questions: *What do you want me to feel? What do you want me to do? Whom do you want me to reach?*

❑ **Day 4 (Voice):** Discussion:
- Share a story of someone you know whose life was radically different after she met Jesus.
- Why do you think we're so uncomfortable with people who are different from us, particularly if they're wealthy or famous?
- What could your church do to reach out to those we assume would not be interested in Jesus?
- Whom in your circle might you be able to influence to follow Jesus?

❑ **Day 5 (Hands):** When will you next be hosting a party? It could be a birthday, graduation, wedding, or anniversary. Find someone outside your Christian circle of friends, and invite that person to the party specifically to introduce him to other Christ followers. The purpose is the same as Zacchaeus's party: to make Jesus famous.

Further Resources: Quest52.org/7

8

Did Jesus Have a Life Purpose? Part 2

Biblical Concept: Life Purpose
Read: Mark 10:32–45 with Matthew 20:17–28;
Luke 18:31–34

One day, when I was twelve, I heard Dad have a deadly serious but short conversation on the phone with my mom. When he hung up, he stoically said to me and my two brothers, "Mom is coming home, and we are going upstairs to talk. When we come down, we'll let you know what's going on. Don't leave the house." Even though I had never seen my parents fight, something inside told me this was the end of their marriage and the end of life as I knew it.

We've all had moments like that—life-altering, life-defining moments. It could be a visit to the doctor, a knock on the door, or a conversation in a car, but you just know that a dark night of the soul is looming and that your grit and character are about to take a herculean leap forward. That is what's happening in the conversation in Mark 10.

The Beginning of the End and
the End of the Beginning

Jesus was marching boldly toward Jerusalem, and the boys were lagging behind. It is as if they instinctively knew a catastrophe was coming. Then Jesus spelled it out in no uncertain terms:

> Taking the twelve again, he began to tell them what was to happen to him, saying, "See, we are going up to Jerusalem, and the Son of Man will be delivered over to the chief priests and the scribes, and they will condemn him to death and deliver him over to the Gentiles. And they will mock him and spit on him, and flog him and kill him. And after three days he will rise." (verses 32–34)

From our vantage point, we can see this prediction is spot on. Jesus identified the place (Jerusalem), the players (chief priests, scribes, and Gentiles), the process (betrayal, spitting, execution), and the promise (resurrection). In fact, had it been written after the fact, not a single detail would be altered. This is not some vague Nostradamus prediction. You would think the disciples would have stood at attention and asked clarifying questions. They didn't. They were paralyzed with fear. Mark noted the tension even before Jesus dropped the bombshell: "They were amazed, and those who followed were afraid" (verse 32).

Apparently, they were unable to respond to Jesus's revelation of his impending death even though he had previously predicted it two other times (Mark 8:31–37; 9:30–32). It was not something they wanted to talk about. The silence was broken by a question, totally unrelated. James and John, with the support of their mother (Matthew 20:20), Salome, came with a request. Little known fact: Salome was likely Jesus's aunt (Matthew 27:55–56; Mark 15:40; John 19:25). Within the kinship structure of their culture, she had a right to make this request.

An Audacious Power Play

These two boys had been with Jesus since the beginning. They were not just apostles; they were the core of the inner three. Their friend and business partner, Peter, completed the trio. If they were to secure their positions as key leaders in the kingdom, they had better work fast. After all, they were approaching Jerusalem, and the competition might beat them to the punch. Peter had already been singled out as the rock and given the keys (Matthew 16:18–19). Judas held the purse strings (John 12:4–6). So there was reason to make a move now as Jesus was heading toward his regal destiny.

Their request is the kind of thing a teenager would try on an unsuspecting parent: "Will you give us whatever we ask?" Who in his right mind would say yes? Jesus asked, "What do you have in mind?" They replied, "Grant us to sit, one at your right hand and one at your left, in your glory" (Mark 10:37). That was a bold move. It did not sit well with the others. Every man in the mix coveted those chief seats. Jesus tried to caution them: "You do not know what you are asking. Are you able to drink the cup that I drink, or to be baptized with the baptism with which I am baptized?" (verse 38). They were confident, of course, that they could. They had no idea that the right and left of Jesus were reserved for two criminals on crosses, not politicians in cabinet seats.

The others were livid—not because of James and John's self-seeking request but because the two had beaten them to the punch. Jesus must have just shaken his head and said, "Boys, you're missing the point!"

Jesus's Advice on Becoming Great

What Jesus said next is the most significant leadership lesson in history. It has taken Western culture nearly two thousand years to catch up. Notice, Jesus did not rebuke them for seeking greatness. If you have a fire in your bones to be a leader, to make a difference, to find significance, that is not a moral flaw. Rather, it's a divine impulse put there by a Creator who wants you to be a change agent in his world. Jesus told them *how* to be great. Mark that well. God wants you to be great; he even explained how and then immediately modeled it.

In his own words, "You know that those who are considered rulers of the Gentiles lord it over them, and their great ones exercise authority over them" (verse 42). That's the way the world does it. They promote themselves and protect themselves with power. There is a subtle but important detail that is difficult to translate. "Those who are considered rulers" is translated as if it is passive. The impression it gives is that the crowds are looking to leaders as their rulers. However, the actual word is active, not passive. It is the rulers who are presenting themselves as rulers. The crowds merely submit. It is the rulers who dress the part, surround themselves with an armed entourage, and manipulate politics to their own advantage. Rulers present themselves as leaders by exercising power over people.

How does that work? Not well. For example, the two rulers of the Gentiles in Mark's gospel are Herod and Pilate. Both are painted in unflattering terms. Pilate caved when the Jewish leaders demanded he kill their Messiah (Mark 15:1–15). He didn't want to. He knew Jesus was innocent, but when they threatened to blackmail him (John 19:12), he gave in to their demands. *He was ruled by his desire to be seen as a ruler.* Likewise, Herod gave in to the heinous request of his pubescent stepdaughter (Mark 6:21–28). After her lewd dance for his lecherous guests, he promised her up to half his kingdom. Her mother, who had put her up to the dance, also told her to ask for the head of John the Baptist. That sobered Herod up quick. He knew it was evil but gave in anyway. Why? *He was ruled by his desire to be seen as a ruler.*

Politics has not changed in two thousand years. Rulers are ruled by their desire to be seen as rulers. Jesus mandated a different path: "It shall not be so among you. But whoever would be great among you must be your servant, and whoever would be first among you must be slave of all" (Mark 10:43–44). In contemporary vernacular, this is called servant leadership. Corporations and CEOs are just now catching up to Jesus's leadership philosophy. We are coming to realize the power of servant leadership for businesses, families, and volunteer organizations. Jesus's model must not be lost on us: "Even the Son of Man came not to be served but to serve, and to give his life as a ransom for many" (verse 45).

We dare not make the mistake of seeing Jesus's actions only as vicarious suffering. Yes, his death on the cross was the singular event that secured our salvation. However, it is so much more than that. It is a model of leadership. Rather than using power for self-promotion and self-protection, we use it only for the benefit of the powerless. By laying down our lives for others (literally or metaphorically), we raise our levels of leadership influence. Christian leaders are not driven by the desire to be seen as leaders. They are driven by the desperation of the least and the lost. The greatest among us must be a servant to the least among us.

The cross of Jesus is not merely what he did for us. It is the model of the life he demands from us. This takes us back to Eden, when God called Adam and Eve to be caretakers of the garden (Genesis 1:28). He created the heavens and the earth and invited us to partner with him in creating the world. Though sin and misery have populated the planet, our call to create a beautiful world is still the same. That's why Jesus's cross cannot be the only cross in our theology. His cross saved sinners. Our crosses save society. When we carry the cross of servant leadership, using our power for the powerless, we will achieve true greatness not only in the eyes of God but also in the presence of a watching world.

Key Points

- Jesus's disciples ignored his predictions of suffering. This illustrates the difficulty of promoting servant leadership.

- Jesus never criticized James and John for wanting to be great. On the contrary, he told them how.

- Servant leadership is the most powerful mechanism for building a life of significance and greatness.

This Week

❏ **Day 1 (Eyes):** Did this essay change how you view your own desire to be great?

❏ **Day 2 (Ears):** What principles of servant leadership can you glean from Joshua 1, particularly since *Joshua* is the Hebrew name for Jesus.

❏ **Day 3 (Heart):** Meditate on the following passages and ask how they reinforce Jesus's teaching on servant leadership: 1 Corinthians 9:19; 2 Corinthians 4:5; 1 Peter 5:2–3.

❏ **Day 4 (Voice):** Discussion:

- Who is the best leader you've ever personally worked with? Why?
- What have you learned about servant leadership from secular sources? Any principles you would like to share or books you could recommend?
- Share about a time when you practiced servant leadership. What was the result?
- Where do you find it most difficult to serve humbly? Why do you think it's hard for you to serve those people or in those ways?

❏ **Day 5 (Hands):** Do one thing this week for someone else that is uncomfortably humbling for you.

Further Resources: Quest52.org/8

9

How Do I Recognize God's Call on My Life?

Biblical Concept: Calling
Read: Luke 5:1–11

When you're a sixteen-year-old boy at summer camp, your mind is narrowly focused—at least mine was. Between the girls at campfire and my buddies at lunch, my brain was pretty much at capacity. So God's call to ministry was a taxing intrusion. I clearly heard him say, *Wouldn't you rather heal souls than brains?* (He knew I wanted to be a brain surgeon.) I thought my answer was clear: "No." The Spirit persisted: *Wouldn't you rather heal souls than brains?* This nuisance went on for *days*. Frustrated, I finally said (rather forcefully), *I've given you 95 percent of my life. All I'm asking for is my own vocation.* I swear I heard the Holy Spirit "humph," then ask, *Aren't you glad Jesus didn't give you 95 percent?* That undid me!

In desperation I conceded: *All right. I'll preach.* Miraculously, from that moment to this day, I've desired to do nothing else. That's my story. Yours will be different. Just so we're clear, I'm not talking about the call to come to Christ. That's about salvation. This call is about service. How can we use the gifts God gave us to make Jesus famous?

It's Bigger than a Boat

The story opens generically: "On one occasion" (Luke 5:1). We don't know exactly when it was. We do, however, know exactly where it was. The story takes place right outside the village of Capernaum on the north shore of the Sea of Galilee. It is the largest lake in the country and was teeming with fish.

By this point, Jesus's popularity was rising, as was his opposition. Crowds were everywhere, jostling to get near Jesus. A few local fishermen were on the shore, mending their nets after a frustrating night of fishing. (I've had a few of those! It can make one sour.) Jesus borrowed Peter's boat, pushed off from shore, and turned it into an amphitheater. Since Peter's servants were occupied mending the nets (Mark 1:16–20), Jesus's preaching was a pretty good excuse to dodge that tedious task.

After his sermon, Jesus turned to Peter and said, "Put out into the deep and let down your nets for a catch" (Luke 5:4). What a dumb idea! It was the wrong time of day to fish, and they had already been skunked that night. You can imagine Peter thinking, *Lord, you're a great preacher, but you obviously know nothing about fishing. You do you and leave fishing to me.* As a carpenter, Jesus was better at building a boat than putting it to use—or so Peter must have thought.

Fortunately, what Peter might have been thinking wasn't what he said: "Master, we toiled all night and took nothing! But at your word I will let down the nets" (verse 5). "At your word" is the right response for Peter and for us. As near as we can tell, Peter met Jesus about nine months earlier when Peter was still following John the Baptist (John 1:35–42). Peter had witnessed the first miracle in Cana. He saw Jesus cleanse the temple. He overheard Jesus's interview with Nicodemus, watched Jesus with the woman at the well, and witnessed a handful of healings in Jerusalem. Peter knew enough to doubt his doubt when it came to Jesus. This Nazarene never ceased to surprise you.

So Peter rowed backward into the deep and let down his nets. His assistants onshore watched with frustration, knowing they would have to clean his nets a second time. Then it happened. As if on cue, the fish leaped into the nets, threatening to drag the boat to the bottom of the lake. The fishermen were frantic. They called to their partners onshore. Actually, they nodded at their coworkers. Luke was right to use this word meaning "nod," because Peter was too far offshore to shout and his hands were full of net so he couldn't let go to wave. He beckoned ferociously with his head to get their attention. James and John jumped into their boat and raced to help haul in the catch. One can only imagine what a financial boon this was after following Jesus for nine months. They were likely behind on some bills, and this single catch would go a long way in catching up.

Appropriate Response

One would think the fishermen, giddy with excitement, would celebrate. This catch would give them bragging rights for years to come. No one had ever competed or could ever compete with this catch, despite the typical spin fishermen use to exaggerate their abilities. This blessing, however, was almost too much to handle. James and John arrived with their boat and ran parallel to Peter's. As they hauled in the net, fish were careening over the edge of both boats. They just kept coming. The more fish landed in the boats, the deeper the boats sank in the water. At some point, they realized this could *drown* them. It was then that Peter understood that the person and power in his boat were no joke.

Many approached Jesus as a magician who could wave a wand and fix their problems. Peter now knew better. Jesus entered *his* occupation. He showed up on *his* shore. He sat in *his* boat and accomplished what Peter never could. Peter became well aware that Jesus wasn't one to be trifled with. He wasn't a would-be business partner; he's the living Lord. In short, Peter was in the presence of God.

He fell to his knees, waist deep in a squirming pile of carp, and cried, "Depart from me, for I am a sinful man, O Lord" (Luke 5:8). When you meet Jesus—I mean really encounter the authentic Christ—it will undo you. Jesus could provide a great catch of fish because he created the lake they inhabited. The moment was overwhelming. Face to face with the Master, Peter came face to face with his own inadequacy.

Perhaps you've had a similar awakening, a spiritual reckoning. If so, you may recognize the coming call: "Do not be afraid; from now on you will be catching men" (verse 10). When Jesus calls you, he calls you to seek and save the lost. Luke used a very interesting word for "catch." It means "to take live captives." The only other time this word is used in all the New Testament is 2 Timothy 2:26: "They may come to their senses and escape from the snare of the devil, after being *captured* by him to do his will."

Whether Jesus calls you to give up your vocation, change your vocation, or use your vocation, the call is the same: to become a fisher of people. We don't catch and release; we release the caught. So many have been snagged by Satan. They have been lured and hooked and are now flailing for freedom. Jesus commissions all his disciples to go on a search-and-rescue mission for POWs of a spiritual war. There is nothing more important in all the world. How did Peter, James, and John respond to such a call? Once onshore, these fishermen "left everything and followed him" (Luke 5:11). Will you? Can you hear his call?

Practical Advice on Hearing God's Call

If you're a Christian, you have a call. Not merely a call to salvation, but a call to service. The Spirit of God has given you spiritual gifts not because he loves you but because he wants to love someone else through you (see *Core 52,* chapter 46). Your spiritual gift may not be something that came miraculously after conversion. It may be a talent given to you at birth. It becomes a spiritual gift not when the Spirit gives it to you but when you give it back to him in service.

You may say, "I have nothing to offer" or "I don't have enough influence or ability." That's nonsense. You can doubt yourself all you want, but don't doubt the Spirit of God. Don't doubt Jesus, who can enter your boat—your vocation, your business—and do something transformational. Here are four principles to help you hear God's call:

1. God is calling you. If you listen, you will hear him ask for both your ability and your availability.
2. He asks some people to give up their occupations; he asks others to give over their occupations. Either way, we are all called to be pastors where we live, work, and play.
3. Often God's call comes through others. You may not hear a divine voice or sense an internal prompting. His call may come through the mundane means of a parent, a coach, or a pastor. When others tell you what they see in you, that's often God speaking to you through them. It may sound like this: "You're incredibly observant of others' feelings." Or "You have a natural gift of leadership." Or "Could you help your peer develop this skill?" Such simple observations and requests can have eternal consequences.
4. Asking Jesus to leave you alone is futile. He's more patient and persistent than you can imagine. So you might as well begin today to find and fulfill his call on your life.

Key Points

- God calls some people to give up their occupations and others to give over their occupations, but all are called to use their lives to rescue captives and draw people to Jesus.

- Jesus enters our boats—our occupations—and overwhelms our expectations.

- God may call you personally or even miraculously. Most often, however, his call comes through others who speak God's truth to us.

This Week

❏ **Day 1 (Eyes):** After reading the essay, are you able to put into words what God has called you to do with your life?

❏ **Day 2 (Ears):** First Samuel 3 describes God's call on Samuel's life. What lessons can you draw from this passage about hearing God's call on your life?

❏ **Day 3 (Heart):** Meditate on the following verses, and ask how they define or describe your call: 2 Corinthians 5:20; 1 Peter 2:9–10; 4:10–11.

❏ **Day 4 (Voice):** Discussion:

- When you think of a person who is called by God, what or who comes to mind?
- Share about a time when you think God was speaking to you. Do you think God ever calls and we don't hear him or we refuse to respond? What would keep a person from hearing God's voice?
- What are some of the mechanisms God could use to speak to us (such as sermons, books, music, nature, children, etc.)?
- Go around the circle, and tell others what you see in them or how they could draw people to Jesus by leveraging their gifts, resources, and abilities.

❏ **Day 5 (Hands):** Write a mission statement for your life. How will you use what God has put in your hands to lead people to Jesus?

Further Resources: Quest52.org/9

10

How Do You Get into Jesus's Inner Circle?

Biblical Concept: Family
Read: Mark 3:31–35 with Matthew 12:46–50;
Luke 8:19–21

Belonging is a universal human longing. That's why rejection is so painful. I remember this feeling from the playground as a skinny kid trying to get picked for kickball. It worsened at the middle school dance. In high school it was varsity squad and student council. In college it was the dean's list and scholarships. In "real life" it is promotions and titles. Selection is a perpetual process of rejection; for each one selected, many are rejected. The odds are always against us. It's more painful for some than others, and even the most fortunate find rejection more common than selection.

Perhaps that's why this particular question is so uncomfortable: How do you get into Jesus's inner circle? Rejection has conditioned us to desire equality but not expect fair play. Most people want God to be impartial but probably secretly doubt that he is. After all, there doesn't seem to be a lot of equality on earth. Still, we hope for a utopia with egalitarian inclusion. Then we run headlong into Mark 3:31–35.

Family Versus Faith

The old saying "Blood is thicker than water" is a claim that family trumps every other allegiance. Jesus rejected this notion in this brief story that has momentous implications. Mark 3:31–32 says, "His mother and his brothers came, and standing outside they sent to him and called him. And a crowd was sitting around him, and they said to him, 'Your mother and your brothers are outside, seeking you.'" Any other rabbi would have rushed to his mother and brothers. After all, they lived in a corporate culture where family ties were much stronger than in our individualist culture. To those raised in the West, individual rights and freedoms are paramount. This is very different in Eastern cultures (as well as in Latin American and African cultures). There your group or tribe is the source of your individual identity, not your personal preferences, gifts, hobbies, or propensities. You are not "I"; you are "we." In corporate cultures your identity derives from family, occupation, and location.

We see this clearly in the biblical genealogies. An individual was identified by three things: who their father was, the occupation he passed on to them, and the village where they were raised. Whom they were connected to determined who they were. Arranged marriages, inherited occupations, and family solidarity were the norm. We have to use a bit of cultural imagination to envision the weight a family carried. That's why it's so shocking that Jesus responded to his family as he did.

We must be clear. Jesus was breaking protocol but not because he was a Western individualist. Rather, he was prioritizing his heavenly Father over his earthly mother. We see the same thing in John 2 when Jesus turned water to wine. He prioritized his vocational call from his Father in heaven over the situational needs of his mother as host of the wedding. Again, after his baptism, Jesus did not move back to his hometown of Nazareth. Instead, he moved his movement to Capernaum, where many of his disciples—James, John, Peter, Andrew, and Matthew—were from. Now he was sitting in a home (perhaps Peter's) on the shore of the lake, teaching his chosen few. Remember, these homes were modest. A dozen would be capacity for most, and even the wealthiest could barely accommodate fifty.

Jesus walked with his disciples, sat in a circle and taught them, and gathered at a table to eat with them. That sounds normal to our ears, even polite. However, their meals showed their solidarity. People in those days didn't go out to eat to get to know someone. Meals were markers for insiders, and the perimeter was mostly fixed along family lines. So to choose to eat with others and ignore your own family was simply unacceptable.

Literary Sandwiches

To fully appreciate what's happening, we should review how this whole incident started. The crowds were swelling and swallowing Jesus. He was mobbed—and not only by the locals: "Jesus withdrew with his disciples to the sea, and a great crowd followed, from Galilee and Judea and Jerusalem and Idumea and from beyond the Jordan and from around Tyre and Sidon. When the great crowd heard all that he was doing, they came to him" (Mark 3:7–8). We read that and say, "Fantastic. He's getting famous." His family, however, would have said, "This is out of control." The people who were monopolizing Jesus were outsiders, not insiders. Some were Jews but from faraway places; others were from non-Jewish places like Tyre and Sidon. That was a problem.

It was actually a big enough problem that the family decided to intervene: "When his family heard it, they went out to *seize* him, for they were saying, 'He is *out of his mind*'" (verse 21). Notice the word *seize*. Mark would use that very word later to describe the soldiers in the Garden of Gethsemane who grabbed ahold of Jesus to arrest him (14:46). This was a full-fledged intervention. In case there is any doubt, listen to what his family said about him: "He is out of his mind." They thought he was crazy, and no, that is not a metaphor.

Mark made this clear by the way he shaped the narrative. Think of it as a literary sandwich. You stack two similar stories like two pieces of bread. Then you slip a story in the middle that's like the meat. The meaning of the middle flavors how you're supposed to read the outer stories. This is a clever device, which Mark used several times in his gospel (4:1–20; 5:21–43; 11:12–25; 14:1–11; 14:53–72).

Notice that Mark 3:20–21 and 3:31–35 are about Jesus's family (that's the bread of the sandwich). Between these two stories is the famous discussion about Jesus casting out demons (the meat): "The scribes who came down from Jerusalem were saying, 'He is possessed by Beelzebul,' and 'by the prince of demons he casts out the demons'" (verse 22). Notice, the scribes accused Jesus of being possessed by a demon. His family accused him of being crazy. These two accusations are different ways of saying the same thing. While our culture attributes mental illness to psychological problems, their worldview attributed mental illness to spiritual warfare. Mark was sending a clear message: Jesus's family was on the same side as his opposition. They believed him to be deceived by the devil. That made them outsiders to Jesus's movement, not insiders. The family was dead set on reining him in, which forced Jesus to force them out.

Getting into Jesus's Inner Circle

The story tells us how insiders became outsiders. Jesus's family treated him in the same way as his enemies. They attributed his power to dark forces and assumed he was heading in the wrong spiritual direction. They even tried to physically take hold of him as the soldiers did when they arrested him. On the flip side, the story also tells us how outsiders became insiders. The people who came from Tyre and Sidon (ancient enemies of Israel) were welcomed into the Jesus movement. The door of his home was open to them, and they had a place at his table. When the knock came at the door and his presumptuous family wanted access, he rebuffed them in favor of those who showed loyalty. Jesus said, "'Who are my mother and my brothers?' And looking about at those who sat around him, he said, 'Here are my mother and my brothers! For whoever does the will of God, he is my brother and sister and mother'" (verses 33–35).

This story is great news, especially to those who have felt left out. We want egalitarian inclusion because we've so often seen the advantage given to the rich, the beautiful, the powerful, or the famous. In God's economy, however, the advantage goes to the pure of heart. The inner circle is reserved for those who respond to Jesus and live along the lines of God's Word. It's true that Jesus prioritizes some people over others, but his metric is our faith, not our biology. He gives unprecedented access to those who give unqualified obedience to God's will. Anyone is welcome, regardless of heritage, biography, or status. Jesus's inner circle is determined not by where you came from but by where you're headed. You can be a part of Jesus's inner circle, and it turns out to be more your decision than his. He has already invited you in.

Key Points

- Blood is *not* thicker than water, at least according to Jesus.

- Mark's story shows how Jesus's family was more similar to his enemies than to his disciples.

- To Jesus, insiders are those who prioritize their heavenly Father over their earthly families.

This Week

❑ **Day 1 (Eyes):** As you read the essay, what was one thing about this story that stuck out to you and might have caused you to think differently about Jesus and his inner circle?

❑ **Day 2 (Ears):** Read Isaiah 49. Look for clues as to how Jesus might have read this chapter in light of his own ministry. If he was to restore Israel, what would be his obligation to other nations?

❑ **Day 3 (Heart):** Meditate on 1 Corinthians 12:13; Ephesians 2:14; Colossians 3:11. Rewrite these verses for your community— what groups have been or should be brought together in your local church?

❑ **Day 4 (Voice):** Discussion:

- How would you answer a child who says, "That's not fair"? Can you give a specific example?
- Share about a time when you felt special because you were in someone's inner circle. What specifically made you feel valued?
- Have you had an experience in church that made you feel like you didn't belong? What made you feel that way? How did you respond?
- Are we sending messages verbally or nonverbally that could make people feel like they don't belong in Jesus's inner circle? What could we do differently to be more open, especially in our smaller groups?

❑ **Day 5 (Hands):** Find a friend that doesn't attend any church and ask her, "Hey, can I get your opinion on something? If you ever decided to go to church, what would make you feel like you were welcome there?"

Further Resources: Quest52.org/10

11

Does My Past Determine My Future?

Biblical Concept: Shame
Read: Luke 7:36–50

One of my most memorable moments preaching was in Oronogo, Missouri. The text was Romans 8:1: "There is therefore now no condemnation for those who are in Christ Jesus." I asked the audience to write on a piece of paper a sin they had been holding against themselves, walk to the front of the auditorium, and slip the paper into a fifty-gallon trash can. From an audience of nine hundred, I expected a dozen or so to come forward. I was *way* off. Nearly every person had some shame to shed.

People stood in line to release the sin that had shamed them for so long. As I knelt in prayer a few feet away, I noticed a seventy-year-old in his Sunday best. When it was his turn, he stepped forward, unfolded the paper, read it one last time, then slipped it into oblivion with the others. I remember praying, *Lord, thank you for using me to release him from decades of self-bondage.* The Holy Spirit said, *What about you?* I asked, *What do you mean?* But I knew exactly what he meant. For more than a decade, I had held secret shame from an act in my past. I didn't want to admit that before the crowd I had just preached to. Ultimately, though, I feared God's opinion more than theirs. So I yielded, got in line with everyone else, and released what I had held against myself for so long.

Trust me when I say I know the power of being liberated from shame. I am just like the woman in this story.

Table, Tears, and Tyranny

The scene is set in a dining room that seated about a dozen. Except they didn't sit on chairs. They reclined on cushions. The table was low to the ground, maybe six inches high, and U-shaped. The host and his honored guest were at the top of the arch. Simon the Pharisee was the owner of the home. His "honored" guest was Jesus. Around the table were Simon's associates—the elite of the community.

In those days, the dining halls held a place of prominence in the home. Because of Simon's social status, lots of locals would come into his courtyard for business and community affairs. When Simon threw a party, those same villagers were allowed to gather in the courtyard and gawk through the window. The more impressed they were with the meal, the more honor Simon gained in the community.

One of the locals was a woman with a bad reputation. Your guess is as good as mine just how she'd earned that reputation. There are few options, though, and sexual promiscuity tops the list. Her sordid reputation as well as her hair being let down in public are clues that she may have been a prostitute. Just so we are clear, that is not any little girl's dream. Most of the time, women are forced into sex trafficking by economic straits or abuse. This nameless woman stepped across Simon's threshold and buckled at Jesus's feet. Tears streamed down her face.

Simon's reaction was visceral. He recoiled in a fetal position. Jesus, on the other hand, watched as her tears rained down on his feet, forming little puddles of mud between his toes. Perhaps instinctively, she cleaned up the mess with the only thing available: her hair. After wiping his feet clean, she opened an alabaster vial of ointment and proceeded to lavishly smear its valuable contents on his feet. Alabaster is a translucent stone, soft enough to bore out as a jar. We know a pint of this stuff was worth a year's wages (John 12:5). According to the scholar Pliny, ointment was an extreme luxury.[1] We don't know how much this woman had, but it was probably a small vial tied around her neck and used as perfume or a breath freshener, common accoutrements of a professional escort. This was likely the only thing of value she owned. Even more striking is that she put this valued ointment on Jesus's feet (considered "unclean" by Jews) rather than on his head, which was standard practice since it was deemed honorable.

Simon thought to himself, "If this man were a prophet, he would have known who and what sort of woman this is who is touching him, for she is a sinner" (Luke 7:39). No one of dignity would allow such a shameful woman to touch him—or so Simon thought. Jesus read his mind, which was not that hard since Simon's body language was shouting rejection (of both the woman and Jesus)! "Simon, I have something to say to you." Simon replied with feigned respect, "Say it, Teacher" (verse 40).

What Love Looks Like

Jesus proceeded with a parable. The main character was a scoundrel—a moneylender. He was somewhere between a banker and a loan shark. One guy owed him five hundred denarii. We're talking two years' worth of salary. The second guy owed a fraction of that: fifty denarii. It didn't really matter, though, since neither could pay him back. The moneylender had legal recourse to throw both in prison until they paid or their family came up with the money (Matthew 18:30). Of course, once they were in prison, that would be nearly impossible! But this moneylender forgave both debts (a ludicrous hypothetical). "Which of them will love him more?" Jesus asked (Luke 7:42). "The one, I suppose, for whom he cancelled the larger debt," Simon said (verse 43). Exactly!

What happened next is stunning. Jesus turned and looked at the woman while speaking to Simon. There she was, still kissing his feet drenched in tears and smeared with ointment. A powerful aroma filled the room, eclipsed only by the love Jesus had for the woman, filling the vacuum of love Simon should have had for Jesus. He said to Simon, "Do you see this woman? I entered your house; you gave me no water for my feet, but she has wet my feet with her tears and wiped them with her hair. You gave me no kiss, but from the time I came in she has not ceased to kiss my feet. You did not anoint my head with oil, but she has anointed my feet with ointment. Therefore I tell you, her sins, which are many, are forgiven—for she loved much. But he who is forgiven little, loves little" (verses 44–47).

Simon had neglected every common courtesy toward a guest in his home. His intentions were exposed. Though Jesus sat at the honored place, Simon dishonored him through neglect. He didn't wash his feet—an expected gesture when guests entered a home so they didn't sully the carpet after walking on dusty roads in Birkenstocks. This woman, however, more than made up for Simon's neglect by washing Jesus's feet with her tears and drying them with her hair. Simon didn't greet Jesus with a kiss on each cheek. If you have ever been to the Middle East, you know how common this greeting is. The woman, on the other hand, had not yet stopped kissing Jesus's feet. Simon didn't put a tablespoon of olive oil on Jesus's head, which was a thing. In contrast, she rubbed costly ointment on his feet.

It is obvious who loved Jesus more. It is equally obvious why: her sins had been forgiven. Notice, she hadn't said a word. She hadn't repented. She hadn't given up her habits . . . that we know of. Yet her tears declared her sorrow. Her ointment professed her repentance. Her kisses indicated her devotion to Jesus. Without words, she said all she needed to demonstrate true repentance. Hence, Jesus, publicly announced her debt canceled.

The Shattering of Shame

Jesus looked at the woman straightaway and stated, "Your sins are forgiven" (verse 48). Oh, that this could be the end of the story. But those around the table muttered, "Who is this, who even forgives sins?" (verse

49). This was not the first time Pharisees (religious leaders of Jesus's day) questioned Jesus's divine ability to forgive sins. The last time, Jesus gave a pretty clear and definitive answer (5:17–26). Here, however, he ignored them. Why? Because there was a woman bearing the weight of shame. Her full freedom was more important than some theological debate. Jesus said with crystal clarity, "Your faith has saved you; go in peace" (7:50).

Let that sink into your soul. If you are bearing the weight of decades of shame, it's time to release it to Jesus. There are no more words to say or sacrifices to make. You don't need more apologies, penance, or self-flagellation. If you have repented of your sin, confessed it to God, and made amends as best you can, then let it go. You are free. Fully. Finally.

We don't know for sure who this woman was. But in the very next passage, we're introduced to Mary Magdalene. If this woman wasn't Mary, she was someone very much like her. The Bible says Mary had seven demons before meeting Jesus (8:2). Clearly, she was a woman with a past. Yet all four Gospels identify Mary Magdalene as the first witness to the Resurrection. She is a splendid example of someone whose past didn't determine her future. Your future can be unfettered from your past if you can correctly answer just one question: How much do you love Jesus?

Key Points

- Religious leaders sometimes justify themselves by comparing their "righteousness" with others' sinfulness.

- Jesus rushes to the downhearted who are truly repentant.

- Jesus does not want you carrying a burden of shame. He has declared your debt paid in full.

This Week

☐ **Day 1 (Eyes):** After reading the essay, do you need to release some sin or regret you've been holding against yourself?

☐ **Day 2 (Ears):** Read Moses's story in Exodus 2:11–4:17. He was the founder of the Jewish nation, yet he began as a fugitive. What lessons does this hold for you about getting past your past?

☐ **Day 3 (Heart):** Meditate on Romans 8:1; 1 Timothy 1:15; 1 John 1:9. How does each of these help you answer the question, "Does my past determine my future?"

☐ **Day 4 (Voice):** Discussion:

- Share a story of someone you know who radically turned his life around.
- Discuss the implications of this statement: sin is not just what you do but also what was done to you.
- Without sharing details that are too personal, can you relate to holding on to shame too long? What are the consequences of this?
- What are some helpful steps to releasing shame? Have others given you any words of wisdom that helped you let go of shame?

☐ **Day 5 (Hands):** Schedule a date with God this week. Write on a piece of paper any sin you are still holding against yourself. Practice 1 John 1:9. Claim Romans 8:1. Release or destroy the paper.

Further Resources: Quest52.org/11

12

Who Are Social Influencers for Jesus? Part I

Biblical Concept: Influence
Read: John 3:1–21

Have you ever had a flight canceled in the airport? A hundred people bull-rush the poor customer service agent as if she personally canceled the flight out of spite. On one such occasion, a long line of frustrated customers stood helplessly as the agent meticulously worked to get each person rerouted. One customer was certain he was more special than the rest. He had clout, high miles, and a name that was apparently important to some. He pushed past the other customers, who gave him angry stares. At the counter he growled at the attendant and asked, "Do you know who I am? *Do you know who I am?*" Unflustered, she grabbed the microphone and made the following announcement: "Ladies and gentlemen, if anyone has lost an adult male in your party, he is at the counter and apparently does not know who he is." The crowd cheered. The "important" man skulked to the back of the line. In a sense, the same thing is about to happen in this text.

In the Dark of Night

Nicodemus was the most influential person Jesus had met up to that point. He sat on Israel's highest court, called the Sanhedrin. It was made up of seventy-one members, making Nicodemus an elite elder statesman. As a Pharisee, he was a staunch defender of conservative Judaism. Unlike his colleagues, however, he liked Jesus. He said, "Rabbi, we know that you are a teacher come from God, for no one can do these signs that you do unless God is with him" (John 3:2). That is a huge deal for an institutional insider. He admitted that Jesus was a rabbi even though Jesus had none of Nicodemus's formal education. He affirmed that Jesus's miracles were legitimate. He was seriously considering whether Jesus was the Messiah and how he might leverage his influence to promote Jesus's ministry.

Nicodemus seems like such a good guy. One would think a fledgling movement like Jesus's could use a friend in high places. Nicodemus's name could go a long way in opening doors, breaking down barriers, and gaining goodwill among the people. So, why did Jesus not welcome him with open arms? Why was he not courted as a potential leading influencer for the disciples? Many pastors would have lunged at Nicodemus the second he set foot in the building.

There are several clues in the text. First, Nicodemus came to Jesus at night. It's not simply that Nicodemus was busy during the day. A man of his standing would have had a flexible schedule, especially with a guy like Jesus, who could become a national hero. Something deeper was going on here. It appears that Nicodemus didn't want his affinity for Jesus to become public.

Furthermore, *night, dark,* and *darkness* occur thirteen times in the book of John (1:5; 3:2, 19; 6:17; 8:12; 9:4; 11:10; 12:35, 46; 13:30; 19:39; 20:1; 21:3). Most of these references are metaphors for spiritual darkness: evil, ignorance, or opposition. Since this passage both begins and ends with darkness (3:2, 19), the night seems to indicate a spiritual condition more than a time frame. "This is the judgment: the light has come into the world, and people loved the darkness rather than the light because their works were evil" (verse 19). The symbol of darkness surrounds this text. Moreover, the final time John mentioned Nicodemus, he reminded us that he came at night (19:39). So, while Nicodemus is painted with white brushstrokes, around him are gray clouds.

Second, Nicodemus's confession of Jesus, while noble, pales in comparison with what others had already affirmed. In the first chapter of John, Jesus had been declared "the Word," "Lamb of God," "Son of God," "Messiah," and "King of Israel" (verses 1, 29, 34, 41, 49). The best Nicodemus could muster was "Rabbi." Was it honorable? Yes. Was it sufficient? Not even close.

There is a third clue that Nicodemus might not have been fully committed. He was pretty engaged in the initial conversation (3:1–8). After all, he was courting Jesus's favor. But Jesus seems to have been uninterested in any high-powered advocate. He told this Sanhedrin superstar that he had to come into the kingdom at ground level like everyone else: "Truly, truly, I say to you, unless one is born again he cannot see the kingdom of God" (verse 3). Nicodemus asked, "How can a man be born when he is old? Can he enter a second time into his mother's womb and be born?" (verse 4). Jesus replied, "Truly, truly, I say to you, unless one is born of water and the Spirit, he cannot enter the kingdom of God" (verse 5).

This would be like telling a US senator he had to take middle school civics. From that point on, Nicodemus was much less engaged in the conversation. He asked only one more question: "How can these things be?" (verse 9). Jesus answered,

> Are you the teacher of Israel and yet you do not understand these things? Truly, truly, I say to you, we speak of what we know, and bear witness to what we have seen, but you do not receive our testimony. If I have told you earthly things and you do not believe, how can you believe if I tell you heavenly things? No one has ascended into heaven except he who descended from heaven, the Son of Man. And as Moses lifted up the serpent in the wilderness,

so must the Son of Man be lifted up, that whoever believes in him
may have eternal life. (verses 10–15)

After that kind of rebuke, is it any wonder Nicodemus stopped talking?

What Do You Do with Nicodemus?

As we focus on the meaning of the meeting, we see that, with Jesus, a
person's prestige carries no weight. You cannot buy your way into the
kingdom or bully your way past faith. Neither fame nor fortune can sub-
stitute for submission to Jesus. For those at the top of the social food
chain, this is *not* good news. For those on the outskirts, for those ostracized, this is great news. We all have equal footing at the foot of the cross.
We all have access to Jesus.

Many would like to be like Nicodemus, a person of power who could
promote Jesus with his influence. After all, no other Sanhedrin member
had affirmed Jesus publicly. Two other times Nicodemus would come to
Jesus's defense—but barely. In John 7, Jesus was getting railroaded. Nicodemus defended his right to a fair trial: "Does our law judge a man without first giving him a hearing and learning what he does?" (verse 51). His
colleagues reacted vituperatively: "Are you from Galilee too? Search and
see that no prophet arises from Galilee" (verse 52). You know what Nicodemus said next? Nothing! He backed down.

We meet Nicodemus one final time, in John 19:39. He joined Joseph
of Arimathea, providing an honorable burial for Jesus. That's good, right?
Well, yes, but it's hardly enough. Joseph is identified as a secret disciple of
Jesus. Therein lies the problem for both Joseph and Nicodemus. They
wanted to be close to Jesus without coming out of the closet. Sorry—that
is not an option. You can't have a personal relationship without public acclamation. That's not just true for Jesus; it's a relational reality. Your dat-
ing relationship won't last if you refuse to update your status on social
media. True devotion requires declaration. As William Barclay observed,

"Discipleship kills the secrecy or the secrecy kills . . . discipleship."[1] If you want to be a secret disciple, the best you can hope for is what Nicodemus achieved. He became the caretaker of Jesus's corpse.

Many so-called disciples are like Nicodemus. They imagine that Jesus is fortunate to have them. After all, they can promote his agenda, even if they do it on their own terms. They want the benefits of being a disciple without the cost. Based on this encounter, that doesn't end well. Jesus's unparalleled sacrifice demands unequivocal devotion. The verse that follows on the heels of this meeting has rightly become the most famous statement in all of Scripture: "God so loved the world, that he gave his only Son, that whoever believes in him should not perish but have eternal life" (John 3:16).

The lesson is clear. In the kingdom of God, one's clout is irrelevant; one's faith is everything. Being good enough just isn't good enough. Jesus isn't impressed with how far you can puff out your chest; he's impressed with the heart inside the chest. Furthermore, he doesn't need your status or influence to further his agenda. So, whom does Jesus prioritize? We'll have to await the next chapter for the full answer. For now, we can say with certainty, it is *not* Nicodemus or anyone else who stands on the pedestal of his own credentials. There is nothing wrong with having influence, moral clout, or positions of authority. They just don't provide a foundation for authentic discipleship. Jesus deserves more. Jesus demands more.

Key Points

- Nicodemus, despite all his credentials, failed to follow Jesus.

- Jesus demands that we all be born again, humbling ourselves and putting our faith in him.

- Trying to be a disciple secretly doesn't work in relation to Jesus. His sacrifice demands our total allegiance.

This Week

❏ **Day 1 (Eyes):** Before reading the essay, had you ever thought that some people had a higher standing with God because of a title, a career in ministry, or some other public recognition?

❏ **Day 2 (Ears):** Read 1 Samuel 10:9–27 and 13:1–15. What lessons do you glean from the life of Saul that are similar to what you learned from the life of Nicodemus?

❏ **Day 3 (Heart):** Meditate on Acts 10:34; Romans 2:11; James 2:1–7. Who are God's favorites?

❏ **Day 4 (Voice):** Discussion:

- When you think of the term *religious person,* who comes to mind? You can either describe a specific person or list the characteristics of such a person.
- What does it mean to be born again? We're asking about the personal experience, not the theological definition.
- What keeps people in general or you specifically from being born again?
- In what areas of your life have you tried to be a secret disciple? Have you ever been embarrassed about your faith or afraid to share it openly?

❏ **Day 5 (Hands):** Do one simple thing or have one simple conversation to make your commitment to Jesus more visible. It could be placing a Bible on your desk, using a scripture as a screen saver, or saying to a friend, "Have I ever told you why I go to church?"

Further Resources: Quest52.org/12

13

Who Are Social Influencers for Jesus? Part 2

Biblical Concept: Influence
Read: John 4:4–42

In the previous lesson, we saw Nicodemus come to Jesus, only to be rebuffed. He held such promise as a social influencer. Yet Jesus showed no interest in courting his favor. In this lesson, we swing the pendulum to the complete opposite side. There was a woman at a well whom no one was interested in *except* Jesus. She was the kind of person you screen when she pops up on your phone. She was a social pariah who wound up being Jesus's greatest advocate! It's worth leaning in to eavesdrop on their conversation.

A Well, a Woman, and Water

Our story begins with a simple statement: "He *had* to pass through Samaria" (John 4:4). Did he really? Actually, no. Many Jews preferred to go down to the Jordan River and follow it up to Galilee. Not only would this provide a constant source of water; it also avoided the racial tensions, which were rife between the Jews and the Samaritans. Jesus was compelled not by geography but by destiny. There was one lone woman he needed to talk to. That is stunning given the cultural separation of men and women, as well as the ethnic tension between Jews and Samaritans.

Samaritans were descendants of the ten northern tribes, the remnant left after the elites were carted off to captivity in Assyria. To repopulate the area, the Assyrians imported other people groups, who then intermarried with the locals. Consequently, the Samaritans were seen as polluted by their Jewish cousins. Furthermore, because they had an alternative temple on Mount Gerizim and an altered version of the Old Testament, they were rejected by "pure" Israelites.

"He came to a town of Samaria called Sychar, near the field that Jacob had given to his son Joseph. Jacob's well was there; so Jesus, wearied as he was from his journey, was sitting beside the well. It was about the sixth hour" (verses 5–6). Here's what we know: this historic well was about two thousand years old, one hundred feet deep, and four feet across. We also know that it was noon—that is, the sixth hour after sunrise. So, why was this woman coming to the well in the middle of the day rather than in the early morning with all the other women of the village? It becomes clear when we learn she had had five husbands and now had a live-in lover. She was the scandal of the community, used by men and rejected by women. Because the well was so small in circumference, there was nowhere to hide. Jesus was right there! She couldn't avoid him, especially when he broke the silence, saying, "Give me a drink" (verse 7).

She was taken aback and asked, "How is it that you, a Jew, ask for a drink from me, a woman of Samaria?" John explained for the reader, "Jews have no dealings with Samaritans" (verse 9). The phrase literally means they "don't use the same [vessel]." This was the cultural equivalent of segregated drinking fountains. Jesus, undeterred, challenged her: "If you knew the gift of God, and who it is that is saying to you, 'Give me a drink,' you would have asked him, and he would have given you living water" (verse 10). Game on! You may not like this woman's biography, but you have to respect her chutzpah. She retorted, "Really? Where do you think you can get living water? You don't even have anything to draw the water with. Do you really think you are greater than our father Jacob?"

Lady, you have no idea! Not only is Jesus greater than Jacob; he's also the source of living water springing up to eternal life! Again, you have to appreciate her honesty: "Well, prove it!" Jesus replied, "Sure . . . as soon as you call your husband." Uh-oh. She didn't have a husband. Up to this point, she had been pretty talkative. In verse 9, she used eleven words (in Greek). In verses 11–12, it increased to forty-two, and in verse 15, she used thirteen words. But when Jesus told her to bring her husband, she used only three words: "Husband don't have."

"That's right," Jesus revealed. "You have had five, and the man you are with now is not your husband." He now had her undivided attention. "Sir," she said, "I perceive that you are a prophet" (verse 19). She was uncomfortable, so she tried to change the subject. Like so many when confronted with Christ, she threw up a theological smoke screen to avoid a decision. She questioned Jesus about the correct location of the temple. The Jews, of course, insisted it was Jerusalem (2 Chronicles 3:1). The Samaritans, on the other hand, maintained it was Mount Gerizim, the very hill in whose shadow they were standing. To make matters worse, the rubble of the Samaritan temple could still be seen in Jesus's day. It had been ransacked by Jewish patriots in 128 BC under the Jewish leader John Hyrcanus. The sight was a powerfully emotive distraction.

Jesus would not be deterred. He drove the conversation back to himself, not as a narcissist but as the Savior. We would do well to follow his lead. A lot of theological questions stir the pot: Why do bad things happen to good people? Did God create the world in seven literal days? Is the Bible historically reliable? Sovereignty of God or free will? The list is long and not completely irrelevant. However, when you get Jesus right, little else matters. Until you get *him* right, nothing else matters. By the end of the conversation, the disciples had returned with lunch, stunned to see their leader interacting with the likes of this woman, who then conveniently raced off to town.

The Villain Becomes the Valiant

She left in such a hurry that she forgot her water jar. Or else she left it on purpose, giving him the drink he had asked for. Her appeal to the villagers was simple and brilliant: "Come, see a man who told me all that I ever did. Can this be the Christ?" (John 4:29). First of all, most dudes would delight in the salacious details of her biography. Second, her question, in the original language, assumed a no. We might ask it like this: "He couldn't be the Messiah, could he?" Knowing her reputation, the locals were likely to disagree with her, regardless of what she said. One wonders whether some of her husbands abandoned her because she constantly outwitted them.

The villagers went out in droves to see the man at the well. As they were coming across the fields, their white robes blowing in the breeze, they had the appearance of a whitened wheat field ready for harvest. This picture led Jesus to say to the disciples, "Do you not say, 'There are yet four months, then comes the harvest'? Look, I tell you, lift up your eyes, and see that the fields are white for harvest" (verse 35).

When they came to Jesus, he taught them about himself. He broke the barriers of the Samaritans and defied the expectations of his followers. He saw the Samaritans as children of God, not enemies of Israel. Perhaps that was why they were so open to his teaching as well as his person. His main message was not global peace, though it would lead to that. It wasn't inclusion, though it implied that. It wasn't moral righteousness, though he modeled that. It wasn't the theology of God, though he embodied that. His message was simply and exclusively this: I am the promised Messiah.

The Samaritans probably couldn't believe that they believed. They wanted more and begged him to stay, which he did but only for two days. In the end, they were convinced that the Samaritan woman was correct. They said to her, "It is no longer because of what you said that we believe, for we have heard for ourselves, and we know that this is indeed the Savior of the world" (verse 42). Savior of the world. Believe it or not, that was the caption on many a coin in the Roman world. It was a designation for the emperor. That puts this confession atop any acclamation Jesus had heard so far, and it came from people far from the center of Judaism.

So, here is the point. If you compare Nicodemus with the woman at the well, your evaluation of social influencers will be turned on its head. By anyone's estimation, Nicodemus was the one who could move the needle for the movement, but he never did. She, on the other hand, went down in biblical history as the single most effective evangelist in all the Gospels. Nicodemus was a Jew; she was a Samaritan. He was a man; she was a woman. He was a famous Sanhedrin lawyer; she was an infamous home-wrecker. *Yet* Nicodemus came to Jesus in the darkness of night, while Jesus "needed" to go to the woman in the noonday light. Nicodemus was commanded to be reborn in water; she was offered living water. Nicodemus's countrymen crucified Jesus; hers hailed him as the Savior of the world.

We are now prepared to answer this question: Who are social influencers for Jesus? You tell me.

Key Points

- The Samaritan woman was the least likely person to influence others for Jesus, yet she did. You can too.

- Jesus didn't avoid her past or judge her for it. Rather, he allowed her to use all of who she was to influence others to come to him.

- The discussion Jesus wants to have with us and wants us to have with others is not about theology but about his identity as the Savior of the world.

This Week

❏ **Day 1 (Eyes):** After reading the essay, what influence do you think you could have for Jesus?

❏ **Day 2 (Ears):** Second Kings 6:24–7:20 tells another incredible story that happened in Samaria. Can you find parallel spiritual lessons between the two stories?

❏ **Day 3 (Heart):** Meditate on Romans 1:16; 1 Corinthians 1:20; 3:18–19.

❏ **Day 4 (Voice):** Discussion:

- Other than Jesus, who would you say are some of the most influential people in history?
- Have you ever known someone who was severely overrated or underrated? Perhaps an athlete, businessperson, or leader?
- What was it about Nicodemus that made him so ineffective as a follower? In contrast, why was the Samaritan woman so influential?
- In your own estimation, what do you think would allow you to be more influential for Jesus?

❏ **Day 5 (Hands):** On a three-by-five card, write down one person you want to influence for Jesus and one specific step you could encourage that person to take toward him.

Further Resources: Quest52.org/13

Section 2

The Power of Jesus

Next we will look at Jesus's miracles. In one sense, they are **wonders** that make us say, "Wow, look at how powerful he is." In another sense, they are **signs** that make us say, "Ahhh, so that is what he wants us to do." And then there are **claims** to which we say, "Oh snap, that's gonna ruffle some feathers." His miracles point to both his identity and his ultimate purpose.

> **Wonders:** chapters 14–17
> **Signs:** chapters 18–22
> **Claims:** chapters 23–26

14

Is Christianity Boring?

Biblical Concept: Celebration
Read: John 2:1–12

For many reasons, I'm grateful for the church I grew up in. There I found my faith, went on my first mission trip, and got my first kiss (our Sunday school teacher wondered where we were). However, the music back then was out of a songbook called a hymnal and was accompanied by the drone of an organ. For a teenager in the seventies, that was akin to the sound of a cat in heat. During communion, soft music would play as the trays were passed and we bowed our heads to "pray," otherwise known as taking a catnap. The preacher spoke for approximately forty-five minutes, but it felt like a day and a half. The wooden pews, I'm convinced, were sadistically designed to keep people awake. That was church as I knew it. So don't hate me for asking, "Is Christianity boring?" It may seem so from our cultural expressions. However, go back in time, walk with Jesus just one kilometer, and you may answer differently. Here is an example.

The Wedding at Cana

Our weddings tend to be less than an hour, and if you're lucky, there's a meal at the reception to go with the cake and butter mints. For the Jews, however, it was a full-throttle affair, lasting up to seven days. The difference is that a Jewish marriage was an alliance between two families, not merely two moonstruck lovers. The groom was showing his ability to provide for the bride's family. If he failed at the wedding, it was a litigable offense since he didn't meet his legal obligation created by the dowry. There was a lot of social freight behind the celebration.

At this particular wedding, the family had enlisted Jesus's mother, Mary, to supervise the food services in Cana, which was about six miles from Nazareth. Both were small villages, and the families were deeply connected. It was not just an honor for Mary; it was a significant obligation. She had to make sure the food and wine would stretch across the entire celebration. If she pulled it off, her clout would rise. This was even more important since it appears that Joseph was deceased. He's never mentioned in the present tense after Jesus turned twelve. If that was the case, Mary, as a widow, had scant opportunities to improve her social standing. This was a chance she couldn't afford to botch.

Jesus had been invited as well. His presence was a big deal for the families. He was a celebrity. For the past several months, he had been kicking off his career down south, making a name for himself and attracting followers. Jesus's entourage added clout to the wedding. It also, however, put pressure on the dwindling supply of food and wine. It may have been this thirsty band that sucked the wine cellar dry.

Mary had a conundrum. She called on Jesus for the solution. It's doubtful that she expected him to do a miracle. Rather, she likely expected him to dip into the apostolic purse and fork over the funds to refill the supply of wine. Just so we're clear, a mother *does* have the right to expect as much, particularly a mother in the Middle East. The power that women wielded over their children was more considerable than what we expect in the West. In fact, she didn't even need to ask. She could merely state the problem and expect Jesus to step up. So she said, "They have no wine" (John 2:3). She expected him to say something like "No problem, Mom. Let me take care of that."

His response must have taken her breath away: "Woman, what does this have to do with me? My hour has not yet come" (verse 4). Notice first that Jesus didn't use a term of endearment like "Mother" or say "Yes ma'am." He curtly said, "Woman." That wasn't an insult back then, but it was far from an endearing appellation. Second, he asked why she would involve him in her affair. She must have thought, *Well, because I'm your mother!* But more was at stake here than family relationships. You see, at the very time God was calling him to his messianic career, she was calling him to family affairs. Since she was a widow, the eldest son should have attended to her needs and provided her with protection. Culturally she had every right to expect him to help her.

Now Jesus had a problem: take care of his earthly mother or follow his heavenly Father? Perhaps that's why Jesus added, "My hour has not yet come." Throughout John's gospel, *hour* is clearly a metaphor for Jesus's suffering (4:21, 23; 5:25, 28; 7:30; 8:20; 12:23, 27; 13:1; 16:25, 32; 17:1). Exactly why Jesus would reference his ultimate end, then go ahead and do a miracle is unclear. However, it was a clear reference to God's call over and above Mary's request. So, as only Jesus could do, he helped his earthly mother *while* following his heavenly Father. His message was crystal clear. It was time for Jesus to break the boundaries of hearth and home. His career as the Messiah had now begun, and there was no turning back.

The Meaning of the Miracle

Mary somehow sensed that Jesus was about to do something big. She ordered the servants to do exactly as he asked. They did. There were six stone jars for ritual washing. Each could hold twenty to thirty gallons. You do the math. That's 120 to 180 gallons. They filled the jars to the brim, then took a sample to the maître d'. He had no idea that this Mogen David had moments before been H_2O. He was astounded at the taste test: "Everyone serves the good wine first, and when people have drunk freely, then the poor wine. But you have kept the good wine until now" (John 2:10). Now, there was a wedding gift worth remembering. It was a blessing you could bathe in!

What does this miracle mean? Well, let's begin with this: John never called it a miracle; he called it a sign. Miracles make you say, "Wow." Signs make you say, "Oooooh." The water-to-wine points to something more than mere power. Just what that something is can be seen only when all the signs are laid side by side. There are seven of them, and that's significant. Seven is a sacred number in Jewish literature and lore. It's a combination of three (representing God) and four (representing humanity). When we meet seven in sacred script, we see that God was making a move among people. He was doing something with us and for us.

Furthermore, each of the seven signs of John is like a chapter in a story. The whole story is how to become a fully devoted follower of Jesus.

#	Text	Miracle	Lesson
1	2:1–11	Water to wine	You are invited to a celebration.
2	4:46–54	Official's son	You have to come with faith.
3	5:1–15	Lame man	You come to Jesus not for healing but for him.
4	6:1–15	Feeding five thousand	Jesus is your sustenance.
5	6:16–21	Walking on water	Jesus overcomes chaos.
6	9:1–41	Blind man	Jesus gives you sight.
7	11:1–44	Lazarus	Jesus restores your life.

It begins with an invitation to a wedding. The next step is to come with faith. Not merely faith that Jesus can help, but faith in Jesus himself (that's sign 3). If we do that, Jesus will become the very sustenance we feed on for spiritual growth. Will following Jesus entail troubled waters? Most certainly. But he will come to us as master of the waves, able to conquer any chaos. Consequently, he can help blind eyes see as never before. Ultimately, he will raise us up from the dead. That is the story Jesus wants to write into my life and yours.

In the conclusion of John's gospel, he wrote, "Jesus did many other signs in the presence of the disciples, which are not written in this book; but these are written so that you may believe that Jesus is the Christ, the Son of God, and that by believing you may have life in his name" (20:30–31).

It all begins with a wedding. And that is how it ends as well. You're called to a lifelong celebration of a lifelong commitment. Jesus is the groom; the church is the bride (Ephesians 5:22–33). When he returns, our first act in eternity will be to participate in the wedding supper of the Lamb:

I heard what seemed to be the voice of a great multitude, like the roar of many waters and like the sound of mighty peals of thunder, crying out,

"Hallelujah!
For the Lord our God
    the Almighty reigns.
Let us rejoice and exult
    and give him the glory,
for the marriage of the Lamb has come,
    and his Bride has made herself ready;
it was granted her to clothe herself with fine linen, bright and pure"—

for the fine linen is the righteous deeds of the saints.

And the angel said to me, "Write this: Blessed are those who are invited to the marriage supper of the Lamb." And he said to me, "These are the true words of God." (Revelation 19:6–9)

So, let me ask again, "Is Christianity boring?" Hardly.

Key Points

- The wedding at Cana demonstrated Jesus's intention to go well beyond the borders of his own family.

- All the signs of John point to our own journey with Jesus.

- Our journey with Jesus begins and ends with a wedding.

This Week

❑ **Day 1 (Eyes):** After reading the essay, consider this question: Have you seen church more as a celebration or as an obligation?

❑ **Day 2 (Ears):** The Song of Solomon is a romantic love poem. Many church fathers, however, read it as an allegory of Christ and the church. Try that. Read Song of Solomon 5, and see what metaphors you could relate to your relationship with Christ.

❑ **Day 3 (Heart):** Meditate on 2 Corinthians 11:2; Ephesians 5:23; Revelation 21:9.

❑ **Day 4 (Voice):** Discussion:

- Share your earliest memories of church. Your favorite memory in church. One time you got in trouble in church.
- If there are married couples, have them share when and where they got married and what their fondest memories are of their weddings. Have singles share what they imagine their weddings will be like.
- Why do you think many people see church as boring or irrelevant?
- What could we do to change the perception that church is irrelevant or boring?

❑ **Day 5 (Hands):** Ask a friend who doesn't go to church what would make it a place she might like to go.

Further Resources: Quest52.org/14

15

Can Jesus Turn My Storm into a Story?

Biblical Concept: Chaos
Read: Mark 4:35–5:20 with Matthew 8:23–34;
Luke 8:22–39

Today is tough for me. Our world is living through a pandemic, and our nation is experiencing social upheaval. On top of all that, I just received some tragic personal news. As I tip-tapped on the keyboard, a dear friend of mine texted that he has stage IV cancer and won't seek treatment during his remaining two weeks. Don't feel sorry for me. You have your own story, and most are more serious than mine. The question is whether Jesus can help us in the middle of our storms. This story is all about the "Yes."

Fear of a Storm

This is the second-longest recorded day in Jesus's life.

- After teaching all day, Jesus set out across the lake with his disciples, right into the teeth of a storm. Jesus stood up in the boat, and the storm stood still.

- On the other side, they met a demoniac near a village called Gerasa. Jesus cast the demons into a herd of pigs.

- The following morning, they returned to Capernaum to find a bleeding woman and a dying girl.

Each event builds on a single theme: fear. The disciples were afraid in the storm. The Gerasenes were afraid of Jesus. The bleeding woman was afraid of being found out. Jairus was afraid his daughter would die. Only the Gerasenes had it right. Jesus is the only one we need fear, for he can calm our storms, cast out our demons, heal our diseases, and rescue us from death. Once we fear Jesus, we can be fearless. Our focus here will be on the middle of the story—the storm and the demoniac.

Jesus said, "Let us go across to the other side" (Mark 4:35). It's not that far—six miles max. However, the other side was a world apart. That's where the Gentiles lived. This is significant. Jesus was going beyond the boundaries of Israel. He had already reached out to those on the perimeter: lepers, lame, deaf, as well as women, children, and tax collectors. He now included foreigners because the kingdom is for all people, not just the "right" people. To quote Jesus, "Those who are well have no need of a physician, but those who are sick. I came not to call the righteous, but sinners" (2:17).

While en route, "a great windstorm arose, and the waves were breaking into the boat, so that the boat was already filling" (4:37). Technically, the storm did not rise up but crashed down. The lake known as the Sea of Galilee sits 692 feet *below* sea level with a rim of hills all around about two thousand feet above the waterline. When the weather patterns move in from the Mediterranean, they sweep down the hills and crash into the "bowl" with incredible speed and force. Peter and company knew them well. That kind of squall had sunk many a ship, reducing fishermen like Peter to poverty. They were afraid for their lives and livelihood. Meanwhile, Jesus was fast asleep in the back of the boat. This perturbed them. "Teacher, do you not care that we are perishing?" they asked (verse 38),

waking Jesus, ostensibly to have him help bail out the boat. He had a better idea.

What Jesus did next was ill advised. He stood up in the boat and rebuked the wind and waves. Of course, if you can walk on water, standing
in a rowboat is less risky. Jesus's command could be translated, "Shut up!"
Interestingly, these were the very words Jesus used to cast out a demon
earlier (1:25). Both the demon and the wind were under his control. It is
one thing to heal someone's sickness. It's quite another to command natural forces and spiritual powers. The wind and waves immediately obeyed.
All creation is under him as Creator (John 1:1–4; Colossians 1:16–17;
Hebrews 1:3).

The boys in the boat were dumbfounded. So was Jesus. He couldn't
believe their unbelief and said as much: "Why are you so afraid? Have you
still no faith?" (Mark 4:40). The word Jesus used for "afraid" was not the
raw word for "terror" but the word for "cowardly." One of the few things
that truly shocked Jesus was people's persistent unbelief (7:18; 8:17–18, 21,
32–33; 9:19). The disciples' cowardice turned to terror when they began
to understand whose presence they were in. Though they had followed
him for the better part of a year, they asked, "Who then is this, that even
the wind and the sea obey him?" (4:41). Fear of Jesus is an indication that
you've caught a glimpse of his true identity.

Fear of a Savior

They were already freaked out over the storm, but it was about to get
worse. It was the middle of the night. They were cold, wet, and spooked.
As they disembarked from the boat at the base of a cliff, a demoniac came
bounding down the cliff from a cemetery. He was a well-known local who
terrorized the villagers. He was homicidal, suicidal, buck naked, and very
loud. He was also so freakishly strong that chains couldn't contain him.
On the plateau high above stood a few spectators. They were the herdsmen on night watch. This was the most excitement they could remember.

Peering over the ledge, they eagerly anticipated the beating this band of Jewish boys was about to receive.

To their amazement, the demoniac came to a screeching halt at the feet of Jesus. He cried, "What have you to do with me, Jesus, Son of the Most High God? I adjure you by God, do not torment me" (Mark 5:7). "Most High God" was a surprisingly kosher title for a demoniac to use. It was a title for Yahweh in the Old Testament (Genesis 14:18–20; Isaiah 14:14; Daniel 3:26). This demoniac had a higher view of Jesus than the disciples had.

He knew Jesus had the authority to order the demons out. The demons begged Jesus to send them into the pigs. When he did, they forthwith destroyed their new hosts. Why? Because demons are naturally destructive. Satan's natural bent is to "steal and kill and destroy" (John 10:10). The demon who had answered Jesus identified himself as "Legion," a term describing six thousand soldiers. If we took that as an exact number (not that we should), it would put three demons in each pig.

The herdsmen raced off to town in the middle of the night. This was an emergency. A herd that large represented the major economy of the entire area. They were wiped out! Some may object to Jesus destroying private property, but let's be realistic. Jesus is Jewish; they were pigs. Humans always trump unclean animals. When the villagers arrived, the local laughingstock was clothed and in his right mind. Where did he get the clothes? Our best guess, knowing Jesus, is that he gave the man the tunic off his own back.

The locals began to plead with Jesus, "Please go away. You frighten us." Note: Jesus is respectful. He will not force himself on any of us. If you demand that he leave, he probably will. Note, too, that when we meet Jesus, we have only two options: kneel before him as Lord or utterly reject him as an imposition. He is not one we can casually ignore. He will be above all or nothing at all.

Faith of a Survivor

Meanwhile, the former demoniac begged Jesus to let him follow. Jesus said, "No." This was stunning. After all, the man had a bad reputation in town, and he had just been responsible for an economic tsunami. What future did he have at home? Jesus told him, "Go home to your friends and tell them how much the Lord has done for you, and how he has had mercy on you" (Mark 5:19). The man did, but he didn't stop at home. He eventually shared his story throughout the entire Decapolis, a league of ten cities in the region. Not only is that commendable; it also had an extraordinary impact. The next time Jesus entered the area, he would feed four thousand (8:1–9). Where did they come from? Our best guess is one lone ex-demoniac shared his story to great effect.

Many of us can relate to the demoniac. After the addiction, after the shame, after the pain, the residual rejection can be worse than the storm itself. Our impulse is to run far from home to get a new start and perhaps a new identity. But Jesus had more in store for the demoniac, and he has more in store for you. Often our deepest pain becomes our highest platform. Your story may be the very thing that brings Jesus the greatest honor. Your story may turn your community's rejection into celebration.

Key Points

- In the storm, Jesus proved to be more than his disciples ever imagined. He is, in fact, Creator God, with the power to order the inanimate.

- Jesus values you above all else in his creation.

- Your story, as painful as it may be, has more potential to bring healing than your past ever had to bring destruction.

This Week

❏ **Day 1 (Eyes):** After reading the essay, think through one simple question: Are you more afraid of Jesus or the storm you face?

❏ **Day 2 (Ears):** Look at the cross-references of Psalm 2 in the margin of a study Bible to discover the three verses of Psalm 2 that are quoted in the New Testament. Each is a prophecy about Jesus. Read them in the context of each New Testament passage. What do they affirm about Jesus and his ability to take us through storms?

❏ **Day 3 (Heart):** Meditate on Ephesians 1:20–21; Colossians 2:9; Revelation 1:17–18. According to these three passages, how do people underestimate who Jesus is?

❏ **Day 4 (Voice):** Discussion:

- Share the story of someone you know whose past pain has been a great encouragement or inspiration to you.
- If you are willing, share the most difficult thing you have ever had to go through.
- What advice or encouragement would you give to the ex-demoniac between when Jesus left in the boat and when he returned home to share his experience?
- Which piece of advice that you just heard do you need to implement to share your story more broadly?

❏ **Day 5 (Hands):** Do this week what Jesus told the ex-demoniac to do: "Go home to your friends and tell them how much the Lord has done for you, and how he has had mercy on you" (Mark 5:19).

Further Resources: Quest52.org/15

16

Can Jesus Provide
for My Needs?

Biblical Concept: Provision
Read: Mark 6:31–52 with Matthew 14:13–33;
Luke 9:10–17; John 6:1–21

Have you ever said, "I wish there were more hours in the day"? Not me, man. I almost always fall into bed beat. You probably do as well, but have you ever been so busy you forgot to eat? That's where I draw the line! In this story, Jesus crossed that line: "They had no leisure even to eat" (Mark 6:31). The apostles had recently returned from their first solo preaching tour (Mark 6:30; Luke 9:10). They excitedly reported how they had cast out demons and preached the gospel. At the same time, a delegation came to Jesus with the sad news of the execution of John the Baptist, Jesus's forerunner and friend (Matthew 14:12; Mark 6:29). This was a heavy emotional blow. Jesus needed some time away with the twelve apostles to take a breath and regroup.

Jesus the Provider

They headed off to Bethsaida, an out-of-the-way village the Bible describes as "a desolate place" (Mark 6:31). But the crowds saw him get into a boat, the kind that taxied people across the lake. They raced along the shore to the next village, asking, "Is Jesus here?" The locals had not seen him that day, but they sure wanted to. So they joined the search party from dock to dock. They ran halfway around the lake—nine miles! When Jesus arrived, he was greeted by an anxious crowd five thousand strong. Well, actually, that was just the men. Counting women and children, it would likely have numbered three times that many.

There are so many things I respect about Jesus, but none more than what he did in this moment. Perhaps it's because I know how cranky I get when I'm overexposed to people's demands. Yet Jesus, in the jaws of a clamoring crowd, "had compassion on them, because they were like *sheep without a shepherd*" (verse 34). This well-worn metaphor of sheep and shepherd comes from the Old Testament. The first great shepherd was Moses, leading Israel in the desert as he had shepherded sheep for forty years before. Other leaders likewise inherited the role of shepherd over God's people (Ezekiel 34:5, 23–24). None could live up to the ideal in Psalm 23: "The LORD is my shepherd" (verse 1). That is, until Jesus arrived. "When he saw the crowds, he had compassion for them, because they were harassed and helpless, like sheep without a shepherd" (Matthew 9:36).

Jesus responded with three actions. The order is important. First, he *taught* them (Mark 6:34). Their most immediate need was not physical but spiritual. Second, he *healed* them (Matthew 14:14), which was likely their immediate concern. Third, he *fed* them, which no one expected. Though all this is literal, it's also spiritually symbolic and so significant that this is the only miracle recorded in all four Gospels prior to the Resurrection.

- The fish (*ichthus* in Greek) became a symbol of the Christian movement because each letter represented the first letter of a word in the phrase *Jesus Christ, God's Son, Savior.*

- The distribution of bread not only represents Jesus as manna (John 6:33) but also foreshadows the Eucharist Jesus would establish the night before he died.

- The twelve baskets of leftovers taken up after the meal represent the regathering of the twelve tribes of Israel.

The disciples suggested that Jesus "send them away to go into the surrounding countryside and villages and buy themselves something to eat" (Mark 6:36). This may sound compassionate, and perhaps it was. However, I know how often I try to avoid obligation out of self-preservation. The disciples were hungry and tired. Jesus, however, never missed a teachable moment: "You give them something to eat" (verse 37). Well, that's just ridiculous. Philip quickly calculated that "two hundred denarii worth of bread would not be enough for each of them to get a little" (John 6:7). That's the financial equivalent of an average person's annual salary. This had to have made Judas Iscariot, the apostolic accountant, squirm.

Peter's brother, Andrew, found a lad who was willing to share his lunch. The only thing we really know about Andrew is he was always taking someone to Jesus. He took Peter to Jesus in John 1:40–42 and a group of Greeks to him in John 12:20–22. This time, it was a kid whose mom had the foresight to send him out with a sack lunch. "There is a boy here who has five barley loaves and two fish, but what are they for so many?" (John 6:9). Undaunted, Jesus ordered the crowd to sit on the green grass. They arranged themselves in groups of hundreds and fifties. The picture Mark painted is that of a military battalion—sitting in groups as ordered troops. That is precisely the right portrait for a Messiah who was to liberate the nation and regather the twelve tribes.

Jesus, like a father, blessed the meal for this extended family. After the prayer, he passed the food. We really don't know whether Jesus reproduced a mountain of loaves in one lump sum as he said "Amen" or whether he dispensed the loaves and fish like a Vegas blackjack dealer. Either way, it got everyone's attention.

This feeding frenzy took place near Passover (indicated by the green grass), which was the Jewish equivalent to the Fourth of July. This was a politically charged event, and John's recent execution didn't help. The crowds were ready to coronate Jesus as king, even by force, and escort him to Jerusalem. Jesus, however, dismissed the crowd and ordered his disciples to get into the boat to go back across the lake. They must have been flabbergasted. They had been waiting for this moment, and Jesus killed the momentum.

Jesus the Protector

Jesus walked to the top of the mountain (actually a hill by our standards) and prayed late into the night. While he was praying, a storm accosted the little boat in the middle of the lake. The apostles were about three and a half miles out. Jesus could see them from the mountain under the full moon around Passover. They were "making headway painfully" (Mark 6:48). It was the fourth watch of the night, which is between three and six o'clock in the morning. They were wet, tired, cold, and frustrated. So Jesus walked out to them *on top of the water*! Freaky.

Mark made a strange observation: "He meant to pass by them" (verse 48). What in the world? Was he going to beat them to the other side so he could shout "Gotcha"? No, actually, this type of phrase is markedly Jewish. It is the way one would describe a theophany (that is, an appearance of God) that passed by a human observer. Mark was portraying Jesus as God on the water. That makes sense of everything that followed: "He got into the boat with them, and the wind ceased. And they were utterly astounded, for they did not understand about the loaves, but their hearts were hardened" (verses 51–52). The divine mystery invaded their space. Jesus cryptically identified himself as Yahweh when he said, "It is I" (verse 50). Translated into Hebrew, it would be pronounced "Yahweh," the great "I Am." They didn't understand, though, because their hearts were hardened. This doesn't mean they were sinful—just human. God concealed the meaning of the moment for the time being.

As readers of the story, we have the advantage of twenty-twenty hind-sight to see what they missed. The feeding of the five thousand portrays Jesus as Creator God, making something from nothing (Genesis 1:1). The walking on water portrays Jesus as the Spirit of God, hovering over the chaotic waters to bring order (verse 2). With that in mind, let's revisit the question "Can Jesus provide for my needs?" Whether it is instruction to make you mature, healing to make you secure, or feeding to help you endure, Jesus is the manna you need day by day.

The real question, I suppose, is not merely whether Jesus can provide for your needs. That seems fairly straightforward: *yes.* The real question is whether you have fed on him. Have you taken advantage of his sustenance so that you are now able to teach others, heal others, or feed others? As followers of Christ, our goal is not simply to glean from him but to make him known so others can have the spiritual resources on which we have come to depend. Our responsibility is much like Andrew's: to introduce people to Jesus. That little boy surely was aware that what he offered was insufficient to satisfy the monstrous needs of the clamoring crowd. How-ever, his radical generosity, his total sacrifice of the little he had to Jesus, was sufficient to generate a miracle so significant that all four gospel writ-ers would repeat it. No other miracle prior to the Resurrection can make such a claim.

What you have in your hand right now is enough. Give it to Jesus and he can multiply it miraculously. He never *needs* what you have, but he can always *multiply* what you offer to meet needs in a way you never imagined.

Key Points

- It is remarkable how the needs of people drove Jesus's ministry. This is a powerful model for us to follow in prioritiz-ing "sheep without a shepherd."

- The feeding of the five thousand is symbolic of Jesus's entire ministry as the Messiah, which explains why all four Gospels tell the story.

- When Jesus fed the five thousand, he demonstrated his deity as described in Genesis 1:1. When he walked on water, he demonstrated his deity as described in Genesis 1:2. He is both provider and protector.

This Week

❏ **Day 1 (Eyes):** After reading the essay, make a list of people you are responsible for in each of these categories: teaching, healing (or physical safety), feeding.

❏ **Day 2 (Ears):** Read Exodus 16, the story of manna in the wilderness. What lessons or guidelines about manna are given in Exodus 16 that you could apply to your relationship with Jesus?

❏ **Day 3 (Heart):** Meditate on Acts 20:28; 1 Peter 2:25; Revelation 7:17.

❏ Day 4 (Voice): Discussion:

- What is the busiest season you have ever been through? What sustained you through it?
- How should this teaching, healing, feeding model of Jesus's ministry inform the way you deal with people you lead?
- What individuals or groups would you describe as "sheep without a shepherd"? What could you do to lead or feed them?
- Are you spiritually hungry right now? How are you feeding on Jesus? What does he do to meet your spiritual, physical, and emotional needs?

❏ **Day 5 (Hands):** Make the time or take the opportunity this week to teach, heal, or feed someone either physically or spiritually.

Further Resources: Quest52.org/16

17

Is Jesus Really Divine?

Biblical Concept: Divinity
Read: Mark 9:2–13 with Matthew 17:1–13; Luke 9:28–36

There are watershed moments that mark the trajectory of your life. When you hear "I do" or "Guilty" or "He didn't make it," you just know that nothing will ever be quite the same. The Transfiguration is one of those moments in Jesus's life. This mountaintop revelation changed everything. Jesus could no longer be viewed simply as a good teacher. He is God's Son.

This was such an important event that it was remembered long after the Gospels. Peter, as an old man, penned these words: "We did not follow cleverly devised myths when we made known to you the power and coming of our Lord Jesus Christ, but we were eyewitnesses of his majesty. For when he received honor and glory from God the Father, and the voice was borne to him by the Majestic Glory, 'This is my beloved Son, with whom I am well pleased,' we ourselves heard this very voice borne from heaven, for we were with him on the holy mountain" (2 Peter 1:16–18). This is *big*!

Timing

The story begins six days after Peter's great confession when he affirmed Jesus as "the Christ, the Son of the living God" (Matthew 16:16). At long last, his most loyal supporters understood he was the Messiah of Israel. Unfortunately, their definition of the Messiah was deficient. You can't really blame them. Virtually every Jewish description of the Messiah portrayed him as militant. He would conquer Israel's enemies, meting out God's wrath with physical violence. That was not, however, the real role of Jesus. On the contrary, Jesus was to suffer for his enemies, not make them suffer. That's why Jesus had to clarify Peter's confession as quickly as it fell from his lips (Mark 8:31).

Only after Jesus laid down his life would God raise him up. Only after his suffering would he be exalted to the highest place. Paul got it right: "He humbled himself by becoming obedient to the point of death, even death on a cross. Therefore God has highly exalted him and bestowed on him the name that is above every name" (Philippians 2:8–9). This moment on the mountain was a glimpse into Jesus's future.

The six days are a literal reference to Peter's confession. They also have a deeper, figurative meaning. In the Bible, big things happen after six days. God completed creation in six days (Genesis 2:2). Then he rested—not because he was fatigued but because his creation would need a weekly reminder of their Creator. God embedded the need for rest and reflection in human biology. That's why he commanded Israel to celebrate Sabbath every week (Exodus 20:8–11).

It was after six days that God spoke to Moses on Mount Sinai, giving him the law. Listen to the description in light of the Transfiguration: "The glory of the Lord dwelt on Mount Sinai, and the cloud covered it six days. And on the seventh day he called to Moses out of the midst of the cloud. Now the appearance of the glory of the Lord was like a devouring fire on the top of the mountain in the sight of the people of Israel" (Exodus 24:16–17). Six days, you see, are more than mere chronology. They are shouting to the reader, *This is huge!*

The witnesses of this majestic moment are familiar: Peter, James, and John—Jesus's inner circle. Two other times Jesus singled them out to witness something special. They got to enter Jairus's house to witness the raising of his daughter (Mark 5:37). Later, they would be with Jesus in the Garden of Gethsemane just before he died (14:33). Ironically, in Gethsemane and here on the mountain, they spent much of their time asleep! Perhaps this is a subtle warning to all of us. We can easily sleep through majestic moments.

Transfiguration

The Gospels report that on the mountain Jesus was changed. The Greek word for "changed" is *metamorphoō,* from which we get our English word *metamorphosis.* That is the right word for such a radical transformation. Jesus's face shone like the sun (Matthew 17:2), and his clothes became dazzling white (Mark 9:3). This shook the drowsy disciples awake (Luke 9:32). It should shake us awake as well, for if we see Jesus unveiled, this very word, *metamorphoō,* is promised to us (Romans 12:2; 2 Corinthians 3:18). We can be transformed by the resplendent Christ.

Not only did Jesus change; he also was no longer alone. The disciples awoke to find Jesus entrenched in a conversation with Elijah and Moses. How the disciples recognized the prophets is never revealed, but their conversation certainly could have given it away. Moses was the founder of the nation of Israel, and Elijah was her greatest prophet. The two were featured in every rendition of Hebrew history. Moses, like Jesus, had a transfiguration story. After he spent time with God, his face temporarily reflected God's glory (Exodus 34:29; 2 Corinthians 3:7). When he died atop Mount Nebo, God buried him in a nearby valley (Deuteronomy 34:1, 5–6). This mysterious end to his life led one ancient Jewish writer to suggest Moses never actually died but was whisked away to heaven by God (see *The Assumption of Moses*). As for Elijah, he was ushered from earth to heaven, and his transport was a chariot of fire (2 Kings 2:11). They were the greatest miracle workers of the Old Testament, and both were predicted to return someday (Deuteronomy 18:16–18; Malachi 4:5–6).

Is it any wonder that Peter wanted to prolong the experience? "Rabbi, it is good that we are here. Let us make three tents, one for you and one for Moses and one for Elijah" (Mark 9:5). That sounds reasonable from a human perspective, but God had an utterly different evaluation. In Peter's defense, "he did not know what to say, for they were terrified" (verse 6).

A week earlier, Jesus had rebuked Peter, calling him "Satan" for trying to dissuade Jesus from the cross (Mark 8:33). This time, *God* rebuked him: "This is my beloved Son; listen to him" (9:7). That had to sting. God seldom spoke audibly during Jesus's ministry—three times to be exact: at Jesus's baptism, during the Transfiguration, and in the temple during the week of the Crucifixion (Matthew 3:17; John 12:28). It's safe to say his words were carefully chosen. Two of the three times, God referenced Psalm 2:7 ("You are my Son; today I have begotten you") combined with Isaiah 42:1 ("Behold my servant, whom I uphold, my chosen, in whom my soul delights").

What God was saying to Peter—and to us—is that no one should be compared to Jesus. As high as Peter's opinion was of Jesus, it was not nearly high enough. Peter wanted to put him on level ground with Moses and Elijah. I'm sure he thought that was outrageously complimentary. After all, Moses and Elijah were revered in Jewish literature. No one dared compare *anyone* to them—until Jesus. However, this moment reveals just how high God holds his Son. There is no person parallel to him, no position comparable to his, none who can stand in his shadow, no name that can be spoken in the same breath. This is the lesson of the Transfiguration, a watershed moment in Jesus's ministry. No more can he be called merely "Rabbi" or even "Messiah." He is God's Son, the divine sacrifice for the sins of the world.

Exodus

Moses and Elijah disappeared. The voice of God went silent. They headed down the mountain. Jesus ordered them to secrecy, not that he had to. This is not the kind of story you could really share even if you wanted to. It would make sense only after the Resurrection. They had so many questions. They didn't know what it meant that Jesus must suffer. They didn't know why Elijah had to come before the Messiah. They didn't realize John the Baptist *was* the embodiment of Elijah. And they certainly couldn't comprehend what it meant that Jesus would rise from the dead. In their theology the Messiah *could not die*! So many questions, all summarized in one word—*exodus,* which is translated "departure" (Luke 9:31), though it means so much more. Jesus fulfilled the entire narrative of Moses's Exodus. He is the Passover lamb, the shepherd of God's people, the giver of the law, the manna, the rock that provided water in the desert. All this would be fulfilled in his death and resurrection.

The Transfiguration is biblical history encapsulated in a single moment. The cloud from which God spoke not only mirrored the cloud that led the Israelites (Exodus 13:21–22) and the Shekinah glory (19:16) but also foreshadowed the future coming of Jesus (Daniel 7:13; Mark 14:62; 1 Thessalonians 4:17). The voice of God takes us back to Jesus's baptism. The six days remind us of creation and the law. The sleepy disciples point forward to Gethsemane, and the talk of the Exodus both reflects the wilderness wandering and foreshadows the Crucifixion. Jesus's transformation forecasts his resurrection; the high mountain, his ascension. If Jesus's whole life was reflected in this moment, perhaps we should reread his entire life against this backdrop: Jesus cannot be compared to the greatest heroes of the faith. He can be compared only to God himself. In a word, Jesus is divine.

Key Points

- The Transfiguration is a watershed moment of Jesus's ministry. From here on, he is God's Son, not merely Israel's Messiah.

- Peter thought he was elevating Jesus by comparing him to Moses and Elijah, but he vastly underestimated the honor God gave him.

- The Transfiguration encapsulates the major events of the Bible.

This Week

❏ **Day 1 (Eyes):** After reading the essay, consider this question: Have you underestimated Jesus's majesty or divinity?

❏ **Day 2 (Ears):** What predictions in Malachi 3–4 were fulfilled by John the Baptist and Jesus?

❏ **Day 3 (Heart):** Meditate on 2 Corinthians 3:7; Philippians 2:8–11; 2 Peter 1:16–18.

❏ **Day 4 (Voice):** Discussion:

- What are some of the popular opinions you've heard about Jesus?
- Share about a time when you helped raise someone's understanding or estimation of Jesus. What did you say or do to clarify his identity?
- How would you respond to a friend who said Jesus is a good moral teacher but he's just human?
- If a Muslim from the Middle East were to watch you for a week, what behaviors or practices would you need to alter to ensure he knew that you actually believe what you say you believe about Jesus?

❏ **Day 5 (Hands):** Identify one area of your life where your devotion to Jesus is less than your confession of Jesus. Confess this to a confidant who can hold you accountable.

Further Resources: Quest52.org/17

18

Does Jesus Care About My Pain?

Biblical Concept: Pain
Read: Mark 1:29–39 with Matthew 8:14–17; Luke 4:38–44

My daughter was probably six at the time. My wife and I went to one of those now-extinct stores where you could rent a video. We're talking the "be kind and rewind" type. As we perused the aisles, we lost track of our daughter. When we went to check out, we found her roaming the aisles, policing the videos. Any video with scantily clad women on the cover she flipped backward so the naughtiness was hidden, at least temporarily.

That is a pretty good picture of Jesus's miracles. He did not offer permanent solutions with physical healings. After all, everyone Jesus healed eventually died. But Jesus did, in the moment, flip the script of Satan. He undid the effect of sin and sickness as a promise of his permanent healing through the Cross. What my daughter did in the video store was merely a statement. What Jesus did through his healings was a prophetic promise of full and final healing. Therefore, each miracle is a window into the world to come. Mark 1:29–39 takes us back to the earliest period of Jesus's healing ministry, before the massive crowds or public confrontations. Here we get a glimpse of the pristine Jesus who took the world by storm.

Peter's Mother-in-Law

Sacred spaces tend to be stable for centuries. In the archaeological site of Capernaum, there is a beautiful fifth-century synagogue built right on top of an earlier synagogue. Chances are very high that this is the very spot where Jesus preached in the first century. About fifty yards from this synagogue stands a Catholic church. It was built in such a way that from the center you can look down through the glass floor past two thousand years into an octagonal stone structure below. It had been a first-century home that later expanded into a humble place of Christian worship. Archaeologists found Christian graffiti as well as fishhooks on the premises. This has led many (or perhaps most) to suggest that Peter lived in this very house with his wife and mother-in-law, as well as his brother, Andrew. It's a strong possibility since the house is just a few yards from the lake where he would have made his living.

While we can't prove these are the structures of this story, it sure inflames one's imagination. Even if we are off, it's not by more than thirty yards. Here we are at ground zero for Jesus's nascent campaign for the kingdom of God. We can picture Jesus worshipping in the synagogue, reading from the Torah scroll, and praying the Shema (Deuteronomy 6:4–9). After the final "Amen," they strolled back to the house, a commute of less than two minutes. Peter's mother-in-law was bedridden with a fever. The Greek word is a form of the word for *fire*. She was in trouble; one might say "a hot mess." Her symptoms may indicate malaria. Today such a sickness would be treatable. In that day, it was frequently lethal.

When Jesus was informed of her condition, he moved into action. Luke said Jesus "rebuked the fever" (4:39). That is interesting because Jesus also rebuked demons, ordering them away (verses 35, 41). He treated this sickness like any other satanic attack. He was flipping Satan's script for humanity. Jesus took her by the hand and lifted her from her sickbed. She immediately began to serve them. The word indicates that she served as a hostess at the table. In other words, not only was she healed of the fever; Jesus also removed the residual fatigue of the illness. When he heals, it is thorough!

Word Gets Out

"That evening at sundown they brought to him all who were sick or oppressed by demons" (Mark 1:32). When the sun set, the Sabbath ended. The village began to bustle. The news of Jesus's healing power spread. People from miles around began carrying cots, hobbling on crutches, running with children in their arms. The bruised, fatigued, bandaged, and beleaguered showed up at the door of Peter's humble home. With little hope, at the end of their rope, with flagging strength and mounting despair, they brought the diseased and demonized. Their frustration must have collided in the narrow street. The jostling would have drawn out groans, accusations, and even tirades from the demonized. It was a cesspool of human pain, and Jesus waded into the middle of it.

What apparently took the better part of the night is tersely stated in a single sentence: "He healed many who were sick with various diseases, and cast out many demons" (verse 34). If we are permitted some literary license, we can imagine the scene. Jesus took his time with each individual as if she were the only one there. "How long have you had this? Who brought you here? Would you like to be well? You know, God loves you, and you are immensely important to him." Each interview was intimate. Each encounter addressed the sick person's concerns. Each healing was personal as Jesus ordered sickness and demons to depart . . . and they did. Moans turned to worship, shrieks to laughter, tears of pain to tears of joy. Each healing created a new wave of celebration, undoing the work of the Evil One.

Here, in the beginning days of his ministry, there was no Pharisaic opposition. There were no theological debates, no skeptics. Just pure love, raw power, and unmitigated praise. Jesus made his way through the street, meticulously tending to each person, caring for the emotional anguish beyond the physical agony. He restored dignity as well as health, hope as well as strength. This is the image of what Eden could look like again.

In the middle of the night, when all was said and done, with the last man standing from his cot, Jesus turned to see an empty street littered with bandages, crutches, and bedpans. He knew it was a drop in a sea of pain. He knew they would all fall prey again to Satan's rude awakening. Yet for this moment, at this place, a sliver of the kingdom broke through the dark night of the soul. It was the beginning of the end of Satan's reign. This world was about to be overtaken by love.

He Took Our Infirmities

Matthew, as he so often did, appended an Old Testament passage to the scene: "This was to fulfill what was spoken by the prophet Isaiah: 'He took our illnesses and bore our diseases'" (8:17). The citation is from Isaiah 53:4. Wait a minute. Isn't that passage talking about our spiritual condition? Peter seemed to think so when he wrote his letter decades after this event: "He himself bore our sins in his body on the tree, that we might die to sin and live to righteousness. By his wounds you have been healed" (1 Peter 2:24). Which is it? Healing of our bodies or healing of our souls? The answer is . . . yes.

The healing of our bodies is a temporary gift of God. Not everyone receives healing, and everyone who receives healing eventually dies. So physical healing is a sign of something more significant, more permanent. Our ultimate healing is the restoration of our souls. That is the power of the gospel. At the same time, God is incapable of caring merely for our spiritual condition and ignoring our physical pain. The two are intertwined. Therefore, as followers of Jesus, we can never be satisfied with someone's spiritual salvation without caring for that person's physical condition. *You can't care for only part of a person!* No mother would put up with that, nor would our great God. He cares for all of you. While the curse of sin will eventually get the best of our bodies, the salvation of our souls will ultimately lead to new bodies, a new Jerusalem, a restoration of Eden. Then we will stand together as they did in the streets of Capernaum that pristine night when the kingdom came to town and the devil was put to flight.

Where Is Jesus When You Need Him?

After the very long evening, the apostles crashed. Rightly so. Early the next morning, the crowds, of course, came knocking. They wanted round two! Everyone was expectant. Jesus, however, was nowhere to be found. The search party was put on alert. He was not in the house, not in the synagogue, not in the barbershop. Finally Peter found him and with a tone of frustration said, "Everyone is looking for you" (Mark 1:37), as if Jesus were missing a great PR opportunity.

Undeterred, he simply responded to Peter, "Let us go on to the next towns, that I may preach there also, for that is why I came out" (verse 38). And that they did, throughout all Galilee, from town to town and synagogue to synagogue. This is not a throwaway statement. It is mission critical. So often we celebrate after a minor victory. Jesus modeled for us that there is no time to rest on our laurels. There are more hurting people to help, more territories to take, more video cassettes to flip over. Does Jesus care about your pain? Yes. *Yes.* And he cares about the pain of others that you may be able to alleviate. Let's get to business.

Key Points

- Jesus's miracles provided momentary relief, pointing to his ultimate agenda of the salvation of body, soul, and spirit.

- Jesus is concerned about the whole person. He desires healing in every area of your life, though your spirit is the priority, for it will result in the healing of your body and soul in eternity.

- We cannot be satisfied with momentary gains like Capernaum. There is still more territory to be taken over from Satan.

This Week

❏ **Day 1 (Eyes):** After reading the essay, consider these questions: Is your greatest need right now physical, emotional, or spiritual? How are these three interconnected?

❏ **Day 2 (Ears):** According to Leviticus 26:1–26, how does (dis) obedience to God's commands relate to disease and disasters?

❏ **Day 3 (Heart):** Meditate on Hebrews 12:12–13; James 5:16; 1 Peter 2:24. How are physical and spiritual healing connected?

❏ **Day 4 (Voice):** Discussion:
- Have you ever experienced miraculous healing or known someone who has?
- Why do you think people often prioritize their physical health over their spiritual health?
- Share about a time when caring for someone physically gave you an opportunity to care for her spiritually.
- Is there anything you have been thinking about doing to care for people's physical needs that could open opportunities to share Christ's love for them? What would you need to take your next step toward that goal?

❏ **Day 5 (Hands):** Do one thing this week to alleviate physical suffering for someone.

Further Resources: Quest52.org/18

19

Can Jesus Make Me Clean?

Biblical Concept: Purity
Read: Mark 1:40–45 with Matthew 8:2–4; Luke 5:12–16

Billy was the most irritating student I ever had. Every day when I called roll, he popped off with some irritating response, pleading for attention. One day I didn't see him in class. I'll admit that I was relieved. I got a day of reprieve. I called his name. He replied from underneath my desk, where he had been hiding. Remember, I taught college, not middle school! I rebuked him sternly. Then the Holy Spirit rebuked me: *You don't even know him.* To which I replied, *Yes, and I plan to keep it that way.* The Spirit urged me to take him to lunch to learn his story. I resisted, but it was futile. At lunch Billy mesmerized me with the story of his life. It was tragic.

Had I been through half as much as Billy, I wouldn't be half the man he is. In that moment, I realized that *people who are unlovely are unlovely not because they are unlovable but because they are unloved.* This truth is at the heart of this leper's story.

Yuck!

Today leprosy is labeled as Hansen's disease. It is a bacterial infection affecting the nervous system. Because it deadens the nerves, damage to the skin and muscles can go undetected and untreated. This often results in disfigurement, crippling of hands and feet, and even blindness. With modern medicine, Hansen's disease is treatable. In the Bible, it was not.

Hansen's disease may be a variant of the bacterial strain of biblical leprosy. However, the clinical description in Leviticus 13 indicates a disease that is far more contagious and dangerous. It was virtually untreatable outside the intervention of God himself. Verse 2 notes several manifestations of the disease: a swelling, a scab, and a bright spot. The hair on the sore spot turns white, and the infected area is subcutaneous (verse 3). Sometimes it leaves raw flesh (verse 14); at other times it results in a boil (verses 18–20). It can affect the hair of your head or beard, resulting in yellowing or thinning hair (verses 29–30). Infected spots may have reddish-white sores (verses 42–43). Worst of all, it is so contagious that it can pass from person to person on surfaces as diverse as leather and plaster walls (verses 48–49; 14:37–41).

Several notable individuals in the Old Testament got leprosy: Miriam (Numbers 12:9–14), Naaman (2 Kings 5:1–27), and Uzziah (2 Chronicles 26:17–23). In the New Testament, there are two more incidents. A group of ten lepers were healed by Jesus in Luke 17:12–19, and the unnamed leper was healed here in Mark 1:40–45. This leper was the first person to ask Jesus to heal him. He saw something in Jesus that put him in the same category as God.

The Direction of Contagion

Leprosy had the reputation not only of being highly contagious but also of being a curse from God for sin. It was a fate as bad as death. Let's eavesdrop on Aaron when his sister, Miriam, was smitten with leprosy: "Aaron said to Moses, 'Oh, my lord, do not punish us because we have done foolishly and have sinned. Let her not be as one dead, whose flesh is half eaten away" (Numbers 12:11–12). Because of her sin, she was cursed with a living death. This idea that leprosy was a curse from God carried through later Judaism and was eventually recorded in the Jewish rule book called the Mishnah, where it is likened to a plague.[1]

So, the Bible commanded that lepers be ostracized. According to Leviticus 13:45, "The leprous person who has the disease shall wear torn clothes and let the hair of his head hang loose, and he shall cover his upper lip and cry out, 'Unclean, unclean.'" This was to keep lepers in quarantine and make them cover their mouths to reduce the spread of the disease. The attitudes of ancient rabbis toward lepers have been well documented. For example, Rabbi Johanan said it was forbidden to walk within six feet of a leper. If the wind was blowing toward you, he said 150 feet would not be enough. Rabbi Meir refrained from eating eggs that came from an area where lepers lived. And Rabbi Lakish boasted that he pelted lepers with rocks to keep them at bay.[2] This was serious social distancing.

It's a fair guess that when this leper approached Jesus, most in the crowd took a step back and gasped. Jesus, to their consternation, stood his ground. The man's presence was physically hazardous and spiritually off putting. They knew he was contagious and believed he was sinful. When Jesus reached out to touch him, it must have been a slow-motion moment with Peter recoiling and yelling, "Noooooo!"

"Immediately the leprosy left him, and he was made clean" (Mark 1:42). This short statement is a fraction of a tweet. Yet it would change religion forever, setting Christianity apart from every other faith. Everyone assumed—I daresay everyone knew—contagion passed from the unclean to the clean. A woman with an issue of blood, a dead body, a leper, a Gentile. They all were pushed away because a mere touch would transgress the boundaries of purity. We see it clearly in the medical community with the use of personal protective equipment (PPE) like masks, gloves, goggles, and hazmat suits. You have to keep the germs out! Religion had always used PPE with spiritual sickness, especially when it seemed to go hand in hand with physical sickness. Religion protected its adherents with sacred spaces where sinners were not allowed. It mandated ritual purification and isolation so people could avoid socializing with sinners.

In one instant, with one touch, Jesus rewrote the laws of spiritual physics: *cleanness is more contagious than uncleanness.* Nobody believed that. *Nobody believed that!* Except Jesus. Rather than a social media tirade or a sermonic filibuster, he simply touched the outcast. The crowd gasped. But then they saw firsthand that Jesus's cleanness had passed to the leper. His skin was restored, and their view of religious purity was turned on its head. The picture Jesus painted silenced a thousand words of argument.

Cure Versus Healing

In sociological terms, there is a difference between a healing and a cure. A cure deals with the physical crisis—that is, the medical aspect of the disease. A healing, however, goes further. Most diseases have social stigma attached to them. That is especially true of skin diseases. Who of us wasn't distraught over acne at some point? Diseases like HIV, other STDs, and leprosy have freight beyond the physical sickness. It's also true of disabilities. Being blind—or worse, being deaf—separates us from loved ones. The list could go on. Sickness and disabilities separate us from those we love, a pain that can be far greater than the physical ailment.

Jesus did two things to move this from a cure to a healing. First, he touched the leper. That was undoubtedly the leper's first human contact since his diagnosis. Jesus didn't just touch him; he grabbed him. The Greek word indicates that Jesus latched on to him. Sometimes a hand on a shoulder or a hug does more for healing than the strongest medications. Notice, Jesus wasn't just concerned about a cure; he was set on healing. That included body, soul, and spirit.

The second thing Jesus did was to send him to the priest. The man was ordered to silence along the way: "Jesus sternly charged him and sent him away at once, and said to him, 'See that you say nothing to anyone, but go, show yourself to the priest and offer for your cleansing what Moses commanded, for a proof to them'" (Mark 1:43–44). Jesus knew that the proof his community needed would come from the official channel of the priest. Leviticus 14 has detailed rules concerning cleansing. Once he passed the test of the priest, he could be restored to his community. Until then, there would be speculation and rejection.

Just in case you're wondering, Jesus has not changed. You may pray for a cure. Jesus will never be satisfied with that. He longs for you to be healed and fully restored to the people you love.

What did the leper do? Exactly what Jesus told him *not* to do. He told everyone everywhere about Jesus's cure. The crowds came running from every direction. So much so that Jesus could no longer enter any town without being mobbed. Just so we are clear, I would have done the exact same thing. If Jesus had touched me like that, there is no way I would *not* have shouted it to the high heavens. At that point, I'm afraid I would have been deliberately disobedient.

Everything changes when purity is more contagious than impurity. It changes how we see Jesus. It changes how we do church, how we become clean, and how we connect with others. We are called to be the hands and feet of Jesus. This requires touching the formerly untouchables, which ultimately turns cures into healing.

Key Points

- Leprosy was a terrible disease not only because of the disfigurement and contagion but also because of the stigma that the person was a sinner cursed by God.
- Jesus proved that cleanness is more contagious than uncleanness.
- Jesus is not satisfied with a cure for your body; he wants to restore your relationships.

This Week

❏ **Day 1 (Eyes):** After reading the essay, consider this question: Are you asking God for a cure or a healing?

❏ **Day 2 (Ears):** Read the story of Naaman the leper, who was cleansed in 2 Kings 5. What lessons can you learn about your own faith and prayer life?

❏ **Day 3 (Heart):** Meditate on 2 Corinthians 7:1; Ephesians 5:26; 2 Timothy 2:21. According to these verses, what does it mean to be clean?

❏ **Day 4 (Voice):** Discussion:

- What kinds of people are avoided today because they are "unclean"?
- Whom do you know is good at including those others might avoid?
- Do you believe that cleanness is more contagious than uncleanness? Can you provide an example? What dangers might this entail?
- Is there a person you deliberately avoid that you could have a positive impact on?

❏ **Day 5 (Hands):** Go to one person you typically avoid, and ask this question: "Would you be willing to tell me your story?" If he asks for clarification, simply say you want to hear a bit about his life so you can understand him better.

Further Resources: Quest52.org/19

20

Is Jesus Impressed
with Me?

Biblical Concept: Inclusion
Read: Luke 7:1–10 with Matthew 8:5–13

Caleb came into my classroom like a whirlwind. He was clearly clever and very entertaining but weird. By *weird,* I mean awkward. I didn't know what to do with him. I liked him, but he was high maintenance. He was the kind of kid that got picked on and pushed out. Only later would I learn that his mother was a lesbian witch and his father came out of the closet when Caleb was in college. What were his chances in ministry?

It turns out his chances were excellent! By sheer tenacity and willpower, he has become a sought-after speaker, a bestselling author, a church consultant, and the single most-connected person I know. In short, he is impressive! How does that happen? We are about to find out.

The Background of the Centurion

Israel was an occupied state in Jesus's day. During his teen years, two Roman cities were built by and for these intruders. One was Zippori, just a few miles from Nazareth. It is likely that Joseph, Jesus's father, helped build that city. The other Roman city built then was Tiberias (named after their sex-addict emperor). Since it was constructed over a Jewish burial site, it was not a favorite haunt of the faithful. Most Jews would have studiously avoided going there.

These kinds of foreign outposts were popping up all too frequently. Major Roman cities like Zippori and Tiberias were galling enough, but when one of the lieutenants in the Roman army was stationed in a bastion of Judaism like Capernaum, that was riot worthy. To his credit, this lieutenant—what they called a centurion—was loved by the locals. These centurions were the backbone of the Roman army, and each led one hundred men—or a century, as the title indicates.

This was the highest rank an enlisted man could hope to achieve in the Roman military machine. Unlike our military, their officers came only from elite families. Consequently, the military careers of the rank-and-file foot soldiers ended with centurion. That put centurions between the troops and the officers. They understood both worlds and were therefore essential to the success of the army.

The centurion of Capernaum is mentioned alongside four other centurions in the New Testament: the centurion at Jesus's crucifixion, who proclaimed him to be "the Son of God" (Matthew 27:54); Cornelius, the first Gentile convert to Christianity (Acts 10); the centurion who halted Paul's scourging when he learned he was a Roman citizen (Acts 22:25–26); and Julius, who accompanied Paul to Rome, showing him honor and kindness (Acts 27). Every centurion in the New Testament is portrayed in a positive light. Think about that. They were lieutenants in the occupying enemy forces yet still respected by those whose land they were invading. That's impressive.

Centurions had learned to balance officers, enlisted men, and local populations. That was critical in places like Capernaum since they would have a skeletal crew of soldiers at their disposal. They provided a symbolic presence more than an occupying force. Because they were vastly outnumbered, they had plenty of incentive to make nice to the citizens. That explains why this centurion built the synagogue in Capernaum, employing his own troops in the construction. Foot soldiers were used for manual labor. It was common for those soldiers to help build Roman roads, some of which are still standing today as footpaths near archaeological sites. By providing free labor, they would have curried favor with the locals, especially the devout, who were the most likely to stir up a riot.

It is also possible this centurion was actually a convert to Judaism— kind of. Many Romans were attracted to the monotheism of Judaism. They admired the ethics embedded in Scripture, which were lacking in their own ancestral religion. This centurion had become a patron of the Jewish synagogue and was possibly what was called a God-fearer. These were converts to Judaism who were not ready to pull the trigger on circumcision. They believed in Yahweh and financially supported the Jews. These God-fearing benefactors were more common than one might guess. In Aphrodisias, eighty-seven miles east of Ephesus, an inscription was found describing those involved in the building of a "soup kitchen" to alleviate the suffering of poor Jews. More than 45 percent of the names were Greek God-fearers. This centurion seems to fit that category.

The Request of the Centurion

This centurion in Capernaum had a servant who fell ill. He wasn't just any servant. He was so highly valued that both Matthew (8:6) and Luke (7:7) used a word that could be translated as "child" and not merely as "servant." It was fairly common for owners to treat certain servants as family members. Many were actually adopted into the family. This poor lad was at death's door, paralyzed and suffering terribly. The centurion was at his wit's end, distraught over his potential loss.

When he heard about Jesus and his ability to heal, he called in a favor. He asked the Jewish elders to approach Jesus on his behalf and request a favor for their patron. "They pleaded with [Jesus] earnestly, saying, 'He is worthy to have you do this for him, for he loves our nation, and he is the one who built us our synagogue'" (Luke 7:4–5). Jesus agreed to go with them.

While Jesus was on his way, a second delegation was sent. This may surprise you. The envoy of the centurion asked Jesus *not* to enter his house. This was not to keep Jesus away from his family but to keep Jesus from defiling himself in the centurion's home. The centurion knew the prejudice these people had for Gentiles like him. He knew that by crossing his threshold, Jesus would be rendered unclean in the eyes of the locals. This would put Jesus in an uncomfortable position with his countrymen. "Lord, do not trouble yourself, for I am not worthy to have you come under my roof. Therefore I did not presume to come to you" (verses 6–7). It was a thoughtful gesture.

The Faith of the Centurion

Not only did the centurion understand Jesus's culture, but he also believed in Jesus's ability. Several months earlier, Jesus healed an official's son in Capernaum while he was in Cana, fourteen miles away (John 4:46–54). It is likely the centurion stationed in Capernaum would have crossed paths with the officials of this village. We can assume he was familiar with the story and this gave him hope that Jesus not only could heal but could also command the healing without jeopardizing his reputation by entering a Gentile's home.

This ability to heal at a distance was attributed only to Yahweh: "He sent out his word and healed them, and delivered them from their destruction" (Psalm 107:20). Consider the implications of this centurion appreciating the position and power Jesus held under the Emperor of the universe. As a military man, he understood what it meant to give a command. The emperor in Rome would give a command, and the generals carried it out on the battlefield far away. This chain of command went down the line to centurions, who not only received commands from above but also sent them out to the troops under their charge. He knew how this worked.

In his own words to Jesus, "Say the word, and let my servant be healed. For I too am a man set under authority, with soldiers under me:

and I say to one, 'Go,' and he goes; and to another, 'Come,' and he comes; and to my servant, 'Do this,' and he does it" (Luke 7:7–8). He assumed that this sickness was part of the unseen army of spiritual forces. He believed that Jesus had the authority to command angels and demons.

His belief in Jesus is unbelievable! No one in Judaism had come close to making this connection. In fact, his faith is so amazing that it amazed even Jesus. "When Jesus heard these things, he marveled at him, and turning to the crowd that followed him, said, 'I tell you, not even in Israel have I found such faith'" (verse 9).

Jesus was amazed. That, in itself, is amazing. Jesus was amazed only twice in all the Gospels. Here with the centurion and in Nazareth, his hometown (Mark 6:6). Oh, Jesus wasn't amazed by his neighbors' faith. No, he was amazed by their *lack* of faith. Those who knew him best had little faith. This centurion, who never actually met Jesus face to face, had faith greater than any Israelite. That's impressive.

What a paradox that those who had the Scriptures rejected Jesus (Romans 3:1–2) but an outsider accepted him. Perhaps that's why Jesus later declared that outsiders would be welcomed in and insiders kicked out (Matthew 11:21–24). Luke is preparing us for the kind of Gentile inclusion that would unfold in Acts 10–11. This is the first shock wave of a seismic shift that Christianity would introduce to the world of religion: *outsiders are often more full of faith than insiders.*

This brings us back to our initial question: Is Jesus impressed with you? If the answer is yes, it has little to do with your background, morality, or even religious devotion. It has everything to do with your belief in him. Such faith will be demonstrated by trust and loyalty.

Key Points

- Centurions in the New Testament are painted in a good light. This shows the paradox that outsiders are often more full of faith than insiders.

- The centurion amazed Jesus by his faith, which is impressive since the only other time Jesus was amazed was by his own hometown's *lack* of faith.

- If you impress Jesus, it will be by your faith in him.

This Week

❑ **Day 1 (Eyes):** After reading the essay, do you think Jesus is impressed with you?

❑ **Day 2 (Ears):** Abraham is known as the father of faith. Read his story in Genesis 12:1–9; 14:1–24. What similarities does this centurion have with Abraham?

❑ **Day 3 (Heart):** Meditate on Acts 10:1–8, 22–23, 28–29, 34–35. How does the story of Cornelius reflect Jesus's encounter with the centurion?

❑ **Day 4 (Voice):** Discussion:
- Share a story of someone who surprised you in a positive way.
- What does Hebrews 11:1 mean?
- Why do you think outsiders are often clearer about who Jesus is than insiders?
- If you are willing to be vulnerable, what is an area of your life that you really have not trusted Jesus with?

❑ **Day 5 (Hands):** Approach someone you think is far from God, and ask this question: "Hey, I was just curious—what do you believe about Jesus?"

Further Resources: Quest52.org/20

21

Can Jesus Restore My Relationships?

Biblical Concept: Restoration
Read: Mark 5:21–43 with Matthew 9:18–26; Luke 8:40–56

Bob was an older mentor and a dear friend. For years, we traveled together, dreamed together, and shared life together. Then, on one trip overseas, I hurt him unintentionally. For a long time, I didn't even know what I had done. When I discovered how I had hurt him, I tried to apologize, but it was too deep and too late. My actions had triggered pain in his past, and it was beyond my ability to fix. We lost contact. Several years later, Bob died. This is one of my greatest regrets. Broken relationships are painful. That's why Jesus's healings are designed not only to cure our ills but also to restore our relationships. This story shows Jesus's desire for relational restoration.

A Twelve-Year-Old at Death's Door

Jesus returned to Capernaum after one of the longest nights of his life. He and the boys were nearly capsized by a storm in the middle of the lake. Jesus ordered the squall into submission. Spooky! Once ashore on the far side of the lake, they were accosted by a raging demoniac. Jesus subdued the demons as easily as he had the storm. After Jesus sent them into some pigs, they rushed into the lake and drowned, along with the economy of the region. The villagers freaked out and asked Jesus to leave. He did. Now he was back home in Capernaum.

As soon as he stepped ashore, he was mobbed. Everybody wanted a piece of him, but only two broke through the crowd. The first was Jairus, a ruler of the synagogue. His only child, a daughter, was knocking at death's door. Jairus implored Jesus to heal her.

What father wouldn't ask for healing for his little girl? But the attentive reader will realize something was awry. We've already seen two local leaders receive a healing from a distance. The official in John 4 found Jesus in Cana. His son was healed in Capernaum, fourteen miles away. Later, the centurion who had built Jairus's synagogue asked Jesus to heal his servant without setting foot in his home. He didn't want Jesus to suffer the scorn of entering a Gentile's home. Very courteous. Each of those men went to Jesus for a child he cared about. Each received a healing without Jesus coming to his home. So, it raises the question, Why did Jairus beg Jesus to come to his house? Where was his faith?

To be fair, this was Jairus's only child. She was twelve years old, which was when she became a woman. At this point, it wasn't likely that Jairus and his wife were able to have any more children. Moreover, Jairus fell at Jesus's feet, showing deference, which was increasingly dangerous for a synagogue ruler as Jesus's fame spread. This kneeling was the same devotion shown by the demoniac the night before and the woman who was about to stop Jesus in his tracks.

A Bloody Interruption

As Jesus made his way to Jairus's home, the mob "thronged" him (Mark 5:24). This word means "to press hard, like a vise." This indicates the potential danger of the crowd. Everyone was jostling for position, pressing forward. Somehow a woman got right next to Jesus. She'd been bleeding for twelve years. This was, most likely, a gynecological problem. Mark noted that she "had suffered much under many physicians, and had spent all that she had, and was no better but rather grew worse" (verse 26)—a detail Luke, the physician, left out. Given the information in the text, we can assume a number of things about her life: (1) Since they lacked disposable sanitary products in those days, the whole village knew about her problem. They saw her daily ritual of going to the lake and washing out her undergarments, bedsheets, and clothes. (2) She was emaciated and weak. (3) A foul odor followed her everywhere she went. (4) She was deemed ritually unclean under Jewish law (Leviticus 15:25–33).

Although she was exhausted and dejected, she recognized that Jesus might be her last hope. She mustered all the energy she had left and muscled through the crowd. Coming up behind Jesus, she grabbed ahold of "the fringe of his garment" (Matthew 9:20). This is likely a reference to the tassels on the corner of Jesus's prayer shawl (Numbers 15:38–39; Deuteronomy 22:12). These tassels had a series of knots that functioned like rosary beads to count prayers. Superstition of the day suggested that the prayers of a powerful rabbi would leave residual "pixie dust" in the tassels. If she could touch the tassels, she could capture Jesus's healing power.

As silly as that sounds, it worked. The moment she touched his garment, "the flow of blood dried up, and she felt in her body that she was healed of her disease" (Mark 5:29). Jesus stopped in his tracks. "Who touched my garments?" he asked (verse 30). Well, lots of people; he was in a crowd! His disciples said, "You see the crowd pressing around you, and yet you say, 'Who touched me?'" (verse 31). However, he knew that someone had touched him with faith and that God had honored that person's effort with healing. As he turned to scan the crowd, it was no secret who the culprit was. She was trembling. She fell at his feet and fessed up.

Why would Jesus out her like that? Why not spare her the embarrassment? Because he knew that she needed more than a cure for her physical problem; she needed restoration of her relationships. Without a public declaration of cleansing, how could she be restored to her husband's arms, her circle of friends, her children's embraces, her worship in the synagogue? Jesus affirmed her faith: "Daughter, your faith has made you well;

go in peace, and be healed of your disease" (verse 34). This word *peace* is the equivalent of the Hebrew *shalom*. Jesus was setting her world right. She was the only person Jesus ever called "daughter." How he loved her! In the meantime, bad news came from Jairus's house.

From Death to Life

Jairus's servants interrupted the procession. The news was jarring: "Your daughter is dead" (verse 35). They were not pulling any punches. How I would have loved to be there in that moment. I can imagine Jesus putting both hands on Jairus's shoulders. Looking into his eyes, Jesus said, "Do not fear, only believe" (verse 36).

By the time they arrived at the house, the funeral was already in progress. Without embalming, you'd better hustle in the balmy weather of Galilee. Jesus stunned the crowd when he declared, "The child is not dead but sleeping" (verse 39). The crowd flipped from mourning to mocking. They might be ancients, but they weren't ignorant. They knew when a person was dead.

Taking only Peter, James, and John, Jesus entered the house. With the parents watching, Jesus took the girl by the hand and said to her in Aramaic, "*Talitha cumi,*" meaning, "Little girl, I say to you, arise" (verse 41). The girl immediately arose and started walking. (verse 42).

What Do These Two Women Mean?

These last two days had been fearful. The disciples were afraid of the storm until Jesus hushed the wind and waves. Then they were terrified of Jesus in their boat (Mark 4:40–41). The townspeople were afraid of the demoniac until Jesus healed him. Then they were afraid of Jesus (5:15). The woman with an issue of blood and Jairus were both afraid in Jesus's presence (verses 33, 36). Fear was in the air. Jesus, who can overcome our fears, is to be feared and loved and worshipped. Why? Because something bigger is at play.

These two women are deliberately linked by the number twelve. The little girl was twelve years old; the older woman had been bleeding for twelve years. Biblical numbers often have symbolic meaning. Twelve is a multiple of three and four. Three represents God; four represents humans. So 3 + 4 = 7; 3 x 4 = 12. Both numbers symbolize God doing something among humans. These two women represent God doing something *extraordinary* in their midst. Together they mean more than their individual healings.

The woman's problem was blood. It defiled her according to Jewish law. The girl's problem was death, which also defiled her according to Jewish law. Question: Where else in the Gospels are blood and death mentioned in the same story? That's right—the cross of Christ. These tandem healings, tethered by twelve years, reflect the greatest story of God restoring relationships. The woman was restored to her husband and children. The girl was restored to her parents and friends. And the cross of Jesus can do the same for us. Jesus's blood overcomes the death we face. It offers forgiveness, but that's not all. The cross of Christ restores us to our heavenly Father *and* typically brings restoration to many of our earthly relationships. These two women offer a promise of what Jesus can do for us all.

Key Points

- The bleeding woman and the dead girl had not just a physical problem but also a social problem of separation from those they cared about most.

- Twelve years tie the two women together, so we read their stories in tandem, knowing they represent God doing something extraordinary in our midst.

- Blood and death point forward to the cross of Christ, which restores our relationship with God and often with others as well.

This Week

❏ **Day 1 (Eyes):** After reading the essay, consider this question: Do you have a relationship that needs to be restored?

❏ **Day 2 (Ears):** Read the story of Ruth. How does she represent redemption and restoration?

❏ **Day 3 (Heart):** Meditate on Luke 8:2–3; Philippians 4:2–3; James 2:25. What do these verses tell us about women, redemption, and restoration in Christianity?

❏ **Day 4 (Voice):** Discussion:
- How do you help people who are separated from those they love: married couples at odds, parents and teenagers, best friends having a tiff, or business partners?
- When there is tension in relationships, do you tend to confront, ignore, or withdraw?
- What do you observe Jesus doing with this woman and with Jairus's daughter that you might use to help restore relationships in your circle of influence?
- Do you have any relationships that you need Jesus to restore?

❏ **Day 5 (Hands):** If you are experiencing any relational separation, offer that person either forgiveness or an apology or both. Share with her that this is prompted by the realization of what Jesus has done for you.

Further Resources: Quest52.org/21

22

Can Jesus Give Me Life?

Biblical Concept: Life
Read: John 11:17–44

Funerals can be awkward. We dress in black but decorate the church with bright flowers. We say the nicest things about the deceased when it's the only time telling the truth wouldn't hurt his feelings. And after the funeral, we eat a potluck meal together. Strange.

Death itself is unnatural. We have this intuitive sense that we were made for eternity. Even non-Christians generally feel an eternal impulse at funerals. God never intended for us to die. But alas, there is sin. Perhaps that's what we are feeling at funerals: the downward spiral of God's good creation because of sin. Jesus seems to feel it too. Let's watch his reaction at one of his best friends' funeral.

The Setting

John gives us a purpose statement for his entire gospel in 20:30–31: "Jesus did many other signs in the presence of the disciples, which are not written in this book; but these are written so that you may believe that Jesus is the Christ, the Son of God, and that by believing you may have *life in his name."* As we saw earlier, John offered seven signs. These aren't merely miracles of power. They're signs pointing to Jesus's ultimate purpose. Each of the seven signs shows a step in discipleship. They culminate in this story of raising Lazarus from the dead. This sign is the epicenter of John's gospel.

The story takes place in a suburb of Jerusalem, just over the Mount of Olives. Here in Bethany was the home of Lazarus and his two sisters, Mary and Martha. Because of their friendship with Jesus, they pop up periodically in the Gospels. The two sisters featured in an earlier story about a dinner party (Luke 10:38–42). John didn't recount that particular story, but he apparently assumed his readers were familiar with it: "A certain man was ill, Lazarus of Bethany, the village of Mary and her sister Martha" (11:1).

The sisters had sent a delegation to Jesus with an emergency message: Lazarus was at death's door; come quickly. They waited until Lazarus was critical, probably because they knew Jesus would be in danger if he showed himself so close to Jerusalem (8:59; 10:31). The Master sent back this message: "This illness does not lead to death. It is for the glory of God, so that the Son of God may be glorified through it" (11:4). Sounds optimistic. However, Lazarus died while the messengers were with Jesus. It appears Jesus's optimism was misplaced. Jesus finally arrived four days after Lazarus died. Since Jews believed that the spirit could linger around the corpse for up to three days, day four meant even the ghost was gone.

Mary and Martha were being consoled by some high-profile friends who made the two-mile trek from Jerusalem. The Jewish period of mourning decreased incrementally from the third day and ended after a year. Their wailing was now reduced to mourning. Martha, the ever-responsible one, went first to greet Jesus.

Jesus Ministered to Martha

Martha's greeting was intended as praise, yet it reveals a veiled complaint: "If you had been here, my brother would not have died" (verse 21). She still believed, however, that Jesus could do *something*. "Even now I know that whatever you *ask* from God, God will give you" (verse 22). This Greek word for "ask" (*aiteō*) is interesting. It's the kind of word you would use for a child asking something of a parent. Jesus, however, never used that word in reference to his own prayers. He used the word *erōtaō,* which refers to a request made to a peer. Martha's faith was great but still not nearly what Jesus deserved.

Jesus was trying to raise her level of faith: "Your brother will rise again" (verse 23). Martha replied, "I know that he will rise again in the resurrection on the last day" (verse 24). She still didn't get it. Jesus replied, "I am the resurrection and the life" (verse 25; see John 6:39–40, 44, 54). You can hardly blame Martha; no theologian of her day projected resurrection before the last day. It was an end-times event, not a present possibility. Jesus was claiming, "I am here right now, the author of life." He asked her, "Do you believe this?" (11:26). She dutifully replied, "Yes," and then made a stellar confession of Jesus as "the Christ, the Son of God" (verse 27). It's beautiful but barren. She was doing what most of us do in crisis. We say the right thing, then walk away without getting from Jesus what he has offered!

Jesus Ministered to Mary

Martha quietly informed Mary that Jesus wanted to see her. Perhaps she was respecting her privacy. Some of her guests noticed when Mary sprinted out of the house, and they charged after her to fulfill their obligation to console her. They might have been concerned for her safety in her grief-stricken state.

As soon as she saw Jesus, she fell at his feet, which was where Mary always wound up when she was with Jesus (Luke 10:39; John 12:3). She repeated the exact words her sister had said to Jesus: "If you had been here, my brother would not have died" (John 11:32). This had likely been the catchphrase in their home for the past four days.

Although their words were identical, Jesus's response to these two women could not have been more different. Martha's statement moved Jesus to a theological discussion; Mary's emotions moved him to tears. Mary's pain moved Jesus deeply. The word translated "deeply moved" (*embrimaomai*) in John 11:33 indicates he was agitated (Matthew 9:30; Mark 1:43). The word translated "troubled" (*tarassō*) is used for roiling water. It is a quaking kind of agitation. But what was it that troubled him? Perhaps it was the sadness of his friends. Perhaps it was death itself. Perhaps it was their lack of faith or his own impending passion. Likely, it was a combination of all these swirling in his soul. This much we know: Jesus does not sit dispassionately on the sidelines. He empathizes with our pain because he has walked our path. He will cry with you. He will sit with you in the pain and whisper, "I know," because he does.

Jesus asked to be shown to the tomb. Standing in front of the stone, knowing what he was about to accomplish, he did the most amazing thing. He wept. The crowds around him wailed (*klaiō*). Jesus, however, shed tears (*dakryō*). Subtly, almost imperceptibly, he wept. It is the shortest verse in the English Bible, yet few are filled with as much meaning. The moment was not lost on the crowd. They said, "See how he loved him!" (John 11:36). From there, the what-ifs began to roll: "Could not he who opened the eyes of the blind man also have kept this man from dying?" (verse 37).

Jesus Ministered to Lazarus

The standard tomb of the day was cut into limestone, approximately six feet wide by nine feet deep by six feet high with niches for as many as eight bodies. After a corpse was laid on a stone slab, a large stone would be rolled across the opening to keep out scavengers. It would take several men to roll the stone away, which is exactly what Jesus asked them to do. Martha protested, "Lord, by this time there will be an odor, for he has been dead four days" (verse 39).

Jesus was undeterred: "Did I not tell you that if you believed you would see the glory of God?" (verse 40). Staring into the darkness of the cave, Jesus lifted up his eyes and prayed. Notice in verse 42, in the prayer, he admitted that this petition was for the sake of the crowd standing there, not for him or his Father. Then he cried, "Lazarus, come out" (verse 43). *And Lazarus did!* Since he was wrapped from head to toe, the only way of escape was to hop up the stairs from the tomb. That must have been a frightful sight. Jesus even had to remind them, "Unbind him, and let him go" (verse 44). This would be hilarious if it were not for this deadly serious observation: Lazarus represents *us*.

What Jesus did for Lazarus was prophetic. It was prophetic of Jesus's own resurrection. It was prophetic of our future resurrection. *And* it was prophetic of the life Jesus wants to give us now. He has called; the tomb has been emptied; life has returned. Yet so many of us continue to be bound by unbelief. Like Martha, we think we are praising him in faith. But he has so much more in store for us if we will simply shed the grave-clothes. It is time to come out!

Key Points

- Martha and Mary both approached Jesus with the same statement yet got totally different responses. Jesus will meet you where you are and with what you need.

- Jesus knew he was going to raise Lazarus yet was swept up in the emotions of the moment. He feels what you feel and will stand with you in your grief.

- The raising of Lazarus is a sign not only of what Jesus will do for us but also of what he has already done for us spiritually.

This Week

❏ **Day 1 (Eyes):** After reading the essay, what area of your life would you like Jesus to breathe life into?

❏ **Day 2 (Ears):** Read 1 Kings 17:8–24 and 2 Kings 4:18–37. What are the similarities between Jesus raising Lazarus, and Elijah and Elisha raising someone from the dead?

❏ **Day 3 (Heart):** Meditate on 1 Corinthians 6:14; 15:20–28; 2 Corinthians 4:14. How do these promises that Jesus will raise us from the dead compare to what he did for Lazarus?

❏ **Day 4 (Voice):** Discussion:

- Do you think most people are afraid to die? How can you tell?
- Have you noticed a difference between Christian funerals and those of nonbelievers?
- Why does death feel so unnatural to us? What can you do to live without that fear of death?
- What area of your life right now could use a bit more life? How could Jesus speak life into that area?

❏ **Day 5 (Hands):** This may seem a bit morbid, but it could provide important insight. Sit down and write your own obituary. What do you want people to remember about how you lived?

Further Resources: Quest52.org/22

23

Can Jesus Forgive Me?

Biblical Concept: Forgiveness
Read: Mark 2:1–17 with Matthew 9:1–13; Luke 5:17–32

Jason is the kind of guy that others envy in the gym. He's also the leader that others respect in the boardroom. His business is booming, and he has contacts all over the world. But he also has a past. Though it made him the man he is today, it took him a while to get past his past. He struggled with accepting the forgiveness Jesus offered him. We sat together on a mountain in Israel overlooking the Sea of Galilee. He was wrestling with his personal history. I sat down next to Jason and said, "God wants you to know that you are forgiven." It's difficult to describe the power of that moment. It was as if he got his legs spiritually. He didn't just walk; he hit a dead run!

How to Break into an Ancient Home

Houses in Jesus's day, at least the wealthier ones, were typically made from mud brick. The building was constructed around a central courtyard, where most of life was lived. Without electricity, the rooms tended to be dark, drafty, and uncomfortable. Each room around the courtyard was designated for a purpose. A house would have simple sleeping quarters, workrooms, storage rooms, a kitchen, and one large banquet hall. An awning typically shaded the perimeter of the courtyard. This allowed people to be outside but sheltered from the rain and sun. There the craftsmen plied their trade, businessmen brokered deals, and women attended to their duties in clusters with servants, friends, and neighbors. It was in one such courtyard that Jesus preached that day.

Jesus had become a familiar figure in the village since making Capernaum the base of operations for his ministry. The locals knew when he came to town and flocked to hear him preach. On this occasion, the place was packed. The single entrance into the courtyard was a logjam, and crowds lined the streets, hoping to get in. There was no more standing room, so no one else was getting in.

This was unacceptable to four particular friends. Their buddy had been paralyzed and needed a healing in the worst way. They carried him on a pallet to the place Jesus was preaching, but there was just no way in, and no one ahead of them was giving way. Being resourceful fellows, they hauled the paralytic to the roof. That's a bit precarious, especially if you're the one lying paralyzed! Though we can't know exactly how they got to the roof, a likely guess is they went next door and climbed the stairs to the roof. From there, they could lay a plank from one roof to the next. This is not the kind of thing you can pull off without making a scene. The crowd in the courtyard couldn't help but notice. Jesus, standing under the awning, knew something was up by the crowd's distraction but couldn't see what these guys were up to.

They dropped down to the awning and started digging. These courtyard coverings were typically thatch—branches woven together and covered with grass and mud. Often they were built in sections. So, once they dug through the edges of the section, it would be easy enough to remove. In the meantime, Jesus would be pelted with debris while trying to make the next point in his message. Suddenly the sunlight broke through the opening, and a cot was slowly lowered. On the rectangular pallet lay a paralytic with an impish grin. His four friends lowered him right in front of Jesus, then peered over the edge to watch.

The Healing We Need Most

Often our prayers reflect the urgent, not the ultimate. Such is the case with this enacted prayer as the friends asked Jesus for a healing. They wanted their buddy to walk. Likely they also wanted to be free from the burden of caring for him. The paralytic would rather work for a living than ask for alms. It was a legitimate need but not his ultimate need.

Seeing their faith, Jesus said, "Son, your sins are forgiven" (Mark 2:5). He gave them more than they bargained for but less than they asked. Notice, it was the *friends'* faith that moved Jesus. This is not to say that the paralytic didn't also have faith. It is to say, however, that our faith in what Jesus can do for others can move him to action. They must have been both confused and delighted. In their culture, they would have assumed that sin caused sickness. His paralysis was a consequence of some secret sin. So to declare his sins forgiven would also have been a promise of healing. Even so, why didn't Jesus just heal the guy and get back to his sermon? Well, because his healing would be the more important message, not merely for the four friends but also for the skeptical scribes.

The scribes in the crowd were professional copyists of the Old Testament Scriptures. They were outraged. Their occupation made them legal experts and watchdogs for false doctrine. Luke 5:17 notes they had come from all over the country, including Jerusalem, the capital city of orthodoxy. They were there to investigate Jesus, and he had just given them something to criticize. "Why does this man speak like that? He is blaspheming! Who can forgive sins but God alone?" (Mark 2:7). To be clear, all of us can—and should—forgive others when they sin against us. Jesus, however, was not forgiving some personal offense. He was taking away this man's guilt, declaring divine deliverance from the law. Only God can do that (Isaiah 43:25).

Jesus knew what they were thinking: "Why do you question these things in your hearts? Which is easier, to say to the paralytic, 'Your sins are forgiven,' or to say, 'Rise, take up your bed and walk'?" (Mark 2:8–9). Well, both are easy to *say*. That's the point! Anyone can say, "Your sins are forgiven," but it matters only when the divine Judge declares it so. Likewise, anyone can tell a paralytic to walk, but to pull it off, you must have God's power.

So, to demonstrate his divine authority to forgive sins, he said, "Rise, pick up your bed, and go home" (verse 11). The paralytic did. The argument ended, giving way to public praise: "They were all amazed and glorified God, saying, 'We never saw anything like this!'" (verse 12).

Matthew and the New Movement

Jesus went straight from the house to the lake, where a man named Matthew (also known as Levi) was collecting duty from the local fishermen. He must have been well known but not well liked by Peter, Andrew, James, and John. A good portion of their business landed in his lap. Matthew's title, *mokhes* (tax collector), is related to the word for "oppression."[1] He was despised.

Jesus stopped in front of his booth. Peter had likely seen this before—that look in Jesus's eye. *No . . . not him!* Before Peter could object, though, Jesus called to Matthew, "Follow me" (verse 14). Peter was perturbed. A despised tax collector would hardly add clout to the movement. Then Matthew did the unthinkable. He left his tax-collection booth and followed Jesus. This is the most impressive vocational call in all the Gospels. Peter and John could always go back to fishing if this Jesus thing didn't pan out (and after the Resurrection, they did!). Matthew, on the other hand, had a line of sharks behind him, eager to take his spot. Once he walked away, there was no going back, no safety net or golden parachute.

Matthew was the least likely candidate to become an apostle. Nonetheless, of all the gospel writers, he quoted the most Old Testament Scripture. He was well versed in the prophecies. Perhaps he learned many of them from Jesus. However, it seems likely that Matthew, so despised by his contemporaries, spent his evenings pouring over Scripture. His alliance with a pagan government made him look uninterested in the Jesus movement. It turns out, however, that he was longing and searching for something more than money could buy. When Jesus offered him the opportunity, he dove in headfirst.

He threw a party that made the other disciples uncomfortable. Matthew invited all his unsavory friends. The local religious leaders stood on the perimeter, muttering critical judgment: "Why does he eat with tax collectors and sinners?" (verse 16). Birds of a feather . . . These Pharisees were the disciples' former teachers. It would have put them back on their heels when their old mentors attacked their new master. All their lives they had honored the Pharisees and dishonored the likes of Matthew. This was a massive shift that they were not quite comfortable with. Jesus intervened on their behalf: "Those who are well have no need of a physician, but those who are sick. I came not to call the righteous, but sinners" (verse 17).

This reminds me of my friend Jason. Several years ago, no one would have guessed he would be a serious Jesus follower. Today I know no one else who leverages his occupation, connections, and experience to introduce more people to Jesus. Like Matthew, he is a party waiting to happen, but his parties have a purpose—to make Jesus famous. Like the paralytic, it was his friendships that put him in a position to receive Christ's forgiveness. Here's the bottom line for you and for me: Don't assume that people far from the church are far from faith. They may be the most open to Jesus *and* his most effective ambassadors. Your friendship and faith may be what they need in order to come to Jesus.

Key Points

- Forgiveness of sins is deeper and more important than physical healing.

- Often our friends are key to leading us to Jesus, who can then fully forgive us.

- Matthew reminds us that those you never suspect may be most open to forgiveness.

This Week

❏ **Day I (Eyes):** After reading the essay, do you believe your sins have been fully forgiven?

❏ **Day 2 (Ears):** Read Psalm 32. Whom do you know who needs to hear this poem?

❏ **Day 3 (Heart):** Meditate on Romans 4:7; Ephesians 1:7; Hebrews 9:22.

❏ **Day 4 (Voice):** Discussion:

- What happens to a person physically, emotionally, and/or spiritually when she is not forgiven?
- Have you ever had a time you felt unforgiven either by God or by another person? What was that like?
- Who in your circle is most like Matthew—a person living outside of faith that you suspect may have interest in faith?
- What drew you to faith? Was it a person, an event, or an experience?

❏ **Day 5 (Hands):** Share the story of Matthew with a pre-Christian friend. Then ask, "Do you think people assume you are less interested in God than you actually are?"

Further Resources: Quest52.org/23

24

What Do We Need
from Jesus?

Biblical Concept: Loyalty
Read: John 5:1–18

One of the most painful critiques I ever received was when a mentor told me that I prioritize people I think I can get something from! It caused me to carefully evaluate my friendships and loyalties. I have done that not just with people; I've done that with Jesus. This story explains why that is such a significant problem.

The Significance of Signs

As we have already seen, signs in the book of John are significant. They are not about Jesus's raw power but about his agenda. The first sign, turning water to wine, signifies the kind of relationship he wants with us. As the second sign (John 4:46–54), Jesus healed an official's son in Capernaum *while he was in Cana* and rebuked him for lacking faith when his son was at death's door. Why? Because what the man needed was not a miracle from Jesus but Jesus himself.

Here is why that matters. When people come to Jesus without faith, they come for what they can get from him. Jesus wants us to come to *him* by faith. The prize is Jesus himself, not some temporary healing or other miracle. This is most clearly seen in the third sign, the healing of a lame man at the Pool of Bethesda.

There's a lot of similarity between this healing and the one in the previous chapter. Both were paralytics. Both were told, "Get up, take up your bed, and walk" (John 5:8; see Mark 2:11). Both times Jesus was accused of blasphemy, and both times the healing proved his true identity. This lame man, however, at the Pool of Bethesda lacked the faith that drove the other paralytic and his friends to Jesus. That's the difference. Faith is the factor that differentiates true followers of Jesus.

Sitting by the Pool

This miracle took place at one of the festivals in Jerusalem. It was probably Passover, the "Fourth of July" for Israel. That would account for why Jesus was visiting the capital. Just north of the Temple Mount (where the Church of Saint Anne is today), the locals came for water. The pool had five covered porticos for people to wait in the shade for the water to emerge. It was called Bethesda, which means "house of mercy." According to a local legend, whenever the spring bubbled up, the first one in the pool got healed. That's probably true; after all, the first one in the pool was likely the least sick. The cool, refreshing water, along with psychosomatic expectation and the rush of adrenaline, may have accounted for a "healing." However, that is hardly how God operates. Why would God heal those who needed it the least? Perhaps you have heard people say, "God helps those who help themselves." That's not biblical. Scripture shows how God helps the helpless.

One of the most helpless that day was a thirty-eight-year-old invalid. This may sound callous, but I don't like him. If I state my case clearly, neither will you. He was just one in a crowd of many sick people labeled as "blind, lame, and paralyzed" (John 5:3), which—read through Jewish eyes—describes their social standing, not just their physical condition. The blind, deaf, and lame were a category of outcasts. Why? Well, as we saw in the previous chapter, sickness was believed to be a curse for some sin. Hence, all these invalids were "bad people." This lame man sat among them, hoping for a healing.

Jesus was prepared to provide what the man had waited for all those years. "Do you want to be healed?" (verse 6). It's a simple question with an obvious answer. But listen to the man's lame answer: "Sir, I have no one to put me into the pool when the water is stirred up, and while I am going another steps down before me" (verse 7). What a whiner! No wonder he had no friends to help him into the pool. He was one of those people who aren't happy unless they have something to complain about.

If I were Jesus (and we're all glad I'm not), I would have said, "Fine. Have it your way," and walked away. Clearly, this healing did not happen because he deserved it, had faith for it, or asked for it. Jesus was making a point we had better not miss. He said, "Get up, take up your bed, and walk" (verse 8). As soon as Jesus said this, the man was healed and did as Jesus ordered. Good news, right? Not so fast! It was the Sabbath, when Jews are forbidden to work. Carrying your mat was considered work. The dude was about to get into trouble. He had no idea that Jesus had just used him to pick a fight with the Pharisees.

Trouble A-Brewin'

As the man bounded home, the Jewish leaders caught him up short: "It is the Sabbath, and it is not lawful for you to take up your bed" (verse 10). After years of a disability and social stigma, his heart had to be pounding out of his chest. This opposition from the religious elite was more than he bargained for. He was used to them looking down on him; he wasn't used to them confronting him face to face. I do kind of feel sorry for him at this point.

The roller coaster of this day took him from pretty low to very high and now was hurtling him toward the ground at breakneck speed. Even so, what he said next is inexcusable: "The man who healed me, that man said to me, 'Take up your bed, and walk'" (verse 11). He flat-out threw

Jesus under the bus! They asked him, "Who is the man who said to you, 'Take up your bed and walk'?" (verse 12). You may not believe this, but the man had no idea who Jesus was. How is that even possible? How can you be healed from a lifelong ailment and *not* find out who changed your life? He didn't know where to send the thank-you note; he didn't even know Jesus's name! Shameful.

Sabbath regulations were unbelievably fastidious. The Bible clearly says to do no work and to carry no loads. However, Jewish literature made an art form out of meticulous specifics. For example, you could carry two acorns. If you had three, you had to eat one and carry only two. If you could latch your sandal with one hand, that didn't count as work. If it took two, you had to go barefoot. Women were not allowed to look in a mirror lest they see a gray hair and pluck it out, which would, of course, constitute work. And it went on . . . and on . . . and on.

Later, Jesus ran across this ex-lame man in the temple: "See, you are well! Sin no more, that nothing worse may happen to you" (verse 14). What in the world? How was this man sinning in the temple? Remember, he hadn't been allowed into the temple court because of his stigma as a sinner. He had been lame for thirty-eight years. Since Jewish boys were not allowed into the temple court until age twelve and since the average life span was less than thirty-five, this was likely the first time he had ever been in the temple. So, how would he be sinning? He surely wasn't stealing or committing adultery. Jaywalking, perhaps? His sin was simply this: rejecting Jesus. It may not seem like much, but there is nothing that will cost you more dearly in the end. Jesus warned him fairly.

What did he do? This is tragic, unbelievable, and infuriating: "The man went away and told the Jews that it was Jesus who had healed him" (verse 15). How can this be? He took the initiative to tell the rulers the identity and whereabouts of Jesus. Why would he do that? I can think of only one reason—he wanted the praise of his leaders even though he had experienced a lifetime of rejection by them. I would not believe it had I not seen so many codependent people seeking approval from those who make their lives hell.

John explained, "This was why the Jews were persecuting Jesus, because he was doing these things on the Sabbath" (verse 16). Jesus said to them, "My Father is working until now, and I am working" (verse 17). Basically, they said to Jesus, "No man has the right to work on the Sabbath regardless of how much good he is doing." Jesus replied, "I'm no man . . . I'm God's Son." Oh boy. That was not gonna go over so well. Verse 18 spells out the consequences: "This was why the Jews were seeking all the more to kill him, because not only was he breaking the Sabbath, but he was even calling God his own Father, making himself equal with God."

That is precisely what Jesus was doing—claiming to be the Son of God. If he really is, that changes everything, especially what he expects from us. We don't come to him as a genie who can meet our needs. Rather, he expects us to come to him for him. For he is the pearl of great price, the grand prize, the Son of the living God.

Key Points

- Typically, the healing of lame men in the New Testament shows what happens spiritually when we demonstrate loyalty to Jesus. In John 5, the lame man is a warning about what happens when you lack loyalty.

- If we are healed physically but not spiritually, we wind up in a worse state.

- Our loyalty to Jesus is driven by who he is, not by what we can gain from him.

This Week

❑ **Day 1 (Eyes):** After reading the essay, do you think you've ever taken Jesus for granted?

❑ **Day 2 (Ears):** Read 1 Samuel 18:1–4; 19:1–7; 20:1–42. How did Jonathan demonstrate loyalty to David?

❑ **Day 3 (Heart):** Meditate on Romans 4:5; Colossians 1:23; 1 Thessalonians 1:3, replacing the word *faith* with *loyalty*. Read the verses again, using the word *allegiance*. Read them one more time, using the word *fidelity*. What did you hear God say to you?

❑ **Day 4 (Voice):** Discussion:

- Have you ever been used by someone as a means to an end? How did that feel?
- What comes to mind when you think of the word *loyal*? Who is the most loyal person you know?
- Whom are you most loyal to? How do you demonstrate that loyalty?
- Do you seek Jesus for who he is or for what you can get out of him? Are there areas of your spiritual life where you are focused more on yourself than on God?

❑ **Day 5 (Hands):** Make a list of your top ten prayers—what you want from God. Now go back and circle those that are more for your comfort than for his glory.

Further Resources: Quest52.org/24

25

Can Jesus Help Me See Clearly?

Biblical Concept: Clarity
Read: John 9:1–41

For twenty-two years I was a professor of New Testament at Ozark Christian College in Joplin, Missouri. It was a great season with many fond memories. However, there was one thing that galled me. Bible college students would sometimes get bitten by the theology bug. They became enamored with deep mysteries. Their debates did more to boost bloated egos than lift the lost. Our own intelligence can become an idol that attracts more attention than the God we claim to be talking about. What you are about to read is one such conversation, which took place nearly two thousand years ago.

The Southern Steps

If you go to Jerusalem today, on the south side of the Temple Mount, you can stand on the very steps where Jesus and his disciples met a blind man. The conversation began as they walked by this blind beggar. The disciples asked, "Rabbi, who sinned, this man or his parents, that he was born blind?" (John 9:2). Why in the world would they ask whether he or his parents had sinned?

One possibility is that they got bitten by the theology bug. After all, Jesus had spent the last two chapters debating the most brilliant theological minds of his day (John 7–8). This may have seemed exciting to these fishermen from the backwaters of Galilee. They asked about this idea that sickness was caused by sin (Job 4:7; 8:20). It could be one's own sin or one's parents'. *Wait a minute,* you might be thinking. *He was* born *blind. Could he sin in utero?* Yes, actually, according to some of the rabbis. They would point to Jacob, who came out of the womb clutching his brother's heel (Genesis 25:22–26). They taught that Jacob attempted to kill his brother in the womb.

Even worse, they taught that a parent's sin could result in a child's blindness. For this they referenced the Ten Commandments: "I the LORD your God am a jealous God, visiting the iniquity of the fathers on the children to the third and the fourth generation of those who hate me" (Exodus 20:5). While a father's sin can cause familial dysfunction for generations, it no longer carries a curse. Jeremiah promised a day when such generational curses would be broken: "In those days they shall no longer say: 'The fathers have eaten sour grapes, and the children's teeth are set on edge.' But everyone shall die for his own iniquity" (Jeremiah 31:29–30).

Jesus came to effect that change, and here his own disciples were, repeating this judgmental theology. Jesus set them straight: "It was not that this man sinned, or his parents, but that the works of God might be displayed in him" (John 9:3). In other words, the blindness would result in God being glorified. Jesus explained, "We must work the works of him who sent me while it is day; night is coming, when no one can work. As long as I am in the world, I am the light of the world" (verses 4–5). Unlike the theological minds of his day, Jesus bypassed the whole question of *why* in lieu of the question of *who.*

Why asks about causes and ultimately leads to frustration, debate, and judgment. *Who* asks about solutions. The right *who* brings healing. As the light of the world, Jesus is more interested in solutions than causes. If you happen to be suffering right now, *why* looms large. However, even if every why question were answered, there is no solution without the *who*. Once we have the *who* right, we, too, can be light in the world (Matthew 5:14). Our role as Christ followers is to be a solution to a problem, not an answer to a question. Let's keep in mind that we are not merely reading about a man who was healed. This story is a mirror to see ourselves and a window to see our world.

The Pool of Siloam

Jesus spit on the ground, made a little mud, and slathered it over the man's eyes. *What in the world?* People of the day believed that a person's saliva could have healing properties. In short, Jesus was healing him in a way he could understand. Then Jesus said, "Go, wash in the pool of Siloam" (John 9:7). It was just down the hill 1,600 feet (or about five football fields). This is interesting: the word *Siloam* means "sent." So the man was sent to "Sent" to wash. As the song says, "I once . . . was blind, but now I see."[1] This man represents everyone who has come to Jesus. He sends us to wash so we can see and so he can send us to share his light.

As soon as the man could see, he wanted to tell his family. So he headed home. That must have been a mind-bending journey. He saw for the first time the paths he had felt along and the people whose voices he had known. His neighbors noticed the delight on the face of this familiar figure but couldn't figure out who he was since he was out of place. They said, "Is this not the man who used to sit and beg?" (verse 8). Some said yes, but others assumed he was someone who looked similar. Imagine the formerly blind man having to defend his identity: "I am the man" (verse 9).

They were, obviously, curious about how he could see. So he told them, "The man called Jesus made mud and anointed my eyes and said to me, 'Go to Siloam and wash.' So I went and washed and received my sight" (verse 11). You would think they would have celebrated their neighbor's good fortune, but no. The very mention of Jesus set off warning sirens in their heads. Their leaders had attempted to arrest Jesus (7:30, 32, 44) and kill him (8:59). The blind man's neighbors knew the penalty of aligning with Jesus: excommunication (9:22). Their standing in the synagogue was in jeopardy, as well as their businesses, families, and community. They were ready to turn Jesus over to the authorities. So they asked the ex-blind man where to find Jesus, but how would he know? When he'd been with Jesus, he'd been blind!

The Trial

The neighbors turned him over to a group of Pharisees who interrogated him. They, too, asked him how it had happened, and he repeated the same story. These leaders were convinced Jesus was a sinner for working on the Sabbath. Yet here was a man healed of blindness. Though Satan could perform some wonders, this was beyond his ability. That was a pretty pickle for these kosher leaders: "'How can a man who is a sinner do such signs?' And there was a division among them" (verse 16).

The Pharisees even interrogated the man's parents: "Is this your son, who *you say* was born blind?" (verse 19), as if the man could have taken part in some elaborate ruse, pretending to be blind all his life to provide Jesus with a false miracle! They affirmed that he was, in fact, their son but claimed ignorance as to how his healing could have happened. They, too, were afraid of being driven out of the synagogue.

This led to a *third* interrogation. They brought the man back in and told him, "Give glory to God. We know that this man is a sinner" (verse 24). In other words, they told him to credit God alone with the miracle since Jesus was bad news. His reply shows how clearly he saw: "Whether he is a sinner I do not know. One thing I do know, that though I was blind, now I see" (verse 25). That was hard to argue with, so they recycled the original question: How were you healed? This was going nowhere, and the blind man saw it. He said, "I have told you already, and you would not listen. Why do you want to hear it again? Do you also want to become his disciples?" (verse 27). Well, that brought a quick end to the discussion. He was kicked out.

Jesus heard what had happened and went to find him. "Do you believe in the Son of Man?" he asked (verse 35). The man's answer is a model for us: "Who is he, sir, that I may believe in him?" (verse 36). In other words, "You tell me who to believe in, and I will." When someone gives you sight, you should listen to him. The man confessed, "Lord, I believe," and he worshipped Jesus (verse 38). Then when Jesus said, "For judgment I came into this world, that those who do not see may see, and those who see may become blind," some of the Pharisees overheard and said, "Are we also blind?" (verses 39–40). Jesus answered, "If you were blind, you would have no guilt; but now that you say, 'We see,' your guilt remains" (verse 41). Here is the warning for us: When you think you can see, you might be blind. When you know you are blind, Jesus can give you sight. As he said, "I am the light of the world. Whoever follows me will not walk in darkness, but will have the light of life" (8:12).

Key Points

- Spiritual arrogance will make you blind. You may sound smart but will miss Jesus.

- The healing of the blind man is a reflection of our own spiritual journeys from darkness to light.

- We don't need to prove everything we believe about Jesus so long as we are clear about this one thing: once I was blind, but now I see.

This Week

❑ **Day 1 (Eyes):** After reading the essay, consider this question: Are you in danger of spiritual arrogance?

❑ **Day 2 (Ears):** Read 2 Samuel 22. How did David use the metaphor of darkness and light to refer to God's saving work? Bonus question: Where else do we find this poem?

❑ **Day 3 (Heart):** Meditate on 2 Corinthians 4:6; Ephesians 1:18; Revelation 3:17.

❑ **Day 4 (Voice):** Discussion:

- How is darkness portrayed in movies and other popular media? What does it represent?
- What was the darkest day of your life? The brightest day of your life?
- Do people in the dark know they are in the dark? Why do people in the dark think people in the light are blind? Extra credit: Read the allegory of the cave in Plato's *Republic*.
- Do you know of areas of your life where you don't think or see clearly? How does spiritual arrogance cause blindness?

❑ **Day 5 (Hands):** Ask someone who knows you well and whom you trust as wise (whether Christian or not) what your blind spots might be.

Further Resources: Quest52.org/25

26

Can Jesus Accept Me?

Biblical Concept: Liberation
Read: Matthew 12:22–45 with Luke 11:14–32

Here is an email I got today: "I was baptized when I was thirteen and got involved with the ministry. However, by my senior year in high school, I fell off the wagon, hard. After a few years and many mistakes, I've now felt a push (quite literally, God gave me a good shove) to return to Jesus. Which brings me to my first question: How does God make things happen in my life if He allows free will? My second question is much more straight-forward and is likely part of the reason I left the church: Dinosaurs?"

Her two questions may seem unrelated, but it's actually a logical sequence. First, she fell prey to Satan's scheme of calling good evil and evil good. As she graduated high school, she was seduced into a lifestyle that was self-destructive. The world promised her liberation but gave her bondage, regret, and shame. Next, she wonders whether God can receive her back or whether she has passed a point of no return. Last, as for her question about dinosaurs, that is an intellectual smoke screen. It's a question about science contradicting the Bible, but the real question she needs to wrestle with is whether Jesus rose from the dead. Each of these three points plays out in today's text.

1. Calling Good Evil and Evil Good

Jesus's miracles were undeniable. For example, on this occasion a blind, mute, and demonized man was brought to Jesus, and Jesus healed him. The man began to speak and see. How could anyone deny that? No one could. As we noted in chapter 10, the Jewish leaders relegated the good Jesus did to the power of the devil: "It is only by Beelzebul, the prince of demons, that this man casts out demons," they said (Matthew 12:24). Beelzebul, a synonym for Satan, was an ancient Canaanite deity.

In one sense, their logic is compelling. Jesus had great power; that was undeniable. However, if that power came from the dark side rather than from God, the people should fear him even more. However, while Satan could perform a false sign to deceive people, what he wouldn't do was destroy his own work. As Jesus pointed out, "Every kingdom divided against itself is laid waste, and no city or house divided against itself will stand. And if Satan casts out Satan, he is divided against himself. How then will his kingdom stand?" (verses 25–26). In short, "If I'm destroying Satan's house from within, why worry?"

Yet there was more. Jesus reminded them their own exorcists were casting out demons. Were they also working for Satan? Hence, their own logic could be used against them. Here is the kicker: "If I'm destroying Satan's work by God's authority, then I should be feared all the more." After all, that would mean "the kingdom of God has come upon you" (verse 28). Jesus continued, "I'm breaking and entering on Satan's turf; I've bound the strong man and you stand against me. You'd better *back off*!" This was serious smack talk: "Whoever is not with me is against me, and whoever does not gather with me scatters" (verse 30). They suggested Jesus should be feared because he did the devil's bidding. Jesus said, "No, *you* should be terrified because I'm doing God's bidding and you oppose me." If Jesus could hog-tie Satan, imagine what he could do to us.

2. Can God Receive Me Back?

At some point, all of us have had the sense that we opposed God. Our sin put us on the wrong side of divine justice. Many of us have questioned whether we could even be saved after our wilderness wanderings. Divorce, addiction, deceit, abuse, sexual misconduct, greed, pride, and a litany of other experiences can leave us feeling unworthy of God. Jesus addressed this directly: "Every sin and blasphemy will be forgiven people, but the blasphemy against the Spirit will not be forgiven. And whoever speaks a word against the Son of Man will be forgiven, but whoever speaks against the Holy Spirit will not be forgiven, either in this age or in the age to come" (verses 31–32). When people are overwhelmed with guilt and shame, they sometimes ask, "Have I blasphemed the Holy Spirit? Am I unsavable?" First take a deep breath and understand this: *blaspheme* is simply a Greek word meaning "to ridicule" or "to revile." The Pharisees attributed the exorcism Jesus performed by the Spirit to the power of Satan. That's not just insulting; it's lethal! Yet why would ridiculing Jesus be forgivable but not ridiculing the Holy Spirit? Is he so much more tender? Vicious? Insecure? No, of course not.

Think of it this way. Imagine you've fallen down a cliff and caught hold of a rope draped from the top. It has several knots to help you climb back up. Each knot represents a gift from God that could save you from falling to your death. One knot is nature, through which God has revealed himself. Other knots include prophecies to warn us, miracles to get our attention, Jesus to teach truth, and the Holy Spirit to convict us. These Pharisees had rejected everything God gave that pointed to Jesus. They even rejected Jesus himself. Their last hope on this rope was the conviction of the Holy Spirit. God had no other tricks up his sleeve to convince them that Jesus was his Son and their Savior. If they rejected the Spirit, there was nothing else to hold on to. Blasphemy of the Spirit is spiritually lethal because the Spirit's conviction represents the last chance to come to God.

What about you? Have you committed the unpardonable sin? No, not if you're asking the question. You see, we never come to Christ of our own volition. If we want to be saved, it's because the Spirit is prompting us to be saved. That means he hasn't abandoned you, which means you haven't fully and finally rejected the Spirit. Anyone who *wants* to be saved has hope to be saved.

3. Smoke Screens and Resurrection

Whenever someone asks me for evidence for faith, I ask, "Do you *want* to believe?" If you want to believe, there is ample evidence. If you don't want to believe, no number of miracles will convince you. The scribes and Pharisees responded, "Teacher, we wish to see a sign from you" (verse 38). Had he not just performed an exorcism? Was that not enough? Actually, no.

This wasn't the only time the religious leaders sought a sign (John 2:18–22; Matthew 16:1–4). Each request came on the heels of clear evidence that Jesus was God's Son. Jesus offered a single sign to bolster their belief: "An evil and adulterous generation seeks for a sign, but no sign will be given to it except the sign of the prophet Jonah. For just as Jonah was three days and three nights in the belly of the great fish, so will the Son of Man be three days and three nights in the heart of the earth" (Matthew 12:39–40). The only sign Jesus offered was his own resurrection. As we will argue in a future essay, it provides a firm foundation for belief. From a historical, theological, logical, and spiritual perspective, it is well beyond sufficient for faith.

If that doesn't convince you, nothing will (Luke 16:31). If the Resurrection *does* convince you, nothing else overwhelms your faith—not dinosaurs, natural disasters, philosophies, politics, or other religions. The nasty Ninevites believed based on the preaching of Jonah. The pagan queen of Sheba traveled the world to see Solomon. Jesus is greater than Jonah and Solomon by an exponential factor. If the Ninevites and the queen of Sheba could believe because of them, how much more are we justified in our loyalty to Jesus Christ?

Going back to the exorcism, Jesus warned them about rejecting his resurrection. If you exorcise your demons but don't fill the vacuum with faith, they will return in force. I've seen this countless times. Like the person who emailed me today, people get lost along the way. They become trapped by an addiction, a habit, or a relationship. Or worse, they are seduced by success, sensation, wealth, or power. The frenzy of our flesh can numb our spirits to God's Spirit. Before you know it, you forget what it even felt like to believe in Jesus, to love his church, to hear his voice.

If you want to believe, then believe now. Don't procrastinate; don't hesitate; don't vacillate. Give your allegiance to Jesus. If you don't, you may find yourself in a wilderness wandering that takes you so far from him, you may doubt your ability to be saved (or God's willingness to save you). Or worse, you may actually pass the last knot on the rope of hope, find that the Holy Spirit has abandoned you, and forget what it's like to want to believe.

Key Points

- When you call good evil and evil good, some very bad things can happen in your life.

- The blasphemy of the Holy Spirit is the full and final rejection of the Spirit's promptings toward faith in Jesus. If you want to believe, you have not blasphemed the Spirit, for that desire comes from him.

- The resurrection of Jesus is the only sufficient evidence for faith. If you believe in that, nothing else matters; if you don't believe in that, nothing else can convince you.

This Week

❏ **Day 1 (Eyes):** After reading the essay, consider this question: Are you in bondage to guilt, shame, or doubt?

❏ **Day 2 (Ears):** Read the book of Jonah. How does his story prefigure Jesus's life, death, and resurrection?

❏ **Day 3 (Heart):** Meditate on Hebrews 6:4–6; 10:26; 1 John 5:16. What do these passages say about willful unbelief?

❏ **Day 4 (Voice):** Discussion:

- Have you ever doubted your salvation?
- Have you ever put up an intellectual smoke screen—a difficult question or an apparent contradiction in the Bible—as an excuse for unbelief? Have you had a friend do that as you were sharing your faith?
- The Pharisees had a hidden motive for not believing in Jesus. What are some hidden motives that have kept your friends or family away from faith? Why did Jesus make his own resurrection the focal point of faith? Why is it such a big deal?
- Since you want to believe, you have not blasphemed the Holy Spirit, but what are some ways you have resisted his promptings to become more obedient to Jesus?

❏ **Day 5 (Hands):** Pray this prayer for five days straight: *Holy Spirit, show me what your next step is in my faith journey.* Share with a mentor or friend the answer you perceive.

Further Resources: Quest52.org/26

Section 3

The Preaching of Jesus

Jesus's preaching was mind blowing. Crowds came to hear his **teaching**, which established new rules for ethics and worship. His **stories** (what we call parables) were subversive in that they told about the kingdom he intended to establish using the most innocent and engaging metaphors. Then there was his **training**, primarily reserved for insiders, coaching them how to carry out his mission.

Teaching: chapters 27–30
Stories: chapters 31–34
Training: chapters 35–39

27

What Did Jesus Say About Social Justice?

Biblical Concept: Justice
Read: Luke 4:16–30

I remember preparing my first sermon: Romans 12:1–2, "Have Your Minds Transformed in Christ." I was a senior in high school, and my pastor asked me to preach on Sunday evening. The audience was sparse but very encouraging. I remember thinking, *This is going to be a powerful message, and I have* so *much to say.* Well, neither turned out to be the case; it lasted seven minutes. Compare that with Jesus's first recorded message in his hometown synagogue. His was shorter than mine (or at least what we read in Luke 4:16–30 is), and his audience was *not* encouraging. After it was over, they tried to kill him. What Jesus said two thousand years ago is still earth shattering. Think of it as his initial Great Commission that set the tone for social justice in evangelism.

Homecoming

Jesus had been away from Nazareth for the better part of a year. That was unusual in a small town. Native sons tended to stay close to home. The locals surely felt a little bit proud and quite a bit jealous of Jesus. Their own local boy had made a name for himself. He had gone off and got baptized by John the Baptist. He had gathered disciples, who followed him around like he was a rabbi. He had done several miracles, cleansed the temple, and even got an interview with Nicodemus, a member of the ruling court of Israel. It was quite a résumé for a backwoods boy from the hills of Galilee.

When Jesus returned home, the folks were delighted to see him. They recounted the tales of his time in the big city, while some might also have wanted to remind him not to get too big for his britches. It's interesting that Luke was the only one to record the message. This was not because he was particularly interested in the synagogue or Jesus's hometown or Jewish culture in general. After all, he was a Greek. He had never been to Nazareth and was not particularly enamored with Jewish peculiarities. No, what attracted Luke's attention was the content of the message. This sermon set a course for the centrifugal force of the gospel to reach beyond the boundaries of Israel. It would eventually have an impact on Luke! This is the Great Commission in embryonic state.

Synagogue Sermon

Services in the synagogue had a standard form. In fact, if you visit a synagogue today, you will notice the same basic contours of the liturgy: prayers, recitations, and public reading of Scripture, followed by a message from the teacher of the day. The text for the sermon was selected by the teacher of the day, who was a trained rabbi, an elder of the community, or a prominent visitor like Jesus.

He deliberately rolled the scroll to Isaiah 61 and read verses 1–2. He picked this passage because it described his role as the Messiah:

> The Spirit of the Lord is upon me,
> > because he has anointed me
> > to proclaim good news to the poor.
> He has sent me to proclaim liberty to the captives

and recovering of sight to the blind,

to set at liberty those who are oppressed,

to proclaim the year of the Lord's favor." (Luke 4:18–19)

Jesus purposefully stopped halfway through Isaiah 61:2, leaving out "the day of vengeance of our God." He will eventually bring about that judgment, but it was too early for that.

This text includes three key claims that Jesus applied to himself. First, he was led by the Spirit of God. This was long before any Christian concept of the Holy Spirit. He was not teaching about the Trinity just yet but merely saying, "The power of God is upon me." He was claiming God's guidance and authority. Second, his ministry was about compassion, specifically for the poor, captive, blind, and oppressed. This sounds about right—Jesus showed compassion to the beleaguered. However, in Jewish literature, the Messiah was militant. The poor, captive, blind, and oppressed represent casualties of war. The Messiah was to rescue Israel, bringing comfort to God's people but wrath to their enemies. Jesus, it turns out, had a totally different take on these texts. Rather than wreaking havoc on his enemies, he suffered for them, bringing spiritual revival instead of national rescue. He would turn enemies into allies.

The final claim Jesus made was that he would bring about Jubilee (Leviticus 25:8–55). God commanded that every fiftieth year would be Jubilee. Just as the Sabbath was a day of rest each week, so Jubilee was a restoration after forty-nine years (seven times seven). All Jewish bondservants would be released. All property sold because of debt would be restored to the ancestral family. All personal debts would be forgiven. It was an economic principle of compassion that ensured natural disaster or personal catastrophe would not be visited on the next generation. It was a brilliant gift of God to the nation. Problem: it was *never* practiced. There is no evidence that Israel ever enacted this law. Jesus did, though, spiritually. Through his death for his enemies, all debts were paid.

Audience Reaction

When Jesus finished reading, he rolled up the scroll and handed it back to the attendant. All eyes were fixed on him. Jesus looked out at the audience and said, "Today this Scripture has been fulfilled in your hearing" (Luke 4:21). That's all we have recorded from his first sermon, and it caught the attention of the congregation. Can you imagine a pastor today reading a portion of Revelation and saying, "That's me! I am the fulfillment of this prophecy"?

Their reaction was about what you would expect: "All spoke well of him and marveled at the gracious words that were coming from his mouth" (verse 22). That's *not* to say they believed in him; they were merely impressed with his oratorical skill. After all, they immediately said, "Is not this Joseph's son?" (verse 22). They knew this kid as the son of a day laborer. They knew his place in their world—or so they thought. Jesus's response is telling: "Doubtless you will quote to me this proverb, "Physician, heal yourself." What we have heard you did at Capernaum, do here in your hometown as well'" (verse 23). They were impressed by his speaking but unconvinced he was their Messiah. That he would have to prove.

Jubilee Extends to Outsiders

Jesus responded to their skepticism with a proverb: "Truly, I say to you, no prophet is acceptable in his hometown" (verse 24). Mark added this interesting insight: "He could do no mighty work there, except that he laid his hands on a few sick people and healed them. And he marveled because of their unbelief" (6:5–6). Their lack of faith impeded Jesus's ministry in their midst. Because his own people rejected him, Jesus promised that Jubilee would extend to outsiders who would be more receptive to his ministry.

He gave two illustrations to prove his point. Elijah was the most famous of all the prophets of the Old Testament. He raised a widow's son in Zarephath (1 Kings 17:8–24). That was in Sidon, *outside* Israel and among their most malicious enemies. Elijah's protégé was Elisha, the only person (other than Jesus) to heal someone with leprosy. However, the man he healed, Naaman, was a military commander in Aram, *outside* Israel (2 Kings 5:1–14). Both major prophets did notable miracles for foreigners. The point Jesus was making is that God has always been interested in outsiders, and outsiders have always been interested in God. That's why Jubilee, which Israel had ignored, would be offered to those outside the perimeter of God's people. This centrifugal movement would become a pattern of Jesus's ministry that extended to the church in the book of Acts.

This story offers three major insights into the Great Commission. First, the expansion to the ends of the earth was always Jesus's intention. Gentile inclusion was never plan B. God's goal has always been global! Second, the preaching of the truth is insufficient if it isn't undergirded with compassion for the poor. There is no authentic Jesus movement without releasing captives, relieving sickness, and reducing debts. It's impossible to care for people's spiritual condition without attention to their physical difficulties. Third, the concern for social justice almost always results in social tension. The episode ends with this shocking response: "When they heard these things, all in the synagogue were filled with wrath. And they rose up and drove him out of the town and brought him to the brow of the hill on which their town was built, so that they could throw him down the cliff. But passing through their midst, he went away" (Luke 4:28–30). Going to outsiders typically creates animosity. It's part of the cost of being disciples of Jesus. If we aren't ready for that, we dare not claim to be his disciples. If our preaching isn't good news to the poor, it isn't the gospel of Jesus Christ.

Key Points

- Jesus's first recorded sermon in Nazareth was a precursor of the Great Commission.

- Jesus always intended for the good news to go to the ends of the earth.

- The gospel isn't merely the message of eternal salvation; it's social justice to the least and the lost.

This Week

❏ **Day 1 (Eyes):** After reading the essay, consider this question: Do you share Jesus's concern about social justice?

❏ **Day 2 (Ears):** Read the story of Elijah and the widow (1 Kings 17:8–24) and the story of Elisha and Naaman (2 Kings 5:1–14). How do they set an expectation of the kind of ministry Jesus would provide?

❏ **Day 3 (Heart):** Meditate on Acts 13:46; Romans 1:16; 2:9–10. Why did the good news of Jesus go to the Jews first and then to the rest of the world?

❏ **Day 4 (Voice):** Discussion:
- Have you personally experienced what Jesus said: "No prophet is acceptable in his hometown"? Why do you think that is?
- What happens when a church is concerned about spiritual needs and not social justice? What happens when a church is more concerned about social justice than spiritual needs?
- What makes a church welcoming to outsiders? What could we do better to make outsiders feel welcome?
- On a scale of 1 to 10, how well are you fulfilling these two sides of the Great Commission? What are you convicted about doing to improve in one of these areas?
    1. Sharing the truth about Jesus
    2. Showing the compassion of Jesus

❏ **Day 5 (Hands):** Schedule a time this week either to share the truth about Jesus with someone you know well or to show the compassion of Jesus to someone you don't know well.

Further Resources: Quest52.org/27

28

What Did Jesus Say About Morality?

Biblical Concept: Ethics
Read: Matthew 5:3–48 with Luke 6:20–36

Albert Einstein is the poster child for genius. People who are merely intelligent can write thick books that are too difficult for most of us to read. True genius takes the complex and puts it on a bumper sticker that the rest of us can wrap our minds around. Einstein did that with the theory of relativity: $E = mc^2$ ("energy equals mass times the speed of light squared"). That simple equation changed physics. It wasn't that physics textbooks merely added an appendix; they had to be completely rewritten.

What Einstein was to physics, Jesus was to ethics—only to a greater degree. In his most famous sermon, the Sermon on the Mount, Jesus changed religious thought five times. Think about that. What Einstein did for science once in his life, Jesus did for religion five times in a single message that takes a mere seventeen minutes to recite. Here are the five ways Jesus restructured ethics.

I. Reversal of Values

This sermon is the Magna Carta of the Christian faith. It opens with a stunning poem we call the Beatitudes (see *Core 52*, chapter 18 for more detail). These short stanzas turn the values of the world on their head. Rather than the rich, the powerful, and the healthy being blessed, it's the poor, the powerless, and the persecuted. That's striking. It shifts God's blessing from success to significance. After two thousand years of history and the rise of the field of psychology, we now see how right Jesus was.

Yet there is more. There is one beatitude—and only one—that Jesus expanded on: "Blessed are those who are persecuted for righteousness' sake, for theirs is the kingdom of heaven" (Matthew 5:10). Being persecuted is not the blessing (obviously!). Being persecuted for the right cause is. Prior to Jesus, Jews considered themselves blessed if they suffered for God's law—the Torah. For Romans it was the empire; for Greeks it was freedom; and for Egyptians it was the dynasty. Even today people consider it honorable to suffer for their nations, their religions, or their ethnic groups. Jesus, however, made it personal. Suffering for *him* was the blessing.

Jesus embodies the law of God. He is the living Torah. As he would say shortly, "Do not think that I have come to abolish the Law or the Prophets; I have not come to abolish them but to fulfill them" (verse 17). Then he concluded the sermon with the parable of the wise man building his house on the rock (7:24–27). That rock is *his words*. He is the new law, shifting morality from philosophy to identity. Jesus himself is the measure of ethics; thus, righteousness requires a relationship. This idea is unbelievably brilliant and can fit in a tweet.

But the kingdom is Christ centered, and the poor know well their need for Jesus. The single parent, the widow, the child, the drug addict—they all realize they have no hope of making it on their own in this world. Their only recourse is to turn to God and plead for help. And he answers them. The rich, on the other hand, hold on to hope in their own prowess.

They have just enough intelligence, power, or savvy to believe the myth that they can be worthy of God. It is this illusion of self-sufficiency that will damn good people to hell. The kingdom of Christ is an upside-down kingdom that makes no sense to this society.

2. Behavior to Motives

This first shift from philosophy to identity led to a second tidal shift in ethics: "I tell you, unless your righteousness exceeds that of the scribes and Pharisees, you will never enter the kingdom of heaven" (Matthew 5:20). How in the world is that possible? If you know anything about the Pharisees, you know how meticulous they were about religious duties. They prayed twice a day, fasted once a week, and tithed their garden herbs.

Who can top that? Fortunately, what Jesus was asking for was not broader religion but better motives. He shifted ethics from your hands to your heart. Jesus gave six specific illustrations:

The Law Says	Jesus Says	Matthew 5
Don't murder.	Don't harbor anger.	21–26
Don't commit adultery.	Don't lust in your heart.	27–30
Divorce legally.	Don't divorce except for adultery.	31–32
Don't break an oath.	Be completely honest.	33–37
Retaliate with equity.	Don't resist your opponent.	38–42
Love your neighbors.	Love your enemies.	43–48

Ethics focuses on behavior. Jesus focuses on motives. Ethics, in Jesus's kingdom, is not about legality but about love. He desires people to desire the good of others. Many "righteous" people never break a command but still break hearts. A person can avoid murder but still destroy another's reputation. You can avoid adultery but still fall prey to pornography. Motives matter. If your motives are pure, your behavior will follow. If your hands alone are pure, there is no guarantee your heart will follow.

Jesus, with unparalleled clarity, made the law simple to understand but arduous to keep. Loving our families and friends is tough enough, but now we have to love our enemies? Honesty under oath is demanding, but now we have to extend that from the courtroom to the courtyard? Controlling our sexual urges is difficult, but to bridle our minds . . . oh boy! Yet in Jesus's kingdom these are not suggestions; these are his laws.

3. Love in Spite Of, Not Because Of

One of these six commands stands out among the rest: "I say to you, Love your enemies and pray for those who persecute you" (Matthew 5:44). In the Middle East, telling people to love their enemies could be interpreted as treason. This is a potentially life-threatening proposition. Love is an action, not a reaction. Jesus is not telling us to feel warm and fuzzy toward those who hate us. He's ordering his followers to love their enemies with actions. Feed them if they are hungry. House them if they are homeless. Protect them from danger. In Jesus's day that could put you at odds with your own family. You could be accused of disloyalty, even harboring a terrorist. This may be the most offensive thing Jesus ever said. Yet it has never been more needed than now. Loving our enemies has been proved sociologically to be the most effective means of reducing violence, restoring peace, and avoiding the loss of life. Mother Teresa, Mahatma Gandhi, and Martin Luther King Jr. demonstrated how sweeping social changes are possible through those who are willing to risk taking Jesus at his word. In the face of racism, terrorism, and tribalism, we need disciples to be true believers and live like Jesus knew what he was talking about. God help us if we don't.

4. God as Father

When Jesus teaches us to pray, it's in a brand-new way. We call it the Lord's Prayer (Matthew 6:9–13). What makes it unique isn't the request for daily bread or the request to avoid temptation. These could be found in other Jewish prayers. What is absolutely unique is the first phrase: "Our Father" (verse 9). Until Jesus, no one prayed like that. Oh sure, some would refer to God as the Father of the nation (though rarely). Jesus, however, *always* prayed to God as Father, with the lone exception of his prayer on the cross: "My God, my God, why have you forsaken me?" (Mark 15:34). He introduced intimacy to prayer with "Our Father." That alone would radically alter our prayers if we could just comprehend the connection we have with God through Jesus (Matthew 7:11).

This concept, however, alters far more than prayer. It affects how we see our influence (5:16), our relationships (5:45), and ourselves (5:48). It affects how and why we practice religious duties (6:1, 4, 6, 8, 18) and whether we offer forgiveness to others (6:14–15). It will lower our anxiety (6:26, 32) and transform our behavior (7:21). If you didn't catch it, that's *seventeen times* the word *Father* was used in this one sermon! It's a big deal and irrevocably alters religious ethics. It's one of the unique things about Christianity: that we see our Creator as our Father, who is both exalted and intimate.

5. From Silver to Gold

The final idea that revolutionized ethics is found in one of the most familiar verses in the Bible: "Whatever you wish that others would do to you, do also to them, for this is the Law and the Prophets" (Matthew 7:12). On one hand this is familiar. As far back as Confucius, you can find this principle: "Don't do to others what you don't want done to you." This is known as "the Silver Rule." But notice the slight variation Jesus made. He took the negative and made it positive in the Golden Rule: "Do to others . . ."

That changes *everything*. The Silver Rule is passive. You can even do it on the beach. The Golden Rule is active. It requires effort everywhere.

Five times in a seventeen-minute sermon, Jesus utterly altered ethics. Therefore, if we are to be ethical by his standards, we need a change of heart, not a change of mind and nor even more efforts to change our behavior. Jesus changes everything.

Key Points

- Jesus is genius, putting earth-altering truth into bumper-sticker statements.
- Jesus's values turn the world's values upside down.
- Jesus altered ethics by shifting the focus from behavior to motives.

This Week

❏ **Day 1 (Eyes):** After reading the essay, consider this question: Which of these five alterations of ethics do you find most challenging?

❏ **Day 2 (Ears):** Read Exodus 20:1–17, the Ten Commandments. How would they be seen differently through the lens of Jesus's ethics?

❏ **Day 3 (Heart):** Meditate on Romans 13:9; Galatians 5:13; 1 John 3:16–18. Christian ethics is based on love. How would you define love based on these passages?

❏ **Day 4 (Voice):** Discussion:
- Can you think of a time when someone kept the letter of the law but still violated the intention of the law? Share an illustration.
- If you grew up in church, would you say your church focused more on the letter of the law or the intention of the law?
- Which of these five alterations of ethics do you think our culture is in most need of now?
- Which of these five is most natural for you? Which is most difficult?

❏ **Day 5 (Hands):** Pick a day this week (or perhaps just an hour), and try to perfectly live out the Golden Rule.

Further Resources: Quest52.org/28

29

What Did Jesus Say About Religious Duties?

Biblical Concept: Piety
Read: Matthew 6:1–18 with Luke 11:2–4

Candles, cathedrals, incense, and offerings. This is the stuff of religious devotion. Right? Not according to Jesus. Piety is not so much about religious devotion as about compassion. The problem with piety (religious devotion) is that it often leads to pride. People are impressed with my worship, enthralled with my offering, and amazed by my performance. As an example, I remember praying in youth group. As my turn approached, I would begin mentally crafting my prayer, scripting it for my friends, not for God. By the time I said "Amen," I could imagine tears gently streaming from their eyes and slight nods in my direction as if to say, "If only I were as holy as he." How often do we all do something similar? Our efforts are not to please God but to impress people. That's why public piety can be so dangerous. Jesus had an important warning about this.

The Problem with Piety

Just as motives matter with morality (as we saw in the last chapter), they are also critical for religious actions. If our devotion is designed to impress people rather than God, it gets squirrely. Here is what happens. Rather than genuinely asking God for help, we pray for others to overhear. We effectively put ourselves on the throne rather than God. Rather than giving generously to make Jesus famous, we give to get noticed. Thus, our "gifts" are investments; they're selfish, not sacrificial. Our "service" becomes performance for which we expect applause. I could go on, but you get the point. Both piety (Matthew 6:1–18) and morality (5:21–48) can be selfish—motivated by people's approval rather than God's. Motives matter.

Jesus made two statements to connect the motives of morality with the motives of piety. We seldom read them in tandem because they are separated by a chapter division: "You therefore must be perfect, as your heavenly Father is perfect" (5:48) *and* "Beware of practicing your righteousness before other people in order to be seen by them" (6:1). At first glance, this seems contradictory. How can I be perfect publicly and also be careful to practice piety in private? It is actually *not* a contradiction.

Perfect does not imply moral perfection. That's impossible. Rather, the word means "mature" or "complete." Since the context is talking about how God loves indiscriminately, we, too, should love others regardless of whether they are Christians or even moral, whether they are like us or even like us. That's what it means to be perfect (in love) as your Father in heaven is perfect. There is no way of doing that without being public with our commitment to other people. That is Matthew chapter 5.

Chapter 6, on the other hand, is talking about our piety (or religious actions). When our motive is to please God, we perform not for others to see but for God as our only audience. Too often Christians (myself included) practice piety publicly and morality privately. We tend to be private with our faith in public, but public with our piety at church. According to Jesus, we should flip the script by making our morality public and our piety private.

Bottom line: public piety is rewarded by people; private piety is rewarded by God. We can choose only one. We will receive praise either from people or from God. This is audience-of-one kind of stuff. Jesus provided three illustrations to make the point: alms, prayer, and fasting. These three could be extrapolated to all our religious actions.

1. **Alms:** "When you give to the needy, sound no trumpet before you, as the hypocrites do in the synagogues and in the streets, that they may be praised by others. Truly, I say to you, they have received their reward. But when you give to the needy, do not let your left hand know what your right hand is doing, so that your giving may be in secret. And your Father who sees in secret will reward you" (Matthew 6:2–4).

   Israel had no governmental social welfare system. The poor were primarily dependent on extended family. Those unfortunate few who were alone in life were forced to rely on benevolence. It seems to have included fourteen meals doled out weekly to the abject poor. Those who provided for the poor wanted everyone to know about their benevolence, so they announced it with trumpets. To be honest, historians are not certain what Jesus was referring to. They might be the trumpet-shaped brass receptacles in the temple where offerings for the poor were collected. Since contributions were made with coins, the clanging of the trumpet-shaped jar would sound out when the offering went in. Or it could refer to literal bugles blown when benevolence was given on any street corner. While this seems arrogantly ostentatious, let's be real. We do the same thing with plaques and awards for those who give big to God's work. Public generosity is sometimes appropriate (Acts 4:36–37; 21:24; Philippians 4:14–18), especially as a challenge to the whole church to join in.

However, it is also always dangerous. Jesus's general principle should be our common practice. Anonymous giving ensures that the approval we seek is from God alone.

2. **Prayer:** "When you pray, you must not be like the hypocrites. For they love to stand and pray in the synagogues and at the street corners, that they may be seen by others. Truly, I say to you, they have received their reward. But when you pray, go into your room and shut the door and pray to your Father who is in secret. And your Father who sees in secret will reward you. And when you pray, do not heap up empty phrases as the Gentiles do, for they think that they will be heard for their many words. Do not be like them, for your Father knows what you need before you ask him" (Matthew 6:5–8).

   Obviously, public prayer is perfectly appropriate (Acts 1:24; 3:1; 4:24). The problem is when prayer is for the purpose of speaking to an earthly audience rather than our Father in heaven. At that point, it's oration, not supplication. We've all seen this, and probably most of us have done it. A flowery public prayer may attract attention from people, but it does little to move the heart of the Father.

   The response to our prayers will always come from the audience to whom they are directed. If we speak to be heard by people, our praise will come from people. But when we speak directly to God, he will hear and answer regardless of others overhearing our conversation. Jesus offered a stellar example of how to pray in Matthew 6:9–13, which we call the Lord's Prayer. (See *Core 52,* chapter 20 for details on how to implement it in your own prayer life.)

3. **Fasting:** "When you fast, do not look gloomy like the hypocrites, for they disfigure their faces that their fasting may be seen by others. Truly, I say to you, they have received their reward. But when you fast, anoint your head and wash your face, that your fasting may not be seen by others but by your Father who is

in secret. And your Father who sees in secret will reward you" (Matthew 6:16–18).

Fasting is a lost art. If you practice it, you know the powerful benefits of telling your body it isn't the boss. Typically it takes me about twenty-four hours of fasting to experience the best benefits. At that point, my physical world gets blurry. My vision is literally blurred; my body is a bit numb; my energy plummets. At the same time, a veil is lifted from my spiritual vision. My prayers become razor sharp, and my spiritual hearing becomes acute. It is a powerful spiritual discipline, but it becomes dangerous if done for public praise.

The law of Moses commanded one fast a year—the Day of Atonement (Leviticus 16:29–31). However, the Pharisees fasted every Tuesday and Thursday. Is it any coincidence that these two days were when the public markets were open? They wanted to prove their piety publicly. Which they did. And they were rewarded, but their reward came from their peers, not their God.

Conclusion

One of the insatiable needs of human beings is approval. That's fine. In fact, it's embedded in us by God's design. The problem is not our need for significance but the source from which we seek it. When we turn to humans for affirmation, we find they can be arbitrary, manipulative, and fickle. The natural desire God put in children to seek approval from parents is a mere stepping-stone to gleaning significance from God. If, however, we never get past our need for people's approval, we will find ourselves in a relentless pursuit of human praise. When we shift to God's approval, we will find an ever-present and inexhaustible source of self-esteem. He will affirm you if you exercise your piety for his eyes only.

Key Points

- Piety (religious actions) performed for other people will lead to pride.

- Alms, prayer, and fasting are examples of religious actions that can garner attention from God or from people. Whom you perform them for will determine whom you receive recognition from.

- God created us with a need for approval. It starts with our parents' approval but should ultimately shift to God's. When we do that, our need for self-esteem is met perpetually and inexhaustibly.

This Week

❏ **Day 1 (Eyes):** After reading the essay, consider this question: Is your need for approval satisfied by God or others?

❏ **Day 2 (Ears):** Read 1 Samuel 13 and 17. How did King Saul and King David differ in seeking the approval of people versus God?

❏ **Day 3 (Heart):** Meditate on Galatians 1:10; Colossians 3:23; 1 Thessalonians 2:4.

❏ **Day 4 (Voice):** Discussion:

- What percentage of people do you suppose have a healthy self-image? What are some of the indications that a person has low self-esteem?
- Often people who appear arrogant are actually insecure. How have you seen that manifested in your experience?
- How do public acts of piety lead to hypocrisy?
- Which acts of religious devotion do you tend to perform for others to see?
- When is it okay to publicly perform religious actions, and when does it become dangerous to your spiritual health?

❏ **Day 5 (Hands):** On a scale of 1 to 5 (1 being completely private and 5 being primarily public), rate the following religious practices in your own life: prayer, giving, Bible reading, church attendance, volunteer service.

Further Resources: Quest52.org/29

30

Why Does Jesus Care So Much About My Money?

Biblical Concept: Wealth
Read: Matthew 6:19–34

Two of the greatest gifts my father ever gave me revolved around money. When I was twelve, he began to give me a monthly allowance. It was a pretty good chunk of change for a kid, but I had to buy *everything* except food. If I wanted to go to the movies, I paid for it. If I wanted to buy clothes, it was on me. Mad money for vacation was my responsibility. He taught me how to establish a budget and live within my means. Delayed gratification set me up for success regardless of my income.

Even more important was my very first financial lesson. Beginning when I was in first grade, if my father gave me a dime, he taught me to give a penny in Sunday school. When it became a dollar, I set aside a dime for the offering. I've carried that lesson through life with every paycheck. It has taught me about stewardship. God owns everything—my house, car, tools, and technology. I'm merely a steward of what God has entrusted to me. That takes all kinds of pressure off financially. The manager of the company always sleeps better than the owner. This lesson is so important for our mental health. Stewards carry responsibility, but they need not harbor worry. If you have high anxiety, what Jesus is about to teach about money can reduce it.

Principle 1: Our Hearts Follow Our Money

Many teach that your money follows your heart. That is, you invest in things that are important to you. You lavish diamonds on your lover, buy tools for your shop, or acquire toys for a hobby. That's true, to some extent. What is *always* true, however, is that your heart follows your money. Your interest follows your investment—always. If you put your money in property or possessions, those things will have your time and attention. That's why Jesus said, "Do not lay up for yourselves treasures on earth, where moth and rust destroy and where thieves break in and steal, but lay up for yourselves treasures in heaven, where neither moth nor rust destroys and where thieves do not break in and steal. *For where your treasure is, there your heart will be also*" (Matthew 6:19–21).

The apostle Paul would say it even more forcefully: "You may be sure of this, that everyone who is sexually immoral or impure, or who is *covetous (that is, an idolater),* has no inheritance in the kingdom of Christ and God" (Ephesians 5:5). Materialism is idolatry. It sounds extreme, but it is true. Jesus knew that the things we put our money into, we put on a pedestal. Instead of serving us, they become objects we serve. That's why the tithe (giving our first 10 percent to the local church) is so important. It orients our hearts toward God. It establishes his ownership of everything.

This makes sense of what Jesus said next: "The eye is the lamp of the body. So, if your eye is healthy, your whole body will be full of light, but if your eye is bad, your whole body will be full of darkness. If then the light in you is darkness, how great is the darkness! No one can serve two masters, for either he will hate the one and love the other, or he will be devoted to the one and despise the other. You cannot serve God and money" (Matthew 6:22–24).

What in the world do eyes have to do with two masters? Well, the ancients perceived the eye as a portal to the soul. Good and evil entered the body through the eye. They were not entirely wrong. If your eyes focus on possessions, the possessions become the object of your affection. If you look to heaven, God will be your focus. We all have a choice about whom we will serve, but to quote Bob Dylan, "You're gonna have to serve somebody."[1] Follow the money, and you'll find your one true master.

Principle 2: Our Worry Reveals
Our Worship

Some people imagine that if they could just make more money, they wouldn't have to worry. Wrong! Wealth *increases* worry. The rich scheme about how to make more money, strategize about how to keep what they have, and dream about how to distribute it to heirs. Wealth does *not* eliminate worry; worship does! When we worship God with our wealth, we realize the other 90 percent is his as well. This doesn't mean we don't work hard, save wisely, or spend carefully. Rather, it means we recognize God as the source of all our good. This takes the pressure off us. Our job is not to create wealth but to manage God's resources. A right view of God allows a proper perspective on wealth. Thus worship erodes worry.

Jesus said, "I tell you, do not be anxious about your life, what you will eat or what you will drink, nor about your body, what you will put on. Is not life more than food, and the body more than clothing?" (Matthew 6:25). Jesus offered two illustrations of the frivolity of anxiety—birds and flowers—as he stood on a Galilean mountain inflamed with flowers. It must have been an extraordinary sight. You've seen your own local versions each spring. Not even the famed Solomon with all his wealth could compare to the transitory raiment of the fields in bloom.

Likewise, the birds of the air sing, seemingly without a care in the world. Both birds and flowers declare God's goodness and lavish provision. Jesus's logic is clear: God cares more about you than birds or flowers, for which his provisions are extravagant. How much more will he meticulously see to your physical, emotional, and spiritual needs? Do you believe that? By and large, we don't!

No mental illness is more common in the United States than anxiety disorders, which affect forty million adults each year. That is 18.1 percent of the population.[2] The US is considered one of the most anxious nations on earth.[3] Our wealth clearly has not reduced our worry. It is estimated that anxiety disorders cost the US $42 billion per year.[4] So it turns out Jesus was right not only theologically but also psychologically and economically.

Worry may increase our activity but never our productivity. As Jesus put it, "Which of you by being anxious can add a single hour to his span of life?" (verse 27). He used a mixed metaphor of time and distance. The word *hour* is literally "cubit," or eighteen inches. He pictured life as a long journey. Worry won't elongate the path of your life by a single step. In fact, modern medicine has conclusively proved that worry actually decreases both the length and the quality of your life.

Worry is practical atheism. It's appropriate only for unbelievers who don't know the Father in heaven. "Do not be anxious, saying, 'What shall we eat?' or 'What shall we drink?' or 'What shall we wear?' For the Gentiles seek after all these things, and your heavenly Father knows that you need them all" (verses 31–32). Worry betrays an ignorance of our provider. To those of us who know the love of God, however, Jesus says, "Seek first the kingdom of God and his righteousness, and all these things will be added to you. Therefore do not be anxious about tomorrow, for tomorrow will be anxious for itself. Sufficient for the day is its own trouble" (verses 33–34).

God's good provision does not eliminate human suffering. Jesus acknowledged that each day has trouble. Christians sometimes suffer even as Jesus suffered (Matthew 5:10–12; Romans 8:17; Philippians 3:10; 4:12). Some of our suffering may even be discipline or training from God (Hebrews 12:7). All of us who live in a fallen world experience the fallout.

Some may even say, "But look at how many go hungry! See? We can't trust God to provide." Not so! Most of the suffering in our world is due not to a lack of provision but to a lack of adequate distribution. When Christians abdicate their responsibility, some of God's children lack the resources he has provided (Matthew 25:42; Mark 10:21; Acts 4:32). Part of the evil of worry is that it reduces distribution to those who need God's provision the most.

Conclusion

Matthew 6 is one of the most brilliant treatises on worry in the whole of human history. Humans tend to worry about two things: significance and provision. Because we need significance, we often perform religious duties for the audience around us rather than for God above us. Jesus's solution in Matthew 6:1–18 is to seek God's approval alone. God will certainly recognize those doing good for his sake. Likewise, because we worry about provision, we hoard the resources God has given us to distribute, and humanity is poorer for it. Jesus's solution in Matthew 6:19–34 is to trust God for provision so we can be generous with those who need it most. This one chapter deals with the two deepest needs of human beings in a way that promotes health, charity, and unity.

Key Points

- Money is spiritual.

- Worry is practical atheism.

- Matthew 6 offers solutions to the two things we worry about most: significance and provision.

This Week

❏ **Day 1 (Eyes):** After reading the essay, how would you rate your own worry on a scale of 1 to 10? What does that reveal about where you need to grow in faith?

❏ **Day 2 (Ears):** Read the following proverbs on wealth: Proverbs 3:27; 6:6–8; 10:4; 11:25; 12:11; 13:11, 22; 14:23; 22:7, 9, 16, 26–27; 24:33–34; 27:23–24; 28:27.

❏ **Day 3 (Heart):** Meditate on Ephesians 5:5; 1 Timothy 6:17–19; Hebrews 13:5.

❏ **Day 4 (Voice):** Discussion:

- Who is someone you respect for his generosity? How would you rate that person's worry?
- Why do you think America has some of the highest rates of worry?
- Discuss the implications of this statement: *the problem of poverty in the world is due not to a lack of provision but to a lack of distribution.*
- What are you worried about right now? It's okay to be honest. Perhaps you have a group that could pray for one another to help reduce anxiety.

❏ **Day 5 (Hands):** Do an audit of your finances. Are you putting God first? If not, what resources does your church provide to help you budget for a tithe?

Further Resources: Quest52.org/30

31

How Does Jesus Feel About Prodigals?

Biblical Concept: Prodigals
Read: Luke 15:11–32

This parable could fit my family well. After my parents' divorce, Mom moved out and we lived with Dad for a couple of months. Then Dad moved out, and Mom moved in for a couple of months. Afterward, the three of us boys (ages eleven, twelve, and fourteen) had to decide whom to live with. My older brother lived with Mom. My younger brother and I stayed with Dad. It was heart wrenching. I kept going to church, and my faith followed suit. My older brother, however, stopped going to church. If we put our own names in this story, he would be the prodigal son, and I would be the one who stayed at home and faithfully served his father. Does that make me better? I would like to think so, but this parable tells a different story. I know how easy it is to get lost at home. As we will see, we all need grace.

Setting the Scene

Jesus had been fraternizing with riffraff—tax collectors, call girls, and scallywags. "The tax collectors and sinners were all drawing near to hear him. And the Pharisees and the scribes grumbled, saying, 'This man receives sinners and eats with them.' So he told them this parable" (Luke 15:1–3). Except it wasn't just one parable; it was a string of five parables! Stories of a lost sheep, a lost coin, and a lost son dominate the landscape of Luke 15. Closely connected to the story of the lost son are two more parables about how to use money to get to heaven (16:1–13) and how to mismanage money and wind up in hell (verses 19–31). Once Jesus started telling stories, he often went on a roll (Matthew 13; 21–22; 24–25; Luke 18).

Why five stories stacked together? Well, the religious leaders attacked the "sinners" around Jesus because, you know, birds of a feather flock together. That ruffled Jesus's feathers! These stories are his response to their hypercritical (and hypocritical) judgment. Five stories indicate how serious Jesus is about the lost and found. He loves the people the righteous tend to avoid. Most men in the audience had, at some point, helped a neighbor find a lost sheep. They could relate to the first story about searching for a stray. The second story resonated with all the ladies who had swept their houses to find lost coins. The third story is about two lost sons. One got lost abroad and one got lost at home. Everyone can relate to this story. Perhaps that is why it is the longest of Jesus's parables. Charles Dickens said it was the greatest short story ever.

The Son Who Got Lost Abroad

We have all known a young man who was fed up with his father. He just had to strike out on his own. Few, however, are as rude as this lad. This arrogant younger brother confronted his father: "Give me the share of property that is coming to me" (Luke 15:12). In the Middle East, the land passed from generation to generation. Thus, he was asking his dad to cash out and give him his share of the estate *prior to his dad's death*! To Jewish ears it would have sounded like this: "Dad, drop dead and give me what's mine!"

If you know anything about the shame-honor culture of the Middle

East, the answer would obviously be "#%@* no!" Not only did his demand guarantee that such a foolish boy would squander the inheritance; it would also have significantly shamed the father among the other elders in the village. No Mediterranean father in his right mind would acquiesce to such a demand from a rebellious son. This one, however, did. You can imagine the shock when Jesus dropped the next line: "He divided his property between them" (verse 12). What on earth was going on? Remember, the father in the parable represents God. The audience knew that. Jesus was portraying Yahweh as a foolish father who capitulated to an insubordinate son. That was shocking!

What happened next is as predictable as the girl falling for the guy in a chick flick: "Not many days later, the younger son gathered all he had and took a journey into a far country, and there he squandered his property in reckless living" (verse 13). That's what we expected. Hard times fall especially hard on hardheaded fools. When his lifestyle consumed his wealth, his "hired" friends disappeared. Then a severe famine hit. He was desperate. So desperate, in fact, that he latched on to a hog farmer and begged for work. That's about as low as a kosher Jewish boy can go.

One day, while feeding the pigs the pods from a carob tree, he thought, *Those don't look half-bad.* How hungry do you have to be for nutritionless roughage to look alluring? It's then that he came to his senses, as if awakening from a trance. He said to himself, "How many of my father's hired servants have more than enough bread, but I perish here with hunger! I will arise and go to my father, and I will say to him, 'Father, I have sinned against heaven and before you. I am no longer worthy to be called your son. Treat me as one of your hired servants'" (verses 17–19). He memorized his speech and set off for home.

His father saw him from a distance and, against all odds, ran to his son. In the Middle East, noblemen never run. That is what thieves and slaves do out of fear. Once again, Jesus was portraying God the Father as throwing caution and dignity to the wind. One of the most amazing things about God is how vulnerable he is willing to become because of his love for us. It turns out that the Father's love is more prodigal than the son's sin.

The lad launched into the speech he rehearsed in the pigsty. The father cut him off with a clap of his hands, barking orders to his servants. "Bring quickly the best robe, and put it on him, and put a ring on his hand, and shoes on his feet. And bring the fattened calf and kill it, and let us eat and celebrate. For this my son was dead, and is alive again; he was lost, and is found" (verses 22–24). The father lavished his son with these three signs of family honor. The signet ring gave him authority over family affairs. The robe and sandals set him apart from the household servants. The father had worried that his son was dead, but now he was alive at home. This metaphor of resurrection is thick in the Epistles (Romans 6:4, 9–11; 7:4; 8:10–11; Ephesians 2:5; Colossians 2:13) and marks the life of the believer.

The Son Who Got Lost at Home

The older brother heard the celebration. Perhaps he thought it was for him? He found it was for his renegade brother, who had shamed the family. He was furious! The father went out to retrieve a lost son for the second time that day. The older brother's anger was legally and logically justifiable. However, Luke 15:29–30 betray the older brother's condition: "Look, these many years I have served you, and I never disobeyed your command, yet you never gave me a young goat, that I might celebrate with my friends. But when this son of yours came, who has devoured your property with prostitutes, you killed the fattened calf for him!" Two statements reveal his heart. "I have served you" indicates that he considered himself a slave, not a son. Second, "this son of yours" suggests "he is not a brother of mine!" Interestingly, in his reply, the father used the same turn of phrase: "this your brother" (verse 32). The father affirmed his elder son: "You are always with me, and all that is mine is yours" (verse 31). The inheritance was not enough for the judgmental older brother. He wanted justice . . . or was it actually vengeance?

Did the older brother ever enter the house to celebrate his brother's return? We don't know. The story isn't finished. Remember, it started in verses 1–2, when Jesus was accosted by the Pharisees for fraternizing with sinners. They were still there in the room. Jesus's open-ended story was an invitation for them (the older brothers) to join the celebration of sinners who had come back home. We're never told whether they did. So the story remains open. The ending is up to you. Will *you* join the celebration of those coming home to the Father? Is justice (or vengeance) more important than celebrating the lost being found?

This is a more serious question than we typically assume. It is not merely a question for individuals. Many churches (perhaps most) are designed for those who never left home. They have been slaving away for God. They talk about inviting sinners. However, lip service does little if the church service is structured to intimidate prodigals or manipulate them with a sense that they are lost. The songs we sing, the clothes we wear, the language we use all signal to prodigals whether this is an insider-out or an outsider-in kind of church. The way we invite, the signage we use, the greetings and glances we employ send silent messages that shout our welcome or rejection of the lost and found.

Key Points

- Rejoicing over the lost being found was so important to Jesus that he told a string of parables about it.

- Prodigals are often shocked when they return home. They are full-fledged sons, not house servants or second-class citizens.

- It's easy for sons or daughters lost at home to be scandalized when their brothers or sisters return.

This Week

❏ **Day 1 (Eyes):** After reading the essay, consider this question: Are you more like the older brother or the younger brother?

❏ **Day 2 (Ears):** What can we learn from 2 Chronicles 7:11–22 about repentance and restoration?

❏ **Day 3 (Heart):** Meditate on Acts 3:19; 2 Corinthians 7:9–10; 1 Peter 2:25.

❏ **Day 4 (Voice):** Discussion:

- Have you known someone who was a prodigal who returned to her community of faith? What was that person's experience like? If it was you, share your story.
- Why do you think it's difficult for "older brothers" to welcome prodigals home?
- Come up with a list of three things your church could do to make prodigals feel more celebrated when they come home.
- What could you do personally to make prodigals more open to attending church with you?

❏ **Day 5 (Hands):** Ask a prodigal you know well, "If you ever did decide to return to church, what would make you feel welcome?"

Further Resources: Quest52.org/31

32

How Do I Hear God's Voice?

Biblical Concept: Parables
Read: Matthew 13:1–23 with Mark 4:1–20; Luke 8:4–15

Hearing loss is common as we age, particularly for those exposed to loud sounds over long periods of time. Higher-pitch frequencies especially become harder to hear. Many men work with machinery, whether shop tools, engines, or construction equipment. Many women have higher-pitch voices. The result is not always good for marriage. As a man ages, he naturally has a harder time hearing his wife's voice. You can imagine how well that goes over. In the same way, over time, we can become deaf to the voice of God. That is not good for our spiritual health. The stories Jesus told helped some people hear better but made others tone deaf.

An Earthly Story with a Heavenly Meaning

Jesus was famous for his parables. He told a total of thirty-eight. We have over two thousand parables from other rabbis, but none of them predate Jesus. So it may well be that Jesus invented this teaching tool and others imitated him. Like the other parables, Jesus's stories involve stock metaphors. Masters, fathers, and kings represent God. Servants and children represent God's servants or prophets. A harvest stands for judgment, and a feast portrays the messianic banquet. Each of these metaphors represents something in real life. Some, in fact, believe that every time Jesus told a parable, he could have pointed to the objects he was speaking about right around him.

While his parables use the same metaphors as other rabbinic parables, two things set them apart. First, every other rabbi told parables to reinforce traditional values. Jesus used parables to explode expectations and teach something new. Second, other rabbis used parables to illustrate points in their messages. For Jesus, the parables *were* the message. Specifically, Jesus's parables were *all* about the presence of the promised kingdom of God. That was new! Matthew 13 is the greatest example of this. He told eight parables in a row. Their arrangement, shown below, is both brilliant and intricate. Think of it as Russian nesting dolls. The first and last parables are a match (like the top and bottom of the largest doll), both illustrating how people receive the message of the kingdom (A and A') accompanied by questions about the parables (B and B'). Inside the first and last parables, we find a matching set of stories (C and C') describing good and evil in the kingdom. Inside that we find two more pairs of parables nested together to illustrate the value of the kingdom (D and D'). This whole intricate arrangement was a common literary device known as chiasmus, and the point of the chiasmus is literally the point in the center of the arrangement. In this case, it is verses 36–43 (E) when Jesus explained the parable of the tares. Watch how it plays out below.

A   (1) Sower—a parable about those who hear the word of the kingdom (verses 3–9)

B   The disciples' question and Jesus's answer about the purpose of parables and the interpretation of the first parable (verses 10–23)

C   (2) Tares—a parable about good and evil in the kingdom (verses 24–30)

D   (3–4) Mustard seed and leaven—a pair of parallel kingdom parables (verses 31–35)

  E Jesus's private interpretation of the tares parable for his
    disciples (verses 36–43)

  D (5–6) Treasure and pearl—a pair of parallel kingdom para-
    bles (verses 44–46)

 C (7) Dragnet—a parable about good and evil in the kingdom
   (verses 47–50)

 B Jesus's question and the disciples' answer about understanding
  parables (verse 51)

A (8) Scribe—a parable about those trained for the kingdom (verse 52)

Parable of the Sower

These parables are kind of like bedtime stories you would tell your children. On the surface they are easy to understand. As you ponder their
meanings, however, you begin to plumb their depths. For example, this
first story is about a farmer scattering his seed indiscriminately. Without modern technology, his best bet was to throw the seed wherever he
could.

  Some of it fell on the path, where the ground was compacted by
human footsteps, making it impenetrable. The birds (representing Satan,
Mark 4:15) snatched the seed away. Some of the seed fell on shallow soil
among the rocks. It sprang up quickly, but the lack of depth meant there
was too little moisture to sustain growth. That was likened to persecution
that causes some to quickly abandon their new faith. Other seed fell on
soil with weed seed. They grew up together, but the weeds won out. These
weeds represent life's worries, riches, and pleasures.

  Some seed, however, fell on good soil and produced a hundredfold,
sixtyfold, or thirtyfold. (A good yield was tenfold, so this is hyperbole,
which is common in parables.) The life lesson is this: All the soil is actually the same. The difference is what is added to it—stones, weeds, or a
good stomping. That's what causes some to hear the message of the kingdom and others to go deaf to spiritual things. Of course, for the Hebrews,

hearing was an action not merely of the ears but of the will. There was no hearing without obedience.

"Why Do You Speak to Them in Parables?"

No one understood what this story meant. At least not until Jesus explained it. So the disciples turned to Jesus in the boat and asked, "Why do you speak to them in parables?" (Matthew 13:10). Jesus's answer was shocking: "To you it has been given to know the secrets of the kingdom of heaven, but to them it has not been given. For to the one who has, more will be given, and he will have an abundance, but from the one who has not, even what he has will be taken away. This is why I speak to them in parables, because seeing they do not see, and hearing they do not hear, nor do they understand" (verses 11–13).

Jesus basically said that parables make the kingdom clear to those who are inclined to believe. Yet to those who reject Jesus, parables conceal the kingdom. Is it fair that to those who have, more will be given and that from those with little, even what they have will be taken away? No, it's not fair. It is, however, reality. When you go out to eat, do you prefer a restaurant with lots of cars in the parking lot or few? When you go to a movie, do you want the theater to be empty or full? Star athletes get product endorsements and famous actors get more offers. It's just the way life works. When it comes to the kingdom, however, the blessed are not those with good looks, physical prowess, or wealth. The blessed are those who believe.

Jesus answered their question with an ancient prophecy from Isaiah. The prophet had a vision of the temple of God. Yahweh was seated high and exalted, the sacred temple was filled with smoke, and the seraphim (flaming angels) flew about, crying, "Holy, holy, holy is the Lord of hosts" (Isaiah 6:3). Their voices shook the foundations of the temple. It was an awesome scene.

God himself spoke: "Whom shall I send, and who will go for us?"

Isaiah, shaken to his core, cried out, "Here I am! Send me" (verse 8).
God commissioned him to preach a shocking message to the people of
Jerusalem:

> "Keep on hearing, but do not understand;
> keep on seeing, but do not perceive."
> Make the heart of this people dull,
>   and their ears heavy,
>   and blind their eyes;
> lest they see with their eyes,
>   and hear with their ears,
> and understand with their hearts,
>   and turn and be healed. (verses 9–10)

What on earth was going on here? God did not want them to repent?
He did not want them to be saved? Well, of course he did. However, their
continual past rejection had shown their unwillingness to obey God. As
they say in business, "Past performance is the best predictor of future performance."

God knows the condition of our hearts. He knows when we are too
cold, too proud, or too selfish to allow him to restore us. At that point,
you know what he did to harden the hearts of his people? This is unbelievable. He sent preachers! The more they heard the message, the less they
heard the message. It is not unlike those who live under the flight path of
an airport no longer hearing the planes. Those who live next to railroad
tracks go deaf to trains. And those who go to church week after week but
don't put into practice the truth of the gospel find themselves deaf to the
Holy Spirit.

This very passage from Isaiah's call is quoted two other times: once by
John in his gospel (12:40) and once by Paul when he preached to the Jewish leaders in Rome (Acts 28:26–27). Each of these three passages says
basically the same thing: people harden their hearts; God calls them to
repentance; they harden their hearts further; God sends them more

preachers until they are totally deaf. Not only does unbelief bring judgment; it also destroys one's ability to perceive truth (Exodus 8:32; 9:12; Deuteronomy 29:4; Isaiah 42:19–20; Jeremiah 5:21; John 3:17–19; 9:39–41; Romans 11:8; 2 Corinthians 3:14).

Spiritual sight is a great gift. We dare not squander it. As Jesus said, "Blessed are your eyes, for they see, and your ears, for they hear. For truly, I say to you, many prophets and righteous people longed to see what you see, and did not see it, and to hear what you hear, and did not hear it" (Matthew 13:16–17). If you are reading these words and want to believe, foster that desire with diligence. It is a gift from God to be cherished, guarded, and acted on.

Key Points

- Jesus told thirty-eight parables. All of them were about the kingdom of God.

- Parables are earthly stories with heavenly meanings— subversive life lessons.

- Parables reveal the kingdom to those who have faith but conceal it from those who reject the opportunity to believe.

This Week

❏ **Day 1 (Eyes):** After reading the essay, consider this question: Do you have eyes to see and ears to hear?

❏ **Day 2 (Ears):** Read Isaiah 6. How can we lose our spiritual sight and hearing?

❏ **Day 3 (Heart):** Meditate on Acts 28:26–27; Romans 11:8; 2 Corinthians 3:14. What actions or attitudes make one spiritually hard of hearing?

❏ **Day 4 (Voice):** Discussion:

- What makes people spiritually hard of hearing?
- Do you think you've always been a good listener when hearing the gospel? When did you listen more carefully, and when were you harder of hearing? What made the difference?
- Are you in a relationship with someone who is hardened to the gospel? How would you assess that person's condition based on the four types of soil?
- Brainstorm ideas for the day 5 exercise. Use your creativity to help each person come up with a story line.

❏ **Day 5 (Hands):** Sit down this week, and write a parable about hearing or seeing—an earthly story with a heavenly meaning.

Further Resources: Quest52.org/32

33

How Can I Be Sure
I'm Saved?

Biblical Concept: Bias
Read: Luke 10:25–37

Yesterday I got an email asking how someone can be sure she is saved. It went something like this: "I attend church. I read my Bible. I pay my tithes. I volunteer. But I just feel like something is missing. How can I be sure I'm saved?" Her question is common and has a fatal flaw. She listed all the good things she's doing to impress God. How on earth are we going to impress God with our goodness? He is already impressed with us simply because we are his creation, his children. In the same way a mother loves her kids, our heavenly Father loves us. In fact, he loved us to the ultimate extent, sending his Son to die for our sins. It is Jesus's death, not our performance, that ensures our salvation. So, the question is not whether God loves us but whether we love him back. That's what the encounter with Jesus in Luke 10 is all about.

Question I: The Query—How Are We Saved?

A lawyer came to Jesus with a question: "Teacher, what shall I do to inherit eternal life?" (verse 25). This man knew the Bible well. Jesus, using a common rabbinic teaching technique, answered his question with a question: "What is written in the Law? How do you read it?" (verse 26).

"Well," said the man, combining Deuteronomy 6:5 and Leviticus 19:18, "you shall love the Lord your God with all your heart and with all your soul and with all your strength and with all your mind, and your neighbor as yourself" (Luke 10:27). That was spot on. We know we are saved when we love God and demonstrate it by loving God's other children, our neighbors. It was a great answer. In fact, Jesus would give this very answer later in his ministry (Matthew 22:37–40).

First John 4:20–21 summarizes this whole idea: "If anyone says, 'I love God,' and hates his brother, he is a liar; for he who does not love his brother whom he has seen cannot love God whom he has not seen. And this commandment we have from him: whoever loves God must also love his brother."

Jesus replied, "Do this, and you will live" (Luke 10:28). Suddenly it was no longer Jesus on trial but the lawyer. Wanting to justify himself, he asked another question: "Who is my neighbor?" (verse 29). He was trying to define *neighbor* as narrowly as possible. Jesus allowed his narrow definition but then told a story that vastly expanded the borders of "neighbor."

Question 2: The Justification— Who Is My Neighbor?

"Once upon a time," said Jesus, "a man went down from Jerusalem to Jericho." This seventeen-mile stretch of highway was so dangerous that it was known as the Ascent of Adummim, the Road of Blood. It was infested with bandits. The road began at the top of the Mount of Olives at 2,710 feet and dropped precipitously (3,574 feet) until it reached Jericho. Sitting 864 feet *below* sea level, Jericho is the oldest inhabited city in the world as well as the lowest on the planet.

Somewhere along the way, bandits attacked the man. They beat him and left him for dead. Before long, a priest happened by. He had probably been at the temple for one of his biannual weeks of service and was returning home to his family and work. Since he had just been in the presence of God during worship at the temple, one would hope his empathy or compassion would be heightened. It was not. He walked right by his fellow Israelite, likely assuming he was already dead. Some have noted that a priest was not to touch a dead body lest he render himself ritually unclean. While that's true, this priest was *leaving* Jerusalem. His duties were over. He would have had more than enough time for ritual cleansing. His fellow Israelite needed him now! Clearly, his motives were *not* pure. Perhaps he was afraid the bandits were still nearby, or worse, he may have simply been apathetic, justifying his inaction as many of us do: *What difference could I make?*

After the priest came a Levite. Same song, second verse. He walked by, distancing himself by crossing to the other side of the road. Then came a Samaritan. We call this story the parable of the good Samaritan, but if you scour the text, the word *good* is not there. There was no such thing as a good Samaritan, according to the Jews. There was bad blood between the two groups.

Samaritans lived in the hills of central Israel. They were the descendants of the northern tribes who remained after the Assyrian captivity of 722 BC. Other people groups immigrated and comingled with the Israelites, resulting in a hybrid group of half Jews (or so the story goes). Samaritans had their own version of the Torah, their own temple on Mount Gerizim, and a nasty rivalry with their more kosher cousins. For example, in 128 BC, John Hyrcanus, a Jewish patriot, destroyed the Samaritan temple. The Samaritans retaliated by sneaking human bones into the Jerusalem temple at night and scattering them to defile the sanctuary. Samaritans were debarred from testifying in a Jewish court of law because you had to be human to do so. And on it went. As you can imagine, *good Samaritan* was an oxymoron in Jewish vernacular.

To show how widespread this sentiment was, one chapter earlier (Luke 9:51–54), Jesus passed through Samaria on his way to Jerusalem. He sent messengers ahead to secure housing for his band of disciples. The locals, however, refused. When James and John saw this, they said to

Jesus, "Lord, do you want us to tell fire to come down from heaven and consume them?" (verse 54). Whoa. That is aggressive (and it's impressive that they actually thought they could pull off what Elijah did with the prophets of Baal!). The antipathy against the Samaritans was widespread, even among Jesus's disciples.

Nonetheless, against all expectations, *this* Samaritan had compassion on the nameless Jew. That is interesting because the only other person in the Gospels to be described as compassionate is Jesus. The Samaritan's compassion was a feeling that translated into action: "He went to him and bound up his wounds, pouring on oil and wine [which had medicinal value]. Then he set him on his own animal and brought him to an inn and took care of him. And the next day he took out two denarii [two days' wages] and gave them to the innkeeper, saying, 'Take care of him, and whatever more you spend, I will repay you when I come back'" (Luke 10:34–35). He may not have liked the Jewish man, but he loved him in practice.

Question 3: The Test—Who Was Neighborly?

Jesus concluded the parable with a question: "Which of these three, do you think, proved to be a neighbor to the man who fell among the robbers?" (verse 36). What Jesus did is subtle but brilliant. Two things, really. First, he changed the lawyer's question. The lawyer asked, "Who is my neighbor?" Jesus asked, "Who *became* a neighbor?" The lawyer's question implies that someone is a neighbor by virtue of his proximity. In other words, "I like them because they are like me." Jesus's question implies that someone becomes a neighbor by showing compassion. It is not being near that makes you neighborly. It's showing compassion.

That led to a second brilliant move by Jesus. He allowed the lawyer's narrow definition of *neighbor* to stand. A person is your neighbor if she is right next to you. How close? Let's say three feet—your arm's reach. People within arm's reach are your neighbors; however, you must take your arm's reach with you wherever you go. Genius.

There was only one right answer to Jesus's question, and the lawyer knew it: "The one who showed him mercy." Jesus replied, "You go, and do likewise" (verse 37). In a moment of brilliance, Jesus changed the question from "Who is my neighbor?" to "Who was neighborly?" With this, Jesus answered both questions: "Who is my neighbor?" (verse 29) and "What shall I do to inherit eternal life?" (verse 25).

Back in the 1970s, a couple of researchers put this parable to the test.[1] They designed a study of forty seminary students who were asked to give a talk either on the best occupations for seminarians or on this parable. They were sent to a nearby building to deliver their talks. On the way, a "victim" was planted to see how the students would react. Sixty percent walked past the victim, some even stepping over him to get to the other building. These were pastors in training! Perhaps this parable needs to be revisited.

Key Points

- Salvation is assured when we respond to the love God has for us. Our love for God is demonstrated by the love we show to fellow humans.

- Your neighbors are those within three feet of you, but that circle moves with you.

- The better question is not "Who is my neighbor?" but "Who is neighborly?"

This Week

❏ **Day 1 (Eyes):** After reading the essay, consider this question: Are you neighborly?

❏ **Day 2 (Ears):** Read the context of these two great commands in Deuteronomy 6 and Leviticus 19:9–18.

❏ **Day 3 (Heart):** Meditate on 1 John 3:15–16; 4:16–21; 5:13. Using these passages, how would you answer the question "How can I be sure I'm saved?"

❏ **Day 4 (Voice):** Discussion:

- Who is the best neighbor you ever had? Any stories of a really bad neighbor?
- Why do you think we can't love God without loving our neighbors?
- What do you think you would have done if you had been a seminary student in the study and had run into someone in need on the way to give your talk?
- Under what circumstances is it most difficult for you to be a good neighbor?

❏ **Day 5 (Hands):** Carry your six feet with you this week, and find one opportunity to make life easier for someone who is unlike you and who cannot repay you.

Further Resources: Quest52.org/33

34

How Did Jesus Lead?

Biblical Concept: Leadership
Read: John 10:1–21

When I was a little tyke, I wanted to be a brain surgeon. Really, right up until the moment God called me to preach. I took all the biology classes I could, read about brains, and practiced tying surgical knots. My motives were not entirely pure. The prestige of the occupation was attractive. I suppose that's what drives most little boys and girls to their dream jobs—firefighter, doctor, astronaut, superhero.

In Jesus's day, little boys didn't dream of an occupation other than what they would inherit from their fathers. If they had, shepherding would not have been high on any little boy's list. After all, the task of leading sheep rendered you ritually unclean. You were often touching blood and dead animals. The pastoral role also made you migrate through other people's property. Consequently, anything that went missing was blamed on the boys leading the sheep. Not to mention that cute farmers' daughters often led to bad blood with the locals.

The Lord Is My Shepherd

The strange thing about shepherds in the Bible is that the *idea* of a shepherd was noble even if actual shepherds were shunned. The ideal Shepherd is God. Psalm 23 is famous for a reason:

> The LORD is my shepherd; I shall not want.
>> He makes me lie down in green pastures.
> He leads me beside still waters.
>> He restores my soul.
> He leads me in paths of righteousness
>> for his name's sake.
>
> Even though I walk through the valley of the shadow of death,
>> I will fear no evil,
> for you are with me;
>> your rod and your staff,
>> they comfort me.
>
> You prepare a table before me
>> in the presence of my enemies;
> you anoint my head with oil;
>> my cup overflows.
> Surely goodness and mercy shall follow me
>> all the days of my life,
> and I shall dwell in the house of the LORD
>> forever.

Throughout the Old Testament, Yahweh is described as a good shepherd. "He is our God, and we are the people of his pasture, and the sheep of his hand" (Psalm 95:7). "He will tend his flock like a shepherd; he will gather the lambs in his arms" (Isaiah 40:11). There are hosts of others (Genesis 48:15; Psalm 28:9; 78:52; 79:13; 80:1; 107:41; Ecclesiastes 12:11; Jeremiah 31:10; Ezekiel 34:15; Zechariah 9:16).

God deputized his key leaders to serve as shepherds over his people. Virtually every major leader of Israel was a shepherd by occupation. Their time in the fields prepared them for their roles as the heads of state. David, for example, was the greatest king of Israel. His training to lead the nation was his time spent in the field with sheep:

> [God] chose David his servant
>   and took him from the sheepfolds;
> from following the nursing ewes he brought him
>   to shepherd Jacob his people,
>   Israel his inheritance.
> With upright heart he shepherded them
>   and guided them with his skillful hand. (Psalm 78:70–72)

Likewise, for forty years Moses led Israel through the desert, where he had already spent four decades leading sheep (Exodus 3:1; Psalm 77:20; Isaiah 63:11). Before Moses there was Jacob (Genesis 29), and before Jacob, his grandfather Abraham (Genesis 13:5–7). This is the who's who of Israel's founding fathers. When Jesus claimed to be the shepherd of Israel, therefore, it was a political claim.

Jesus Is the Good Shepherd

John 10 comes at the tail end of the Feast of Tabernacles, which began clear back in John 7 and had been white-hot with controversy. Jesus's biological brothers insinuated he was a false prophet (7:1–4). When he showed up late to the feast, the Jewish leaders already had a BOLO out for his arrest (7:11). The crowds were divided over him (7:12, 31, 40–43; 8:30; 9:16; 10:19). Some called him a deceiver (7:12, 47; 8:13), a Samaritan, and demon possessed (7:20; 8:48, 52; 10:20). The Jewish leaders attempted to arrest him (7:30–32, 44–45; 8:20), entrap him with a woman caught in adultery (7:53–8:11), and intimidate the crowds with the threat of excommunication (9:22, 34). An assassination plot was afoot at the beginning of the feast (7:25) and at one point erupted into an attempted stoning (8:59).

All that background makes sense of Jesus's opening foray: "Truly, truly, I say to you, he who does not enter the sheepfold by the door but climbs in by another way, that man is a thief and a robber" (10:1). This is a gloves-off, no-holds-barred, heavyweight bout. Jesus stood in the temple, face to face with the "shepherds" of Israel. He accused them of being illegitimate, even satanic, while he is the one true shepherd of Israel. What chutzpah!

Both Jesus and the Jewish leaders claimed to be shepherds of Israel. The crowds were divided. Some sided with the establishment: the chief priests and teachers of the law. After all, these had been their recognized leaders all their lives. Some sided with Jesus, in large part because of his unprecedented miracles. The miracles caused many to conclude, "These are not the words of one who is oppressed by a demon. Can a demon open the eyes of the blind?" (verse 21).

This was nothing new. In the same way, centuries before, God criticized the religious leaders through his prophet Ezekiel: "Ah, shepherds of Israel who have been feeding yourselves! Should not shepherds feed the sheep? You eat the fat, you clothe yourselves with the wool, you slaughter the fat ones, but you do not feed the sheep. The weak you have not strengthened, the sick you have not healed, the injured you have not bound up, the strayed you have not brought back, the lost you have not sought, and with force and harshness you have ruled them" (34:2–4). His critique concluded with a promise: "I will set up over them one shepherd, my servant David, and he shall feed them: he shall feed them and be their shepherd" (verse 23).

Jesus's claim to be the good shepherd has a prophetic precedent. How could the crowds determine whether his claim was valid? Jesus offered a series of tests for the true shepherd:

- **He knows his sheep.** The true shepherd enters by the door rather than by climbing over the wall (John 10:1–2). In other words, he shows legitimacy through transparency. The good shepherd does not hide from his sheep but is with them openly, just as Jesus was with the people constantly. The sheep recognize the voice of the shepherd (verses 3–5, 14–16). Unlike shepherds in other parts of the world who drive their sheep, Palestinian shepherds call their sheep. Each one has a name, and the shepherd knows them all.

- **He sacrifices himself for his sheep.** The shepherd lays down his life for the sheep (verses 9, 11, 15, 17–18). In verse 9, Jesus said, "I am the door." The sheep pen was simply a low rock enclosure with an opening on one side. It didn't actually have a door. Rather, when the sheep were put in the pen to sleep, the shepherd lay in the doorway. He was saying, "No one gets to my sheep except over my dead body."
  - In Jesus's case, however, even his dead body was an entrance into God's protective fold. To borrow his own words, "If anyone enters by me, he will be saved and will go in and out and find pasture" (verse 9). His self-sacrifice authenticates his identity as the good shepherd: "For this reason the Father loves me, because I lay down my life that I may take it up again. No one takes it from me, but I lay it down of my own accord. I have authority to lay it down, and I have authority to take it up again. This charge I have received from my Father" (verses 17–18).
  - In contrast, Jesus accused the religious leaders of falsely claiming to be shepherds since they didn't sacrifice for the sheep: "He who is a hired hand and not a shepherd, who does not own the sheep, sees the wolf coming and leaves the sheep and flees, and the wolf snatches them and scatters them. He flees because he is a hired hand and cares nothing for the sheep" (verses 12–13).

- **He improves the lives of his sheep.** Jesus said, "The thief comes only to steal and kill and destroy. I came that they may have life and have it abundantly" (verse 10). We saw false shepherds in action over the past few chapters. Remember how they treated the lame man in chapter 5, the woman caught in adultery in chapter 8, and the blind man in chapter 9. Jesus, however, healed, freed, and loved those abused by their own religious system.

These are the very tests we should use for leaders of our own day. Do they make your life better, or do they use you to make their lives better? Do they sacrifice the sheep or sacrifice for the sheep? Do they know their sheep by being among them? Whether someone is a business owner, a CEO, a teacher, a coach, a parent, or a pastor, a true shepherd lives as Jesus did, for the benefit of those God has put under his care.

Key Points

- Shepherds have always been a symbol of godly leadership—from Yahweh, to the heroes of the Bible, to Jesus himself.

- Jesus's words in John 10 mirror the ancient prophecy of Ezekiel 34 that a new shepherd would come to feed the flock of God.

- The three tests of a good shepherd that Jesus introduced are still valid for testing good leadership today.

This Week

❏ **Day 1 (Eyes):** After reading the essay, identify your own flock, the people you have influence over.

❏ **Day 2 (Ears):** After reading Ezekiel 34, underline all the similarities between this passage and John 10.

❏ **Day 3 (Heart):** Meditate on Hebrews 13:20; 1 Peter 2:25; 5:4. What do these passages add to our understanding of Jesus as a shepherd?

❏ **Day 4 (Voice):** Discussion:

- Who is the best leader you have ever had outside your own family?
- Why is knowing your flock so important for a leader?
- How can you tell if a leader is sacrificing for you or using you for her benefit?
- Identify one thing a leader is doing to make your life better.

❏ **Day 5 (Hands):** Do one thing this week to make life a little bit better for those God has put under your care.

Further Resources: Quest52.org/34

35

How Can We Share Our Faith Effectively?

Biblical Concept: Evangelism
Read: Matthew 10:1–42 with Mark 6:7–13; Luke 9:1–6

In middle school I ran around with three guys. None of them were Christians. I felt obligated to tell them about Jesus, but I was afraid of rejection. Peer pressure during puberty is heavy! One day I ran across Matthew 10:32–33: "Everyone who acknowledges me before men, I also will acknowledge before my Father who is in heaven, but whoever denies me before men, I also will deny before my Father who is in heaven."

I read it like this: if you *live* for Jesus, he will acknowledge you before God; if you *verbally* deny him, he will deny you. I soon discovered, however, that the word *acknowledge* in Greek specifically refers to verbal acclamation, whereas the word *deny* implies lifestyle. I remember thinking, *I had better figure out this evangelism thing if Jesus takes it that seriously.* That's why Jesus provided practical guidelines for sharing our faith:

1. **Offer help.** Jesus will never send you on a mission he has not prepared you for. "He called to him his twelve disciples and *gave them authority over unclean spirits,* to cast them out, and to heal every disease and every affliction" (verse 1). Hone the skills Jesus

has given you to benefit your community. When the apostles met real needs (verse 8), people were far more open to the message of the kingdom.

2. **Go in teams.** Jesus sent the apostles out in pairs. If you read verses 2–4 closely, you will notice each pair is identified between the semicolons: "The names of the twelve apostles are these: first, Simon, who is called Peter, and Andrew his brother; James the son of Zebedee, and John his brother; Philip and Bartholomew; Thomas and Matthew the tax collector; James the son of Alphaeus, and Thaddaeus; Simon the Zealot, and Judas Iscariot, who betrayed him." This was a model invariably followed in the book of Acts. Follow their example. Don't go it alone. Team up with others to share the good news of Jesus.

3. **Be strategic.** Surprisingly, Jesus told the Twelve, "Go nowhere among the Gentiles and enter no town of the Samaritans, but go rather to the lost sheep of the house of Israel" (Matthew 10:5–6). Why didn't Jesus want them preaching to Gentiles and Samaritans? Aren't we supposed to go to the ends of the earth? We are. However, it was too soon for that. This fits the pattern of "to the Jew first" (Romans 1:16; see Acts 13:46; 18:6; 28:25–28). They needed to go first to the places where they would have the greatest potential for success. You also should go first to the people and places most open to the gospel, unless the Holy Spirit directs you otherwise.

4. **Keep the main thing the main thing.** Often people want to debate about creation, other religions, or politics. Don't. Here's what Jesus told them to talk about: "Proclaim as you go, saying, 'The kingdom of heaven is at hand'" (Matthew 10:7). Talk about Jesus as the King, specifically his death for our sins and resurrection to life. Focus on Jesus.

5. **Keep your motives pure.** Jesus warned the Twelve, "You received without paying; give without pay. Acquire no gold or silver or copper for your belts, no bag for your journey, or two

tunics or sandals or a staff, for the laborer deserves his food" (verses 8–10). The only benefit we are seeking is the honor of Jesus. We don't share our faith with ulterior motives.

6. **Find the influencer.** Jesus said, "Whatever town or village you enter, find out who is worthy in it and stay there until you depart" (verse 11). Missionaries call that individual "the person of peace." He is an influencer in a particular place who shows openness to the gospel (or at least to you) and might multiply your efforts. If that person comes to Christ, he will influence others to follow. It could be a leader at work, a fellow teammate, a community organizer, or a social influencer.

7. **Bring God's blessing.** We typically don't think about bringing a spiritual blessing to people. However, as Christians, our very presence brings the Spirit of God. Jesus told the Twelve, "As you enter the house, greet it. And if the house is worthy, let your peace come upon it, but if it is not worthy, let your peace return to you" (verses 12–13). Paul raised the stakes when he said, "We are ambassadors for Christ, God making his appeal through us. We implore you on behalf of Christ, be reconciled to God" (2 Corinthians 5:20). Your status with God brings a blessing to anyone who welcomes you. Look at Matthew 10:42: "Whoever gives one of these little ones even a cup of cold water because he is a disciple, truly, I say to you, he will by no means lose his reward." The context makes it clear that the "little ones" are those of us who dare to brag about Jesus publicly. God's commission to speak comes with his authority to bless.

8. **Know when to "fold 'em."** There comes a time when our preaching is counterproductive. If people are unreceptive, at some point you just leave (either literally or figuratively). This doesn't mean they will never be open to the gospel. But if we keep preaching before people are ready to listen, we waste our energy and push them further away. It takes discernment to know when to back off, but Jesus told us pretty clearly, "If any-

one will not receive you or listen to your words, shake off the dust from your feet when you leave that house or town. Truly, I say to you, it will be more bearable on the day of judgment for the land of Sodom and Gomorrah than for that town" (verses 14–15). There is a time to fight (Acts 8:1; 16:37–40; 21:13) as well as a time for flight (8:1; 13:51; 14:6, 20).

9. **Be ready to suffer.** Preaching Christ makes people uncomfortable. They have to face their sin and confess their need for a savior. Some react violently. If they mistreated Jesus, should we expect anything different? As he said, "A disciple is not above his teacher, nor a servant above his master" (Matthew 10:24). Some of the worst treatment, in fact, will come from your own family: "Brother will deliver brother over to death, and the father his child, and children will rise against parents and have them put to death" (verse 21; see verses 24–37). Hopefully it doesn't come to that. If it does, however, there are three principles to keep in mind. First, the judgment of God is to be feared over the violence of humans. While humans can kill the body, Jesus warns us that God "can destroy both soul and body in hell" (verse 28). Second, carry your cross: "Whoever does not take his cross and follow me is not worthy of me. Whoever finds his life will lose it, and whoever loses his life for my sake will find it" (verses 38–39). Third, finish the race: "But the one who endures to the end will be saved" (verse 22; see Matthew 24:13; Mark 13:13; Hebrews 3:14; Revelation 2:26).

10. **Be shrewd.** Jesus warns us to be ready: "Behold, I am sending you out as sheep in the midst of wolves, so be wise as serpents and innocent as doves" (Matthew 10:16). There could hardly be a more pathetic picture than a sheep surrounded by wolves! Unless, of course, you are standing next to the Shepherd. Therefore, we need to be both wise and innocent. Christians often are better at being innocent. We talk a lot about morality. In the last days, it is just as important to be shrewd as to be pure.

11. **Trust the Spirit.** We may find ourselves in situations where we don't have the answer and lack the clout or courage to speak to "governors" or "kings." It is then that the Spirit in us can give us just the right words. "You will be dragged before governors and kings for my sake, to bear witness before them and the Gentiles. When they deliver you over, do not be anxious how you are to speak or what you are to say, for what you are to say will be given to you in that hour. For it is not you who speak, but the Spirit of your Father speaking through you" (verses 18–20). Believe it!

12. **Remember God's love.** God loves us more than we can imagine. "Are not two sparrows sold for a penny? And not one of them will fall to the ground apart from your Father. But even the hairs of your head are all numbered. Fear not, therefore; you are of more value than many sparrows" (verses 29–31). That's incredible and universal. Nonetheless, for those of us who dare to represent him on this earth, not only does he love us; he also provides us with the resources and protection we need to complete the commission he has given us. When anyone speaks up for Jesus, he takes it personally.

Key Points

- Being a witness for Jesus requires speaking up for him.

- Jesus gives us specific guidelines about how to effectively bear witness to him.

- Our ultimate power to preach comes not from our skills, knowledge, or training but from the guidance of the Spirit and the love of God.

This Week

❏ **Day 1 (Eyes):** After reading the essay, consider this question: How well are you doing speaking up for Jesus?

❏ **Day 2 (Ears):** Read Exodus 3–4. God called Moses to speak with Pharaoh; he had all kinds of excuses why he couldn't. How many of Jesus's talking points can you find in his story?

❏ **Day 3 (Heart):** Meditate on Romans 10:9–10; Hebrews 13:15; 1 Peter 3:15. What do these verses say about speaking up for Jesus?

❏ **Day 4 (Voice):** Discussion:

- Who told you about Jesus? What did that person do right? What could she have done better?
- We're all afraid to speak up for Jesus at some level. What do you think is the worst that can happen?
- Whom would you like to tell about Jesus? What is your main concern about how he might respond or what you might do to offend him?
- Which of the twelve points do you need to work on to be more effective in speaking up for Jesus?

❏ **Day 5 (Hands):** Put into practice one of the twelve points this week.

Further Resources: Quest52.org/35

36

Do You Ever Doubt
Your Doubts?

Biblical Concept: Resilience
Read: Matthew 11:2–11 with Luke 7:18–28

We all have our doubts. Try this with your pastor if you doubt he doubts. Ask this simple question: Are there any stories in the Bible you find hard to believe? Most will have a ready answer. For some it would be Jonah and the "whale" or the Virgin Birth—miracles that are scientifically difficult to believe. For others it would be exclusive statements that suggest Jesus is the only way to salvation. Some might be uncomfortable with women submitting to their husbands. For me it would be the genocides of the Old Testament when God ordered the execution of whole people groups. If you are looking for a reason to doubt, you won't have to look long. If, however, you want to doubt your doubts, that is just as easy. Look to Jesus, and you will find enough to hang on to during any season of doubt.

Doubt Your Doubts

John the Baptist was Jesus's forerunner. He announced the coming Messiah and baptized Jesus when he showed up at the River Jordan. Later,

John's disciples came to him with a report that Jesus was baptizing more disciples than he was. They asked, "What can we do to put you back on top?" "Nothing," said John. "He must increase, but I must decrease" (John 3:30). He was a true believer.

Fast-forward a year. John continued to preach in the wilderness about sin and social injustice, and one of his targets was the king. Herod had seduced his brother's wife and married her. Both left their spouses to climb the political ladder. When John railed against such immorality, the king did not take too kindly to John's negative PR campaign. His wife was worse. She convinced her hubby to have John arrested. According to one contemporary historian, Josephus, Herod was concerned that John's popularity was ready to explode into an uprising.[1]

There John sat in a prison cell in the fortress of Machaerus. It was a stronghold in the desert on the northeast shore of the Dead Sea. John had been there for ten months with lots of time to think. Jesus turned out to be different than John had imagined. The Messiah, according to the prophecies, was to release prisoners (Isaiah 61:1). Jesus knew that. He had even preached that very passage in his first sermon in Nazareth (Luke 4:18). So, why was John sitting in a cell? He sent a delegation ninety miles north to ask Jesus. "When John heard in prison about the deeds of the Christ, he sent word by his disciples and said to him, 'Are you the one who is to come, or shall we look for another?'" (Matthew 11:2–3).

We've all had those moments when Jesus doesn't meet our expectations. Perhaps it is the pain of a broken relationship. Maybe it's sickness or the loss of a job or the death of a dream. All of us have been there. Jesus's response is not just for John; it's for all of us who have experienced disappointment that birthed doubt: "Go and tell John what you hear and see: the blind receive their sight and the lame walk, lepers are cleansed and the deaf hear, and the dead are raised up, and the poor have good news preached to them. And blessed is the one who is not offended by me" (verses 4–6).

Jesus simply described his ministry. His actions spoke for themselves. His reply is pretty much a quote, combining Isaiah 35:5–6 and 61:1. He was telling John, "I may not have freed you from prison, but look at my résumé." Here is where it gets really interesting. He added a statement to his quotation that is not found in either Isaiah 35 or Isaiah 61: "the dead are raised up." Why would he add that line?

Directly across the Dead Sea from John's prison cell stood a community called Qumran. He could see it on a clear day. That settlement is famous today for the Qumran scrolls, a cache of eight hundred scrolls rediscovered in 1947. One of them quotes from Isaiah 35 and 61, the very passages Jesus combined. In that scroll, there is one line added that is *not* in the biblical text: "the dead are raised up." It appears that Jesus quoted from that scroll, saying to John, "I know where you are, and I know what is going to happen to you. I won't free you from prison, but I will raise you from the dead. I'm not what you expected; I am more than you imagined." This is precisely what Jesus did and precisely what he wants to say to you today: "I am more than you imagined."

Jesus was not bothered by John's doubts, but he did take the opportunity to warn him, "Blessed is the one who is not offended by me" (Matthew 11:6). Jesus will not *meet* your expectations; he will *exceed* them.

Don't Doubt Your Value

Sometimes we doubt God because we doubt ourselves. Jesus doesn't meet our expectations, so we are pretty sure we can't meet his. Not so. Jesus followed his mild rebuke of John with a wild affirmation: "What did you go out into the wilderness to see? A reed shaken by the wind? What then did you go out to see? A man dressed in soft clothing? Behold, those who wear soft clothing are in kings' houses" (verses 7–8). John was a man's man. He was no weakling, shaken by the wind. He was no prissy prince pampered in an ivory tower. His doubts did not diminish Jesus's respect for him, nor do yours. Jesus continued, "What then did you go out to see? A prophet? Yes, I tell you, and more than a prophet. This is he of whom it is written, 'Behold, I send my messenger before your face, who will prepare your way before you'" (verses 9–10, quoting Malachi 3:1). John was predicted in Scripture.

That's a big deal, but there is more. What Jesus said next is breathtaking. "Truly, I say to you, among those born of women there has arisen no one greater than John the Baptist" (Matthew 11:11). Really? The greatest man ever born? Why? Because of his proximity to Jesus. John announced his coming, baptized him in the Jordan, and sent his own disciples to follow him. It was his proximity to and promotion of Jesus that made him greater in God's eyes than Abraham, Moses, and David.

That's what Jesus said about John. What do you suppose he would say about you? We actually know. Verse 11: "The one who is least in the kingdom of heaven is greater than he." Are you a follower of Jesus? Then you are in the kingdom. Even if you are least in the kingdom, you are greater than John the Baptist. By extension, that makes you greater than Abraham, Moses, and David. How? By your proximity to and promotion of Jesus.

This is a *lot* to take in. Let's take a moment to think through the reality of our standing with God. We're greater than the saints of old for at least four reasons. First, we are filled with the Holy Spirit. Jesus said, "Whoever believes in me, as the Scripture has said, 'Out of his heart will flow rivers of living water.'" John explained, "This he said about the Spirit, whom those who believed in him were to receive, for as yet the Spirit had not been given, because Jesus was not yet glorified" (John 7:38–39). As Christians, we have the Spirit of God in us. The Spirit came on the prophets and patriarchs, but he never dwelt *in* individuals until the blood of Jesus atoned for our sins.

Second, we have a better covenant. Hebrews 8:10 (quoting Jeremiah 31:33) describes the difference:

> This is the covenant that I will make with the house of Israel
>   after those days, declares the Lord:
> I will put my laws into their minds,
>   and write them on their hearts,

and I will be their God,

    and they shall be my people. (see 2 Corinthians 3:7–18)

Third, we are children of the promise. "This means that it is not the children of the flesh who are the children of God, but the children of the promise are counted as offspring" (Romans 9:8; see Galatians 4:21–31). God planned all along for his blessing to go to the whole world. It is not the physical descendants of Abraham he prioritizes but those who imitate Abraham's faith.

Finally, we introduce Jesus to others in more personal and powerful ways! John was great because he announced Jesus's coming; we get to announce Jesus's second coming. John baptized Jesus in the Jordan River; we baptize people into Jesus. John announced Jesus as the Lamb of God; we proclaim him as the risen Savior.

You may be excited to see Moses in heaven. He is *more* excited to see you. You may ask, "What was it like to cross the Red Sea on dry ground?" He will respond, "Forget the Red Sea. What was it like to lead someone through the waters of baptism?" King David will ask about worshipping God in Spirit and truth. Abraham will inquire about birthing spiritual heirs. You see, you really are greater than they were because of your proximity to and promotion of Jesus. Go ahead and doubt your doubts; just don't doubt God's love.

Key Points

- Everyone has doubts, even John the Baptist.

- Our doubts do not diminish our value to God, and he is not offended by them.

- John was great because of his proximity to and promotion of Jesus. That's why the least in the kingdom is even greater than John the Baptist.

This Week

❏ **Day 1 (Eyes):** After reading the essay, consider this question: Do you ever doubt your doubts?

❏ **Day 2 (Ears):** There are four servant songs in Isaiah: 42:1–4; 49:1–6; 50:4–9; 52:13–53:12. What do we learn about Jesus's true nature from them?

❏ **Day 3 (Heart):** Meditate on how the Holy Spirit in us makes us closer to Jesus: Romans 8:14–17; 2 Corinthians 3:17–18; Ephesians 1:13.

❏ **Day 4 (Voice):** Discussion:
- What are your greatest doubts about God, Jesus, or the Bible?
- What makes you doubt your doubts?
- How has Jesus been different than you expected but better in the long run?
- How does the Holy Spirit help you personally connect with God? Are there places, experiences, or people that help you connect with Jesus and his Spirit?

❏ **Day 5 (Hands):** Write a declaration of who you are to God based on the verses in day 3.

Further Resources: Quest52.org/36

37

What Makes You a Good Person?

Biblical Concept: Morality
Read: Mark 7:1–23 with Matthew 15:1–20

Different people groups have very different ideas of "clean." For example, in India, you should never shake hands with your left hand. Why? Well, let's just say it is reserved for personal hygiene in a country that often does not use toilet paper. In Japan, the idea of carrying around a handkerchief in your pocket is disgusting. They cannot fathom why the British would want to blow their noses and keep the contents. Here is a bit of TMI: after living in Europe, I purchased a bidet, having been convinced of the superiority of touchless cleaning. My friends are disgusted with me when they discover this, but they are just wrong!

In this episode, Jesus got into a heated debate about clean and unclean. Of all things, it was an argument over handwashing. The stakes were way higher than when Mama says to wash up before supper. This short story may seem silly to some, but it has far-reaching ramifications, as we will see.

A Dinner Party with Baggage

Human beings are the only creatures that eat communally. God put that impulse in us. This makes our tables theological. It is at the table, more than any other place, where we reinforce roles in family, establish relationships with siblings, and set boundaries between insiders and outsiders (see Further Resources: "Table Fellowship"). In fact, each of Jesus's meals had some spiritual result. This meal was no exception.

> When the Pharisees gathered to him, with some of the scribes
> who had come from Jerusalem, they saw that some of his disciples
> ate with hands that were defiled, that is, unwashed. (For the
> Pharisees and all the Jews do not eat unless they wash their hands
> properly, holding to the tradition of the elders, and when they
> come from the marketplace, they do not eat unless they wash.
> And there are many other traditions that they observe, such as the
> washing of cups and pots and copper vessels and dining couches).
> (Mark 7:1–4)

Mark, writing to the church in Rome, had to explain some of the finer points of Jewish practice. The Jews had lots of rituals that only insiders understood (Leviticus 15 records a long list of them). For example, they washed their hands with an eggshell's worth of water. Their fingers had to point downward. If, however, they had been to the market and might have inadvertently bumped into a Gentile, they washed twice. First they poured the water over their hands with their fingers pointing upward to cover their hands down to their wrists. Then they reversed the process, rinsing their hands with their fingers pointing downward. What in the world?

We must understand that these washings were rituals; they were not for hygiene. They knew nothing of microbes. They were not washing off dirt; they were washing off cooties. You remember those from recess in the third grade? They are supposedly germs transferred by the touch of a girl. The Jews believed that the mere touch of an outsider could cause a spiritual infection. If you didn't wash, the cooties could get on your hands and, as you ate, be transferred to your mouth. Once inside you, they caused a spiritual infection. That's the reason for the double washing if you had been around outsiders.

This may sound silly. I assure you, it is not. Every culture, including our own, has rules about whom you can hang around with and the dire consequences of cross contamination. These rules may be political, religious, socioeconomic, or racial. All of them, however, are designed to keep your in-group pure from "contamination." Think of it as a physical means of virtue signaling. The reason these rituals so often surround food is that your table is a boundary marker between insiders and outsiders. The people you eat with are those you deem fully human.

In the Old Testament, God commanded his people to be separate from outsiders. They were particularly warned about intermarriage with unbelievers (Deuteronomy 7:3). The apostle Paul, of course, gave the same warning: "Do not be unequally yoked with unbelievers. For what partnership has righteousness with lawlessness? Or what fellowship has light with darkness?" (2 Corinthians 6:14). The rabbis, however, extended the marriage prohibition to their tables. After all, if you have a foreign guest at your table, your daughter may fall in love, then marry, then reproduce little reprobates. They actually called this "the hedge about the law." The same idea is behind installing a railing a few feet from the edge of a cliff. Kids may still climb on the railing, but if they fall over, they don't plummet to their deaths.

Clean Hands and Dirty Hearts

The Pharisees criticized Jesus's followers for not following their rules: "Why do your disciples not walk according to the tradition of the elders, but eat with defiled hands?" (Mark 7:5). Jesus criticized the Pharisees for replacing God's commands with human traditions: "Well did Isaiah prophesy of you hypocrites, as it is written, 'This people honors me with their lips, but their heart is far from me; in vain do they worship me, teaching as doctrines the commandments of men.' You leave the commandment of God and hold to the tradition of men" (verses 6–8).

That was gonna go over about as well as pork rinds at Passover. How dare he accuse them of not following the law? They were professionals in the Mosaic law! Jesus, however, cited a specific example they could hardly deny. It's called Corban (verses 9–13). This was a stipulation in the Mishnah (*Nedarim* 1:2–4) that stated that anything devoted to God could not be used for any other purpose. If my parents need a house to live in but I don't want to give them my vacation home, I simply devote it to God. Now, obviously, I can use it while I'm alive, but I can't give it away. In this way, I use my "religious devotion" to avoid one of the most sacred duties: honoring my father and mother (Deuteronomy 5:16).

Jesus halted the party, called for everyone's attention, and flipped the script. "Hear me, all of you, and understand: There is nothing outside a person that by going into him can defile him, but the things that come out of a person are what defile him" (Mark 7:14–15). The problem is not unwashed hands; the problem is an unclean heart.

The disciples were befuddled. When they got him alone, they asked what in the world he meant. His reply was not gentle: "Then are you also without understanding? Do you not see that whatever goes into a person from outside cannot defile him, since it enters not his heart but his stomach, and is expelled?" (verse 18–19). Yes, this was potty talk. He was saying exactly what it sounds like he was saying.

Lest you find this off putting, you should know that this is one of the most important things Jesus ever said. Mark, in fact, added a parenthetical comment to explain the impact: "Thus he declared all foods clean" (verse 19). Dietary restrictions (along with Sabbath observance and circumcision) were what identified a good Jew as a good Jew. Keeping kosher ensured that most Jews would keep to themselves and thus would be undefiled. This was necessary so the Messiah could come from a people who honored God's laws.

Now that the Messiah had come, however, such regulations were becoming obsolete. Why? Because God now wanted the message of Jesus to go to the ends of the earth. Dietary restrictions and rules about purity hindered the mission. In fact, table fellowship was *the* issue when Cornelius became the first Gentile to come to faith in Jesus (Acts 10–11). You cannot read his story without coming back to this moment when Jesus declared all foods clean. This is a colossal shift in Jewish religion, not because it changed the food on the table but because it opened the front door to the whole house (Acts 10:14, 28; 11:8; 15:20; Romans 14:14).

Christians often look at these Jewish laws as if they were frivolous: diet, Sabbath, circumcision. However, these were identity markers. Christians may have different markers, but they have them for sure: abstinence from alcohol and certain media, political affiliations, dress. I call it box morality. You get to the center of the box by digging deeper and deeper into the rules. The most righteous are at the center of the box. In this encounter, however, Jesus upended ethics by destroying the box. According to Jesus, morality is not about getting to the center of the box, but rather moving beyond your own boundaries. We can no longer tolerate artificial signs of spiritual significance.

If the church is to go global, only internal markers, not external signals, will suffice to include all tongues, tribes, and nations. To quote Jesus, "What comes out of a person is what defiles him. For from within, out of the heart of man, come evil thoughts, sexual immorality, theft, murder, adultery, coveting, wickedness, deceit, sensuality, envy, slander, pride, foolishness. All these evil things come from within, and they defile a person" (Mark 7:20–23). If we are to be clean Christians, we must guard what comes out of us, not what goes into us. Jesus's goal for the church is sanctification, not sanitation; he is about people over purity.

Key Points

- Table fellowship is socially and spiritually significant.

- Dietary restrictions became obsolete when the Messiah came because God wanted the gospel to go to the whole world.

- Jesus upended ethics by declaring all foods clean. This shifted morality from external rules to the motives of the heart.

This Week

❏ **Day 1 (Eyes):** After reading the essay, consider this question: What personal markers signal to others that you are a good Christian?

❏ **Day 2 (Ears):** How does Isaiah 58 answer the question "What makes you a good person?"

❏ **Day 3 (Heart):** Meditate on how these principles could apply to other areas of your life: Acts 15:20; Romans 14:14; 1 Corinthians 8:7.

❏ **Day 4 (Voice):** Discussion:
  • Share about your favorite meal—not what you like to eat but a memory you made at a specific place and time.
  • Why are meals so important for building relationships with people?
  • Did you grow up in a church that had external markers of morality—ways to signal your righteousness? What were they?
  • How could you use meals to open the door to a relationship with someone far from God?

❏ **Day 5 (Hands):** Schedule a meal with one of your neighbors whom you don't know well and who doesn't know Jesus well.

Further Resources: Quest52.org/37

38

Who Do You Say Jesus Is?

Biblical Concept: Declaration
Read: Matthew 16:13–28 with Mark 8:27–38; Luke 9:18–27

Every relationship must have the DTR talk—to define the relationship. At some point, you have that uncomfortable conversation: What are we doing here? Are we just friends, or are we really committed to each other? This is especially true with romantic relationships, but it also applies to business partnerships, friendships, and—believe it or not—your faith. Two years into his ministry, Jesus had the DTR with his apostles. He asked them, "Who do you say that I am?" (Matthew 16:15). At some point, he will have that conversation with you. Perhaps he already has. How you answer will determine more than you can imagine.

A Distant Place for a Close Conversation

Jesus wanted to have this important conversation in just the right place. He chose the area of Caesarea Philippi, twenty-five miles north of Capernaum. That is the farthest Jesus ever traveled outside Jewish territory. The place itself underscored the gravity of the question. Caesarea was a beautiful area with an ugly tradition. It was a center of worship for the god Pan, a nasty little pervert of a god. However, Jesus took his disciples there not because of Pan but because of Dan. Dan had become a ghost town by Jesus's time.

In the days of King David, Dan was a prominent city because it was the northernmost point of the kingdom. It became even more important after David, when his grandson Rehoboam provoked the people to rebel (1 Kings 12). The ten northern tribes seceded from the two southern tribes. Jeroboam, the leader of the rebellion, set up two altars to replace the temple so that the northern Israelites never had to venture back to Jerusalem in the south. One altar was in Bethel, on the southern border; the other was on the northern border in Dan. Each altar had a golden calf, which Jeroboam thought would be kosher. The prophets, however, considered them idols.

Dan represented the moment when Israel was broken and began to recognize their need for a Messiah. That made Dan the perfect place for this DTR. The site itself, where the base of the altar still stands today, would have reminded the disciples just what was at stake. It gave gravitas to the question "Who do people say that the Son of Man is?" (Matthew 16:13).

The answers offered were John the Baptist, Elijah, Jeremiah, or one of the other prophets. Each of these had two things in common. First, they all confronted Israel's leaders. Second, they were all dead. That pretty much describes where Jesus's ministry was heading. His coming confrontations would lead to martyrdom. I'm sure the apostles thought this was a compliment, comparing Jesus to the likes of Elijah. However, to equate Jesus with even these greats is to damn him with faint praise. He is far more than a formidable prophet.

The Most Important Question
You'll Ever Answer

The disciples hadn't revealed anything Jesus didn't already know. He had heard all the gossip. So he asked the real question: "Who do *you* say that

I am?" (verse 15). That's what really mattered, and it matters just as much for us. At some point, we will all have to give our own answers, whether here on earth or in eternity.

Peter spoke for the group: "You are the Christ, the Son of the living God" (verse 16). That's huge. After two years, they finally gave voice to their dreams. Jesus was the long-awaited Messiah. In Jewish vernacular, that meant Jesus was to be the king of Israel. The predictions of this Messiah were not of the humble, self-sacrificial savior we find in the Epistles. Rather, the Messiah in Jewish literature was a violent warrior who would brutally destroy all enemies of the state. That was Peter's expectation (and hope). A correction was coming.

Just as Peter had affirmed Jesus's parentage (Son of God) and position (Messiah), Jesus affirmed Peter's parentage (son of Jonah) and position (foundation stone of the church): "Blessed are you, Simon Bar-Jonah! For flesh and blood has not revealed this to you, but my Father who is in heaven. And I tell you, you are Peter, and on this *rock* I will build my *church,* and the gates of hell shall not prevail against it. I will give you the *keys* of the kingdom of heaven, and whatever you bind on earth shall be bound in heaven, and whatever you loose on earth shall be loosed in heaven" (verses 17–19).

This declaration is dense. Three words require a bit of explanation. First, Peter is the rock on which the church is built. It is a clever play on words since *Peter* actually means "rock." There is some debate as to whether Peter himself is the rock or whether his confession carries that weight. Whatever this might mean, however, it at least suggests that Peter represented the apostles as the foundation of the church. This is true in some sense of all the apostles since the church is "built on the foundation of the apostles and prophets, Christ Jesus himself being the cornerstone" (Ephesians 2:20). By extension, all Christians are included since we are "living stones" in the "spiritual house" of God (1 Peter 2:5).

Second, *church* (*ekklēsia*) means "those called to an assembly." It is a Greek word used for a civic gathering (Acts 19:32). When God calls the assembly, it becomes sacred. In the Old Testament, his assembly was called the *qahal*—the nation of Israel. In the New Testament, the ekklēsia is a spiritual kingdom, not an ethnic nation, called through faith in Christ.

Finally, the *keys* Jesus gave Peter represent the authority to lock or unlock the door of salvation. Peter, of course, is not the only one with that authority. In John 20:23, the same authority was given to all the apostles, and Matthew 18:15–18 extends it to Christian leaders in general. In fact, as a believer, you share that authority and responsibility to preach Jesus and announce his forgiveness to those who repent and make him Lord (2 Corinthians 5:20). Peter held the first set of keys, but all of us open the same set of doors, giving others access to Jesus.

That's a lot of authority vested in the church. Consequently, the Lord is invested in the church. He ensures its ultimate victory: "The gates of hell shall not prevail against it" (Matthew 16:18). This simple statement is the book of Revelation in miniature. In fact, it's a pretty good summary of the whole Bible.

I'm Not Who You Think

Jesus clarified Peter's confession. Virtually every prediction describes the Messiah as a conquering king. But two outliers give us a glimpse of the suffering Savior: Isaiah 53 and Zechariah 12. Little wonder, then, that Peter could not fathom Jesus dying. As soon as the confession dropped from Peter's lips, Jesus course corrected: "From that time Jesus began to show his disciples that he must go to Jerusalem and suffer many things from the elders and chief priests and scribes, and be killed, and on the third day be raised" (Matthew 16:21). He identified the specific place he would be killed and the people who would kill him. This was the clearest Jesus had ever been about his death. However, it wasn't the first time he had alluded to his impending suffering (Matthew 9:15; 10:38–39; 12:39–40; John 2:19; 3:14). Why did they miss it?

A victorious king *and* a suffering servant seemed contradictory. Peter took Jesus aside and rebuked him: "Far be it from you, Lord! This shall never happen to you" (Matthew 16:22). Let that sink in—Peter rebuked Jesus. That was not going to end well for Peter. Jesus rebuked him: "Get behind me, Satan! You are a hindrance to me. For you are not setting your mind on the things of God, but on the things of man" (verse 23). Oh snap! He just called Peter "Satan" (which means "adversary"). It may seem harsh, but it's not inaccurate. Peter was tempting Jesus to short-circuit the cross. That was the very thing the devil tried to do during Jesus's wilderness temptations (Matthew 4:8–10).

Jesus then turned to the other apostles (and to us!) and gave this crucial command. It is, in fact, the most frequently cited saying of Jesus. We dare not disregard it. "If anyone would come after me, let him deny himself and take up his cross and follow me. For whoever would save his life will lose it, but whoever loses his life for my sake will find it" (Matthew 16:24–25). Jesus's call to a cross, understood in his social context, means getting caught and punished as a rebel. He is calling us to die to ourselves and trust him for our resurrection.

So often Christians talk about the cross as Jesus's sacrifice. That's correct but insufficient. One-third of all cross talk in the Gospels is about the cross we take up in following Jesus. Hence, the cross is not only Jesus's sacrifice but ours as well. When Jesus died on the cross, he saved the world from her sins. When we die on the cross, we save society from hers. Therefore, not only is the cross Jesus's path to victory; it is ours as well. If we lay down our lives, God will raise us up.

Key Points

- Who do you say Jesus is? There is no more important question.

- Jesus's suffering as a servant was the precursor to his victorious reign as king.

- The cross of Jesus saves the world from her sins; the cross of Christians saves society from her sins.

This Week

❏ **Day 1 (Eyes):** After reading the essay, who do you say Jesus is?

❏ **Day 2 (Ears):** Read the story of Rehoboam and Jeroboam in 1 Kings 12. How might Jesus think about his own royal career in light of this history?

❏ **Day 3 (Heart):** Meditate on 2 Corinthians 4:10–12; Galatians 2:20; Philippians 3:10–11. What do these verses say about being crucified with Christ?

❏ **Day 4 (Voice):** Discussion:

- Share how you came to faith in Jesus. Was it through a process or a crisis (or both)?
- What is the difference between believing in Jesus as Lord and believing in him as Savior? Can you really do one without the other?
- In what ways do you think the church has misunderstood or misrepresented Jesus's true identity?
- How is it that Christians taking up their crosses leads to salvation for society? Can you offer an example of how that works?

❏ **Day 5 (Hands):** Think carefully about how to answer this question: Who do you say Jesus is? Write your answer in a single sentence. Now find someone to share that with this week.

Further Resources: Quest52.org/38

39

What's Worth Worrying About?

Biblical Concept: Anxiety
Read: Luke 10:38–42

Anxiety disorders have increased 1,200 percent in the last four decades.[1] They have now surpassed depression and all other disorders as the most common mental illness in America, affecting forty million adults each year.[2] That's one in five. Since many people never seek help for mental health, some professionals estimate that it's actually closer to 30 percent (or one-third) of adults who suffer from some form of anxiety disorder. That counts as a pandemic.

Most anxiety disorders are more prevalent among women than men, two to one, in fact. Even though most anxiety disorders are highly treatable, only 37 percent of people suffering are actually diagnosed and treated.[3] Some anxiety disorders will require medication or counseling if they pass a certain threshold of severity. So, please, if you need medical or psychological support, get the help you need to be healthy. At the same time, we should recognize that all mental health disorders have at their root a spiritual component. Therefore, faith in Jesus Christ should be at the core of any treatment for mental health issues. For anxiety, in particular, faith is often the most formidable antidote. Let's take a look at one example from the life of Jesus.

Two Sisters

Mary and Martha were sisters. Their brother, Lazarus, was one of Jesus's best friends. We meet them from time to time in the Gospels. In fact, sometime after this event, Jesus would raise their brother, Lazarus, from the dead (see John 11). The sisters, of course, played a crucial role. In this passage, Luke shared the prequel, a story from earlier in Jesus's ministry.

If we piece together the chronology of the four Gospels, Jesus was invited to Mary and Martha's home after the Feast of Tabernacles. They lived just over the Mount of Olives from the capital city. One can imagine the women sending daily invitations: "Hey, Jesus, since you're in the area, you simply *must* come to our home for dinner." They were surely aware of the pressure Jesus was under. There was an assassination plot afoot, which he knew full well (John 7:25, 30–32, 44–45; 8:20, 59). Yet they kept applying pressure for Jesus to come. When the feast was over, he finally did. (John 7–10 describes the Feast of Tabernacles, offering some color commentary on what Jesus must have been feeling as he went to Mary and Martha's home.)

The sisters planned a retreat at their table. Undoubtedly, they fussed over menus, recipes, seating arrangements, and hors d'oeuvres. After their extensive preparations, shopping, and sweat equity in the kitchen, Jesus arrived with the boys. All was set for a memorable event, which it was, but not for the reasons Martha had imagined.

Martha executed her plan to perfection. Mary, on the other hand, got swept up in Jesus's teaching. She sat at his feet in rapt attention. Martha picked up the slack. She worked double time to make sure the banquet went off without a hitch. With every dish and drink she served, her anger increased. Martha was doing everything she could to be a Martha Stewart, but her sous-chef was negligent, sitting down on the job. That is bad enough in our culture, but in hers, women were to be seen and not heard.

Never had a rabbi allowed a woman to sit as a student. Jesus was simply ignoring Mary's irresponsible behavior! To make matters worse, meals in the Middle East were traditional events where roles and rules were established and reinforced. Mary was *out of line,* and Jesus was letting her get away with it, setting a very bad precedent. Something had to be said.

Martha was beside herself, while Mary was beside Jesus. Martha finally snapped, asking Jesus to order Mary back into the kitchen: "Lord, do you not care that my sister has left me to serve alone? Tell her then to help me" (Luke 10:40). The word translated "left" is a Greek word with a melodramatic meaning: "Mary *abandoned* me!" Oh brother! Jesus's reply was just as "reckless" as Mary's actions. He deliberately ignored their cultural mores in the hope of establishing new and better priorities. "Martha, Martha, you are anxious and troubled about many things, but one thing is necessary. Mary has chosen the good portion, which will not be taken away from her" (verses 41–42). Rather than supporting Martha's traditional values, Jesus rewrote the script of what was most important.

Why We Worry

Jesus simply told Martha, "Don't worry." Or more accurately, "Stop worrying, and start focusing on the one thing that really matters." He was right; there is only one thing necessary, and it is Jesus himself. Mary had the proper priority. It is clear from our perspective. We see how incredibly fortunate Martha was to have Jesus in her home, and she was missing the moment, fussing over the insignificant. If Jesus showed up at your house right now, would you worry about the dishes? (Well, honestly, some would.) Martha was missing the majesty of Jesus's presence because she was trying to impress him with her hosting prowess. As nonsensical as that seems, we all do that very thing. We worry more about impressing God than experiencing him in the moment. We are more concerned about our social status than our spiritual health. Worry has snared us through public opinion, which is magnified by social media.

As we saw in chapters 29 and 30, worry comes from two concerns: (1)

social approval and (2) physical needs. That may sound like an oversimplification, but it really is not. Matthew 6 shows how God is more concerned than we imagine about our two greatest concerns. He provides magnificently for birds and flowers yet loves us far more than he loves them. He privately approves us every time we perform a good deed with pure motives. There is simply no reason we should worry, unless, of course, we doubt God's love or question his power. Worry is practical atheism.

For most, their primary worry is not about food or clothes but about others' opinions. Here is my personal confession: virtually every time I experience anxiety, it is because I fear someone's disapproval. When I get an aggressive email or miss an appointment or deadline, my mind shifts into overdrive. I concoct all kinds of conversations in my head. I script out my defensive response, my justifications and rebuttals. Why? Because I don't believe God has my back. Even while typing this, I'm embarrassed by my miniscule faith. Like Martha, I'm trying to manipulate God's opinion of me rather than experiencing the love God has for me.

Jesus told Martha not to worry. The word Jesus used, *merimnaō,* is found nineteen times in the New Testament. If we trace every use of that word, we find that worry has not changed in two thousand years. What worried them then still concerns us today. All our worry can be reduced to three categories: resources, reputation, and relationships:

1. **Resources.** Nine of the nineteen times, this word refers to resources (Matthew 6:25–34; Luke 12:22–26). These are the famous passages where Jesus warns us not to worry about clothes and food. God knows our needs and proves his ability to provide as he cares for birds and flowers.

2. **Reputation.** Two of the nineteen times are in Matthew 10:19 and Luke 12:11. Jesus said, "When they deliver you over, do not be anxious how you are to speak or what you are to say, for what you are to say will be given to you in that hour" (Matthew 10:19). We don't have to worry about being embarrassed in public because of the overwhelming approval God gives us in

private. If our motives are noble, we never have to fear God's disapproval.

3. **Relationships.** Four of the nineteen times are in one passage. Paul tells single people to remain unmarried if possible so they will be able to give full attention to spreading the gospel rather than worrying about a relationship (1 Corinthians 7:32–34). The implication is that it is right to worry about relationships. He affirmed that in Philippians 2:20 when he bragged about Timothy: "I have no one like him, who will be genuinely concerned for your welfare." If you are going to worry about anything, worry about your marriage and about the people of your church. That's fair.

Worry incapacitates warriors. For those who want to fight for God, Paul offered an antidote to worry: "Do not be anxious about anything, but in everything by prayer and supplication with thanksgiving let your requests be made known to God" (Philippians 4:6). Is it really possible to remove all anxiety? No, of course not. But we can reduce it significantly. The story of Martha tells us how: get your priorities right. How do we do that? Philippians 4:6 tells us: prayers of thanksgiving. When we thank God for all he's done for us, we are reminded of his meticulous care for us. Therein is the secret to a worry-free life.

Key Points

- Martha was worried about impressing Jesus. Mary chose to be impressed by Jesus.
- The antidote to worry is prioritizing Jesus.
- Prayers of thanksgiving set your priorities right.

This Week

❑ **Day 1 (Eyes):** After reading the essay, consider this question: Do you have the right priorities to minimize worry in your life?

❑ **Day 2 (Ears):** Read Psalm 37. Underline each verse that speaks to your present situation.

❑ **Day 3 (Heart):** Meditate on Philippians 4:6. Take time to actually memorize it with this video: https://core52.org/week/week-48.[4]

❑ **Day 4 (Voice):** Discussion:

- As a group, make a list of things you are worrying about, perhaps on a whiteboard (or a window in your living room with erasable markers). Now put them in three columns: resources, reputation, and relationships.
- As an anti-anxiety exercise, make a list of things you are grateful to God for.
- Is your worry in your head or in your body? True anxiety disorders have physiological manifestations such as shortness of breath, insomnia, extreme fatigue, and/or heart palpitations. If you have anxiety in your body, you may need to consult with a physician or counselor.
- Worst-case scenario exercise: Have the group take one item on your list. Play it out to the ultimate extreme. What is the worst thing that can happen? How do the scriptures in the New Testament address the worst-case scenario?

❑ **Day 5 (Hands):** Read Philippians 4:6. Now do it.

Further Resources: Quest52.org/39

Section 4

The Passion of Jesus

Leading up to the Cross, we want to look at historical, political, and social aspects of Jesus's **preparation** for his sacrifice. We will then look at the **suffering** itself, both spiritually and physically. This takes us beyond the grave to Jesus's **victory** in the Resurrection and Ascension, which point to his ultimate return when our quest will finally end in eternity.

Preparation: chapters 40–43
Suffering: chapters 44–48
Victory: chapters 49–52

40

Was Jesus Political?
Part I

Biblical Concept: Politics
Read: Luke 19:29–44 with Matthew 21:1–11; Mark 11:1–11;
John 12:12–19

What does it mean to be political? Let's start with a definition. The word *political* comes from the same Greek root as *politeuomai,* meaning "to live as a citizen" (Philippians 1:27). At its core, politics is the creation of a community. Therefore, to be a political figure, one must meet four specific criteria. She must (1) be **public,** not private, (2) have an identifiable group of **followers,** (3) have a social **agenda,** and (4) exercise **power** over people.

Did Jesus fit the description? Absolutely. You may say, "But he didn't have a political position of power in the establishment." True, but neither did Martin Luther King Jr. or Mahatma Gandhi. Being political is not always the same as being a politician. What really throws us is not Jesus's lack of position but his use of power. Politicians are known for using power to promote and protect themselves. Jesus, in contrast, used power only for the powerless. His brand of being political subverted politics itself.

Jesus Claimed to Be King

Although Jesus never verbally claimed to be king (which would have been suicide), his actions spoke louder than words. His selection of twelve apostles showed his intention of restoring the twelve tribes. His commissioning of seventy-two evangelists (Luke 10:1) mirrored the seventy-one members of the Sanhedrin (the Jewish Supreme Court). He compared himself to Moses, who founded the nation, as well as David, her premier king. He claimed to be a shepherd, a judge, and the Messiah, all leadership roles in Israel.

One incident, however, was more overtly political than any other. The Triumphal Entry was straight-up political theater. Its importance is seen in the fact that it is only the second event recorded in all four Gospels. The first was the feeding of the five thousand, which was also political since it caused the crowd to clamor for Jesus's immediate coronation, by force if necessary (John 6:15).

The Triumphal Entry began in a suburb of Jerusalem known as Bethphage. Jesus commissioned two of his men to get a colt. The details sound like an eyewitness account: "Those who were sent went away and found it just as [Jesus] had told them. And as they were untying the colt, its owners said to them, 'Why are you untying the colt?' And they said, 'The Lord has need of it'" (Luke 19:32–34). We can only guess that the colt's owners knew Jesus. It is possible that he had healed one of their relatives during one of his frequent speaking engagements in the area.

Matthew added two interesting details in his rendition. First, they sequestered both the colt and its mother. Those who know about livestock will see the wisdom in this. Both mother and baby would be far calmer if they could walk together through a clamoring crowd. The second detail is more significant. Matthew identified the moment as a fulfillment of prophecy:

Say to the daughter of Zion,
"Behold, your king is coming to you,

humble, and mounted on a donkey,

on a colt, the foal of a beast of burden." (21:5, quoting

Zechariah 9:9).

Donkeys make us think of Don Quixote; Jews, however, thought of kings (Judges 5:10; 1 Kings 1:33). If we continue reading Zechariah's prophecy, we find it pregnant with messianic predictions:

- **The thirty pieces of silver** Iscariot was paid to betray Jesus: "The LORD said to me, *'Throw it to the potter'*—the lordly price at which I was priced by them. So I took *the thirty pieces of silver* and threw them into the house of the LORD, to the potter" (Zechariah 11:13, fulfilled in Matthew 27:9–10).

- **Jesus pierced at his crucifixion:** "I will pour out on the house of David and the inhabitants of Jerusalem a spirit of grace and pleas for mercy, so that, when they look on me, on *him whom they have pierced,* they shall mourn for him, as one mourns for an only child, and weep bitterly over him, as one weeps over a firstborn" (Zechariah 12:10, fulfilled in John 19:34, 37).

- **Strike the shepherd,** and the sheep will scatter: " 'Awake, O sword, against my shepherd, against the man who stands next to me,' declares the LORD of hosts. *Strike the shepherd,* and the sheep will be scattered; I will turn my hand against the little ones' " (Zechariah 13:7, fulfilled in Matthew 26:31; Mark 14:27).

- **The Mount of Olives** and the appearance of the Messiah: "On that day his feet shall stand on *the Mount of Olives* that lies before Jerusalem on the east, and the Mount of Olives shall be split in two from east to west by a very wide valley, so that one half of the Mount shall move northward, and the other half southward" (Zechariah 14:4). This happens to be the exact spot of the Triumphal Entry.

Clearly, there is more here than meets the Western eye. The timing of Passover, the location of the Mount of Olives, and the colt on which Jesus rode were all clear signs that he was claiming to be king. Interestingly, that was the second triumphal entry that week. You see, Pilate, who normally resided in Caesarea, came to town to calm the crowds during this particularly patriotic holiday. When governors visited important cities, the populace were obliged to greet them royally. Pilate's grand entrance, however, would have been on the opposite side of the city since he was coming from the northwest. The compass points were not the only thing opposite with Jesus. His whole approach to political power can be summed up in a simple observation: all earthly politicians use power for self-promotion and self-protection; Jesus used his power only for the powerless. So began a brand-new kind of leadership.

The Crowds Affirmed Jesus as King

Jesus's intentions could not have been clearer. He was the Messiah, and now was the time for his coronation. The crowds were equally clear. We may not see it through the lens of our own culture. But if you put on the lens of the Middle East, their actions shouted their acclaim of their new king:

- The disciples spread their cloaks on the colt for Jesus to sit on (Luke 19:35). The crowds spread their cloaks on the road for the donkey to walk on (Matthew 21:8; 2 Kings 9:13).

- They cut palm branches and waved them and laid them on the ground as a red carpet (Mark 11:8; John 12:13). Waving

palm branches was a sign that royalty was in the room (Revelation 7:9).

- They started singing Psalm 118:25–26:
  a. "*Hosanna* [which means 'save now!'] to the *Son of David*!"
     (Matthew 21:9). This was clearly a reference to the messi-
     anic King.
  b. "Blessed is he who comes in the *name* [meaning 'author-
     ity'] of the Lord!" (verse 9).
  c. "Blessed is the coming *kingdom* of our father David!"
     (Mark 11:10). John added this interpretation: "even the
     King of Israel" (12:13). That's pretty clear.
  d. "Hosanna in the *highest*!" (Matthew 21:9). That's where
     God dwells and from whence his salvation comes.

Even if we read only the italicized words above, we cannot miss the
political rhetoric. The Pharisees understood exactly what both Jesus and
the crowds were claiming. They said to one another, "You see that you are
gaining nothing. Look, the world has gone after him" (John 12:19). Then
they said to Jesus, "Teacher, rebuke your disciples" (Luke 19:39). Yeah,
right! Like *that* was gonna happen. Here is his reply (get ready to giggle):
"I tell you, if these were silent, the very stones would cry out" (verse 40).
It was a magnificent moment. That's why what happened next was so
unexpected.

Jesus wept over the city. He didn't just shed a tear; the word Luke used
indicates deep, audible sobs: "Would that you, even you, had known on
this day the things that make for peace! But now they are hidden from
your eyes. For the days will come upon you, when your enemies will set
up a barricade around you and surround you and hem you in on every
side and tear you down to the ground, you and your children within you.
And they will not leave one stone upon another in you, because you did
not know the time of your visitation" (verses 42–44).

In a moment when most politicians would revel in their accolades,

Jesus wept for his people. He knew full well that his coronation would be with a crown of thorns. He knew that a terrible price would be paid for rejecting him. Yet he walked straight into the teeth of suffering and death, knowing the power of the Resurrection.

This sets a new gold standard for leadership. A leader's goal is no longer accolades and power. Rather, leadership is measured by service and sacrifice. The endgame of leadership is not power but a legacy of love. Jesus was political by any reasonable definition, but he altered the purpose and practice of political leadership so as to require a whole new metric of success. As his followers, subjects, and servants, our promotion of our king should reflect his political methodology of using power only for the powerless. By this we will win the world and make Jesus famous.

Key Points

- Jesus does not appear political to us because we are used to politicians using power for self-promotion and self-protection. Jesus used power only for the powerless.

- Though Jesus never verbally claimed a political title, his actions clearly indicated his intent to be the king of Israel.

- The Triumphal Entry was the most politically charged event of his career. He clearly claimed to be king, and the crowds overtly declared their support.

This Week

❏ **Day 1 (Eyes):** After reading the essay, consider this question: What difference would it make to you if Jesus really were the president of the world, not merely the Savior of your soul?

❏ **Day 2 (Ears):** Psalm 118 was quoted by the crowds at the Triumphal Entry. What other verses in this poem reflect the life of Jesus?

❏ **Day 3 (Heart):** Meditate on Acts 17:7; 1 Corinthians 15:24–25; Revelation 11:15. How do these verses portray the politics of Jesus?

❏ **Day 4 (Voice):** Discussion:
- Had you ever thought of Jesus as a political figure? Does that resonate with you or seem unsettling? Why?
- If Jesus were the president of the world, what do you think his agenda would look like?
- What is the difference between claiming Jesus as Savior and acclaiming him as Lord?
- If you were campaigning for Jesus, what would your strategy be to make him famous?

❏ **Day 5 (Hands):** Pull out one item from your campaign strategy this week, and put it into practice.

Further Resources: Quest52.org/40

41

Was Jesus Political?
Part 2

Biblical Concept: Authority
Read: Mark 11:12–25 with Matthew 21:12–22;
Luke 19:45–48; John 2:13–22

When I'm hungry (or hangry), I'm not a nice person. My sweet wife knows this. If I have to wait more than an hour for dinner, I get all kinds of cranky. It's sad, but it helped me appreciate one of the weirdest moments in Jesus's ministry. He cursed a fig tree for not providing breakfast. His motives were nobler than mine. So there has got to be more to the story than meets the eye. There is—a *lot* more.

A Fit over Figs

The final Sunday before the Crucifixion, Jesus had ridden down the Mount of Olives in what is now known as the Triumphal Entry. It was a watershed moment of his ministry. He proclaimed himself as the King of the Jews. When the dust settled, the boys returned to Bethany, where they were lodging during Passover.

"On the following day [Monday], when they came from Bethany, [Jesus] was hungry. And seeing in the distance a fig tree in leaf, he went to see if he could find anything on it. When he came to it, he found nothing but leaves, for it was not the season for figs. And he said to it, 'May no one ever eat fruit from you again'" (Mark 11:12–14). Matthew noted that the tree withered immediately (21:19). Mark revealed that it actually took twenty-four hours (11:20). That seems rather rude to the unsuspecting fig tree. Perhaps a bit of background would make more sense of this.

Jews typically ate two meals a day (ten o'clock in the morning and six o'clock in the evening). Given the gravity of the previous day's events, it's reasonable to assume that Jesus might have missed supper as he often did when he got too busy (Mark 3:20; 6:31). This would explain why he would eat figs before they were ripe. Since it was only April, all he could hope for were green bulbs. They would be bitter but edible. The fact that there were none meant there would not be any in the future. This fig tree was fruitless.

T. W. Manson was critical of this cursing: "It is a tale of miraculous power wasted in the service of ill-temper (for the supernatural energy employed to blast the unfortunate tree might have been more usefully expended in forcing a crop of figs out of season); and as it stands it is simply incredible."[1] With all due respect, Manson's eco-friendly commentary misses the point entirely.

Mark shaped the story so it is hard to miss the message. He told about the cursing of the fig tree, followed by the cleansing of the temple. He then circled back to the fig tree the following day when the apostles actually noticed its demise. Mark was making a literary sandwich. The incident in the middle is the meat, flavoring the bread on either side. Bottom line: Jesus's action against the fig tree is a prophetic parable, parallel to the cleansing of the temple. Both show the destiny of a fruitless nation because of their rejection of their Messiah.

The "Cleansing" of the Temple

This title in our Bibles is a bit of a misnomer. Jesus did not exactly cleanse the temple. Rather, he threatened it: "He entered the temple and began to drive out those who sold and those who bought in the temple, and he overturned the tables of the money-changers and the seats of those who sold pigeons. And he would not allow anyone to carry anything through the temple" (Mark 11:15–16).

Again, a bit of background will help us mentally map this moment. First, the buying and selling in the temple was not the problem. The chief priests profiteering from the piety of pilgrims was. Annas, the high priest, had set up a system to traffic in the sacred precincts. Specifically, the sacrificial lambs were sold at exorbitant prices. If you brought your own lamb, it had to be without defect. Some priests were tasked with inspecting the lambs to make sure they were worthy. They would not pass inspection, of course. The priests would, however, offer to buy the lamb at a reduced rate (it could later be sold to another unsuspecting pilgrim at the inflated price). Furthermore, the priests would accept payment only in the temple shekel, which could be obtained from the money changers—with an exchange fee, of course.

Is it any wonder Jesus disrupted their bazaar? But how did he get away with it? He attacked the establishment in the pocketbook, and he did so in the temple, where they had home-field advantage. That seems brazen. At least three factors likely allowed Jesus to pull it off. First, the Pharisees, who were respected by the populace, actually sided with Jesus on this issue. Their support would have mitigated the aggression against him in the temple. Second, the temple courts covered an area roughly the size of thirty football fields. Jesus did not necessarily stop all trade and certainly not for any significant length of time. He could engage quickly, toss a few tables, and disappear back into the crowd. Third, the Roman garrison (approximately nine hundred men) was stationed in the Tower of Antonia, which literally overlooked the northwest court of the temple. These soldiers were eager for an excuse to knock a few heads. The chief priests would have gone to great lengths to keep that from happening. Ignoring Jesus's infraction (for now) would avoid a catastrophe during Passover.

Jesus explained his motive: "Is it not written, 'My house shall be called a house of prayer for all the nations'? But you have made it a den of robbers" (Mark 11:17). This is actually a quote combining Isaiah 56:7 and Jeremiah 7:11. Both texts were carefully chosen, and together they send a powerful and threatening message.

Isaiah 56 opens with this promise: "Thus says the LORD: 'Keep justice, and do righteousness, for soon my salvation will come, and my righteousness be revealed'" (verse 1). The prophet then listed those who would receive salvation: the one who kept the Sabbath and did good (verse 2) and the foreigner who showed fidelity to Yahweh (verses 3, 6), even if he was a eunuch (verses 4–5). In other words, all outsiders who believed in the Messiah would have equal standing, even inside the temple. You know where the chief priests set up the bazaar? Not in the court of the Jewish men. No, it was in the court of the Gentiles, the only part of the temple complex in which foreigners could worship.

The second passage Jesus quoted was Jeremiah 7:11. Jeremiah was known as "the weeping prophet" for good reason. He preached against the powers that be and got punished for it. In Jeremiah 7, he stood in the temple court, the very ground where Jesus was now. He railed against their oppression of foreigners, the fatherless, and widows (verse 6), against their theft, murder, adultery, and perjury (verse 9). The people believed that they were safe from judgment because they maintained the temple for God. Jeremiah warned them that God would tear it down if they did not repent. Their own false prophets asserted that God would *never* destroy his own temple. But Jeremiah said, "Do not trust in these deceptive words: 'This is the temple of the LORD, the temple of the LORD, the temple of the LORD'" (verse 4). He warned that God *would* destroy the temple if their worship was false. In 586 BC, God did.

Taken in context, Jesus's quotation was a stern warning: repent or repeat your history. This temple would be destroyed. Two days later, Jesus detailed for his disciples just how it would happen (Matthew 24; Mark 13; Luke 21). In AD 70, his prophecy was fulfilled down to the smallest point. It was tragic, and to this day, the physical temple has never been rebuilt. It has been replaced, according to the apostles, with the spiritual temple of the body of Christ (1 Corinthians 6:16–19; 2 Corinthians 6:16; Ephesians 2:19–22; 1 Peter 2:5). This reminds us of an earlier incident. At the beginning of his ministry, Jesus also cleared the temple courts. This threat to the temple bracketed his ministry. Back then he told us exactly what he was up to: "Destroy this temple, and in three days I will raise it up" (John 2:19).

His body is the new temple. This very threat to the old one would be brought up at his trials as the reason for his execution (Matthew 26:61). His resurrection not only proved he was right but also launched a new era of the temple. He is now able to incorporate foreigners into his body, this renewed kingdom where citizenship is open to every tongue, tribe, and nation. That kingdom of God is the temple of Christ, where true worship and sacrifice are performed. This is the epicenter of the politics of Jesus. A new nation of people whose citizenship is in heaven even as we spread his fame to every corner of the earth.

Key Points

- The cursing of the fig tree is an enacted parable predicting the destruction of the temple.

- Jesus quoted from Isaiah 56 and Jeremiah 7, threatening the temple because the nation was fruitless like the barren fig tree.

- Jesus himself is the temple. It was destroyed and raised up again in three days, launching a new era of a global temple we call the body of Christ. This defines the politics of Jesus.

This Week

❏ **Day I (Eyes):** After reading the essay, how would you describe Jesus's political agenda?

❏ **Day 2 (Ears):** Read Isaiah 56:1–8 and Jeremiah 7:1–11. How does this context help you see more fully what Jesus was up to?

❏ **Day 3 (Heart):** Meditate on 1 Corinthians 6:16–19; 2 Corinthians 6:16; Ephesians 2:19–22. What do these verses say about Jesus's politics?

❏ **Day 4 (Voice):** Discussion:

- What is the difference between cleansing the temple and threatening the temple?
- We often hear, "Your body is the temple of God," meaning your own physical body. How would it change your view if you read *body* as "the church"? (See the verses in day 3.)
- After reading Isaiah 56:1–8 and Jeremiah 7:1–11, consider these questions: How does your church align with the social priorities of Jesus? How do you personally align?
- What social concerns would be part of Jesus's political agenda? Lean into Isaiah 56 and Jeremiah 7 for your answers.

❏ **Day 5 (Hands):** Take up one item from Jesus's political agenda, and develop an action plan for carrying it out where you live, work, or play.

Further Resources: Quest52.org/41

42

Was Jesus Full of Himself?

Biblical Concept: Humility
Read: John 13:1–20

Can I confess something to you? I'm not a particularly humble person. Now you might think, *Well, that's because you are preaching at a large church, you write books, and you have a social media following.* Nope. My bravado does not come from public accomplishments. It comes more from my private insecurities. I am constantly tempted to present myself as more than I am because I fear I'll be found out to be less than others imagine.

As long as I can remember, I've struggled with this question: *Am I enough?* Now that the cat's out of the bag, I might as well tell you, all my achievements have had a very short shelf life of gratification. Don't get me wrong—I do honor Jesus with every fiber of my being. It's not like I'm a self-seeking narcissist. I serve as I do to make Jesus famous. Yet there is always an internal battle. Do I defer all honor to Jesus or retain a bit of the limelight for myself?

Perhaps that's why this chapter and the next are so important to me. Jesus's self-esteem was as high as anyone can imagine. He made unbelievably self-aggrandizing statements: I am the bread of life, the light of the world, the good shepherd (John 6:35; 8:12; 10:11). Without me, you can do nothing (John 15:5). I will be the judge of the world (Matthew 25:31–32). I am the Son of God, the Lord of the Sabbath, and even the embodied temple, the very Word of God (Matthew 12:8; John 2:19; 10:36). Talk about bravado! If you look at his language, you will never get the impression that he was humble. However, if you look at his actions, none can equal his service to the least and the lost. His high view of himself and his humble treatment of others seemingly run in opposite directions. Yet this single, simple observation will clarify the apparent contradiction: *in the Bible, humility is not how you feel about yourself but how you treat others.* No incident proves that more than Jesus washing his apostles' feet.

Setting the Table

The scene takes place at Passover. This is the most important feast in Israel, celebrating the birth of the nation (kind of like our Fourth of July). The meal mirrors Israel's last night in Egypt, complete with a Passover lamb and unleavened bread (see Exodus 12 for full details). This particular Passover was Jesus's last, at least prior to his return (Luke 22:16; Revelation 19:1–9). He was well aware that this was his Last Supper: "Jesus knew that his hour had come to depart out of this world to the Father, having loved his own who were in the world, he loved them to the end" (John 13:1). Within twenty-four hours, Peter would deny him, Judas would betray him, the chief priests would condemn him, and the Romans would crucify him. Jesus predicted each detail.

Jesus was brooding; the Twelve were tense. Something was wrong. No one could put his finger on it, but it lingered in the air. John let his readers in on the secret: "The devil had already put it into the heart of Judas Iscariot, Simon's son, to betray him" (verse 2). There was a traitor at the table. Think about that. Jesus knew the Cross was coming, he knew Peter would deny him, and he knew Judas would betray him. Under the mounting pressure, Jesus demonstrated humility when it was least convenient. It is even more remarkable when we realize that washing his disciples' feet was not merely an act of humble service; it was a precursor to the Cross. There is a lesson here for us: if humble service is beneath you, the ultimate sacrifice is beyond you. True greatness in a single moment is the culmination of humble habits over a lifetime.

Washing of Feet

Because people in Jesus's day walked on dusty roads in sandals, it was customary to wash one's feet before a banquet. You never wanted to sully your host's expensive carpets. This was not the kind of job *anyone* enjoyed. It wasn't so much the smell of the feet; ancient cities were permeated with unpleasant olfactory assaults. Rather, in a shame-honor culture, the feet were the least honorable of the "touchable" body parts. That is why it was a task relegated to the lowest servant in the house.

It comes as no surprise that none of the Twelve volunteered for the job. After all, they were vying for positions of honor. Since they believed Jesus was about to be inaugurated, they were posturing for cabinet positions in the soon-coming kingdom. Jesus volunteered. You could have heard a pin drop when Jesus disrobed down to his loincloth. This made him appear as a slave (John 19:23–24; Philippians 2:7).

Peter became unhinged by the thought of Jesus washing *his* feet. "You shall never wash my feet" (John 13:8). Jesus answered, "If I do not wash you, you have no share with me" (verse 8). Checkmate. Peter, in a typical overreaction, said, "All right, then. Give me a sponge bath" (a rough but accurate translation of verse 9). Jesus, perhaps with a wry smile, replied, "Peter, you've already had a bath; you just need your feet washed."

As Jesus continued, whatever wry smile he might have had faded. "You are clean, but not every one of you . . . are clean" (verses 10–11). He was even clearer in verses 18–19: "I am not speaking of all of you; I know whom I have chosen. But the Scripture will be fulfilled, 'He who ate my bread has lifted his heel against me.' I am telling you this now, before it takes place, that when it does take place you may believe that I am he."

Jesus had read the prophecies about Judas (Psalm 41:9; 69:25; 109:8; Zechariah 11:12; Acts 1:20). He knew Judas was about to betray him—that very night. Yet he still washed his feet in one last attempt to recover him. If that is what Jesus did for Judas, imagine the patience he has with you. Do not underestimate how far Jesus will go to recover you as his disciple.

The Lesson of the Basin and Towel

Foot washing was bigger than the basin and towel. It was about humble service. That applied to every area of life and even to sacrificial death. The basin and towel would be replaced by a cross the very next day. If that is how Jesus lived and died, then we, his followers, must follow suit. Jesus is calling us to a lifestyle of service, not a single act. Here is how he explained it:

> When he had washed their feet and put on his outer garments and resumed his place, he said to them, "Do you understand what I have done to you? You call me Teacher and Lord, and you are right, for so I am. If I then, your Lord and Teacher, have washed your feet, you also ought to wash one another's feet. For I have given you an example, that you also should do just as I have done to you. Truly, truly, I say to you, a servant is not greater than his master, nor is a messenger greater than the one who sent him. If you know these things, blessed are you if you do them." (John 13:12–17)

Foot washing is a cultural artifact with little relevance in the West. However, the humble service it modeled has never gone out of style. It is the perpetual call for a Christian CEO, parent, coach, pastor, teacher, mentor, neighbor, and friend. There are unlimited expressions of humble service, but none of us are exempt if we call Jesus Lord. Simple, right? Not so fast. What happened next shows us how difficult it is to humble ourselves to serve others.

The Debate at the Table

If we fast-forward past the foot washing, the meal, and the institution of the Lord's Supper, an unbelievable debate took place over which of the apostles was the greatest (Luke 22:24). They'd had this argument several times. The first time was over a year before (Matthew 18:1–5; Mark 9:33–37; Luke 9:46–48), and they argued again about it just a week prior (Matthew 20:20–28; Mark 10:35–45). All three arguments came right after Jesus predicted his death. They were vying for positions of power in the shadow of Jesus's suffering. That total lack of self-awareness would be unbelievable if we didn't see it so often in the mirror.

In the moment, they were arguing about who should sit closest to Jesus. Such banquets had strict seating arrangements according to each person's prominence. They were posturing for positions of power in Jesus's kingdom, without recognizing his crown would be made of thorns.

As I apply this lesson to my own life and my own struggle with humility, I realize that my quest for position and power is usually due not to arrogance but to insecurity. Only those confident in their relationship with God can fully embrace humble service. For many of us, humility is threatening to our fragile self-esteem. The solution is to fully embrace the love of God through Jesus Christ. When we grasp *whose* we are, we know *who* we are. Then we can serve others without worrying about our position in the community.

Key Points

- Washing feet was a sign of humble service. It foreshadowed the Cross, which was humble sacrifice in death.

- If we claim to follow Jesus, we must also imitate his actions.

- The disciples' argument about who was the greatest shows just how difficult this lesson is to apply in real time.

This Week

❏ **Day 1 (Eyes):** After reading the essay, consider this question: Do you have confidence in who you are before God?

❏ **Day 2 (Ears):** Read Daniel 4. Contrast this story of King Nebuchadnezzar with the story of Jesus.

❏ **Day 3 (Heart):** Meditate on Romans 7:6; 2 Corinthians 4:5; Galatians 5:13. Can you be humble without self-sacrifice?

❏ **Day 4 (Voice):** Discussion:

- As a kid, what was your least favorite household chore? What is it today?
- Do you tend to think of humility as your attitude about yourself or your actions toward others? What difference does that make in how you define humility?
- Make a list of actions that would be equivalent in our culture to foot washing in Jesus's day.
- Do you find doing these kinds of things easy or hard? Why?

❏ **Day 5 (Hands):** Identify and do one act of humble service for someone you live with. Do not say anything to anyone about what you have done.

Further Resources: Quest52.org/42

43

What Did Jesus Think About Himself?

Biblical Concept: Sacrament
Read: Mark 14:1–25 with Matthew 26:1–29; Luke 22:1–23;
John 12:2–8

There is a tattoo shop in the Old City of Jerusalem that has been in the same family for twenty-seven generations. They have been practicing this art since 1300. One year I was there with my two best friends, and we marveled at a five-hundred-year-old stamp of the Jerusalem cross. It had been marking pilgrims since before the Reformation. My friends looked at me and asked, "Are you ready to get a tattoo?" And that is how it happened. It's a symbol on my calf of my love for God and for my friends that share this mark of faith. It's cool, but it's just a symbol, like a flag or a wedding ring. A sacrament? Well, that's a whole other level. Not only do sacraments represent something; they also reflect divine realities. In the church, we have two sacraments: baptism and the Lord's Supper. Power beyond the elements connects us to God in ways our eyes cannot see. That's why the Lord's Supper has been so important to every church in every country for the entirety of church history.

Preparations for Passover

This was the beginning of the end. Jesus was on a collision course with the cross. From the eyewitnesses' perspective, it must have seemed like a derailed freight train careening off a cliff. From God's bird's-eye view, it was a carefully orchestrated symphony.

Preparation by enemies (Matthew 26:1–5, 14–16; Mark 14:1–2, 10–11; Luke 22:1–6). Two days before Passover, the Sanhedrin (the Jewish Supreme Court) convened an emergency meeting. They wanted to get rid of Jesus, but he was wildly popular. They had been plotting his demise for two years (John 5:18). If they grabbed him from the temple, they risked a riot. Little did they know that one of Jesus's own would give them the opportunity they were seeking. Judas showed up on their doorstep, offering to hand over the Master. This is the kind of secret plot you expect from a spy novel, but it was all too real. None of this took Jesus by surprise; he had already predicted it in meticulous detail. They offered Judas thirty pieces of silver, the price of a slave (Exodus 21:32). Just what his motives were, none may ever know. But one thing seems clear: God's sovereign design was at play (John 17:12), as well as satanic possession (Luke 22:3; John 13:27) and Judas's own greed, which was about to be revealed.

Preparation by friends (Matthew 26:6–13; Mark 14:3–9; John 12:2–8). Five days earlier, Mary, in stark contrast to Judas, offered Jesus an extravagant expression of devotion. She anointed his feet with valuable ointment poured from an alabaster jar. It was worth about a year's wages. The apostles, led by Iscariot (John 12:4–5), objected to her lavish love. Jesus came to her defense: "Leave her alone. Why do you trouble her? She has done a beautiful thing to me. . . . She has done what she could; she has anointed my body beforehand for burial" (Mark 14:6, 8). She saw that Jesus was about to die and anointed him for burial while she had the chance. She saw what the apostles had missed, perhaps because she humbled herself before Jesus while they exalted themselves before one another. (Sidebar: Every time we see Mary, she is at Jesus's feet [Luke 10:39; John 11:32]. She got it.)

Preparation by Jesus. "On the first day of Unleavened Bread, when they sacrificed the Passover lamb, his disciples said to him, 'Where will you have us go and prepare for you to eat the Passover?'" (Mark 14:12). Rather than returning to Bethany, they secured a home in the sacred city of Jerusalem. They used the upper room of the house, which was typically reserved for guests. Our guess is that it was the home of Mary and her son John Mark, friends of Jesus. If we are correct, this was also the home where the church would gather after the Resurrection (Acts 1) and pray for Peter's release from prison (Acts 12). Jesus was secretive about it, which makes sense since he knew there was a warrant out for his arrest. They found the house by following a man carrying a jar of water (which men typically would not do). This looks like a prearranged secret meeting place; everything was already set up (Mark 14:12–17).

The table was arranged with U-shaped seating. The host reclined at the head of the U. The chief seats were directly behind Jesus (Judas) and in front of him (John) as he reclined. The conversation began like a shot from a cannon: "Truly, I say to you, one of you will betray me, one who is eating with me" (verse 18). Judas gave the subtlest clue. While each apostle asked, "Is it I, *Lord*?" he could bring himself to say only, "Is it I, *Rabbi*?" (Matthew 26:22, 25). Jesus replied, "It is one of the twelve, one who is dipping bread into the dish with me" (Mark 14:20). That narrowed it down to two, maybe four. A bit later, John leaned back against Jesus's chest and asked, "Who is it?" In a conversation only John and Judas could hear, Jesus said, "'It is he to whom I will give this morsel of bread when I have dipped it.' So when he had dipped the morsel, he gave it to Judas, the son of Simon Iscariot" (John 13:25–26). Now John knew, but it was too late to stop him. Judas left quickly.

The Fulfillment of Passover

Passover is the most important Jewish holiday. This seven-day celebration culminates in a meal where each item on the table tells part of the story of how Israel became a nation. The meal is a kind of pop-up book of Exodus, recounting Moses leading God's people out from Egypt and up to the promised land. He wrestled with Pharaoh through the ten plagues. He parted the Red Sea, and they passed through on dry ground. He delivered the Ten Commandments at Sinai and constructed the tabernacle, where they could worship God. Every detail reflects Jesus. He is the sacrificial lamb and the firstborn Son. He is Moses, the law, the tabernacle, even the promised land. As the table is set, it is telling *his* story, not merely history.

Two elements are particularly important: the bread and the wine. The unleavened bread is a reminder of the haste with which Israel fled captivity. There was no time for the bread to rise with leaven. Since leaven sometimes represents the pervasive influence of sin, the unleavened bread signifies sinlessness. Jesus is the sinless one through whose suffering we find freedom. That is why "as they were eating, he took bread, and after blessing it broke it and gave it to them, and said, 'Take; this is my body'" (Mark 14:22). Luke said, "When he had *given thanks,* he broke it" (22:19), using the Greek word *eucharisteō,* from which we get the word *Eucharist.* The bread represents his body on the cross, torn to release us from slavery to sin. This is the institution of the Lord's Supper, or communion. However, Jesus talked about this moment in one of his longest sermons (John 6:53–58). Paul would later give specific instructions on this important sacrament of the church (1 Corinthians 11:17–34).

"He took a cup, and when he had given thanks he gave it to them, and they all drank of it. And he said to them, 'This is my blood of the covenant, which is poured out for many. Truly, I say to you, I will not drink again of the fruit of the vine until that day when I drink it new in the kingdom of God'" (Mark 14:23–25). The wine, of course, represents his blood, shed for our forgiveness. The symbolism is richer than our own communion suggests. Luke indicated that Jesus passed two cups around the table (22:17–20). The seder actually has four cups of wine. With each toast, one line is recited from Exodus 6:6–7:

- Cup 1: "I am the LORD, and *I will bring you out* from under the burdens of the Egyptians."

- Cup 2 (Luke 22:17): "*I will deliver you* from slavery to them."

- Cup 3 (Luke 22:20): "*I will redeem you* with an outstretched arm and with great acts of judgment." This is the cup of communion representing what Jesus did on the cross.

- Cup 4: "*I will take you to be my people,* and I will be your God" (see Revelation 21:3). Jesus did not drink this cup with them. It would await the marriage supper of the Lamb (Revelation 19:7). This is what Jesus meant when he said, "I tell you I will not drink again of this fruit of the vine until that day when I drink it new with you in my Father's kingdom" (Matthew 26:29).

This miniature meal contains a world of meaning. It represents our new covenant, promised back in the days of Jeremiah (31:31–34). In the new covenant, you don't make a sacrifice for God; rather, he offered a sacrifice for you (Isaiah 53:12; Mark 10:45; John 1:29). This mystical meal has the power to look in four directions at once. It looks inward to examine your heart (1 Corinthians 11:27–32). It looks outward to connect you to your brothers and sisters in Christ (10:17). It looks backward at the history of Israel (11:25). And it looks forward in faith to the return of our Redeemer (verse 26).

Key Points

- God meticulously orchestrated the events surrounding the Lord's Supper.

- Passover told the story of Israel's beginning, but it was ultimately fulfilled by Jesus.

- The Lord's Supper is a sacrament through which we celebrate and connect with the sacrifice of Jesus.

This Week

❑ **Day 1 (Eyes):** After reading the essay, consider this question: How did Jesus view himself?

❑ **Day 2 (Ears):** Read the story of the Passover in Exodus 12. How do you see the life of Jesus reflected in this story?

❑ **Day 3 (Heart):** Meditate on 1 Corinthians 5:7; 1 Peter 1:19; Revelation 5:12.

❑ **Day 4 (Voice):** Discussion:

- Can you give an example of how history repeats itself?
- What is the difference between a symbol and a sacrament? Feel free to use Google for some basic definitions. Can you give examples of each?
- Go to www.biblegateway.com. Type in the word *lamb*. Find out which New Testament book contains the most uses of that word, and read each verse.
- Share why the Lord's Supper is meaningful to you. What could you do to make it more meaningful?

❑ **Day 5 (Hands):** Prepare a meal with family and/or friends. Celebrate communion at that meal.

Further Resources: Quest52.org/43

44

How Can I Survive Difficult Days?

Biblical Concept: Hope
Read: John 14:1–31

I was living overseas when I got some earth-shattering news. It could have changed my life trajectory and definitely would damage a relationship dear to me. It was my dark night of the soul. Overwhelmed and alone, I called my best friend in Texas. He listened intently. When I was done, he said only one thing, and it made all the difference in the world: "Do you need me to come?" He was ready to put his life on pause and fly halfway around the world to be with me. Presence is more important than solutions. That is Jesus's promise to you.

Let's eavesdrop on a conversation Jesus had with his disciples the night before he died. John 14 begins and ends with an identical line: "Let not your hearts be troubled" (verses 1, 27). Jesus comforted his disciples while he himself was troubled (John 12:27; 13:21). He was about to die a torturous death, betrayed by the hand of a friend. He would leave the mission to imperfect men who faced overwhelming odds. So, where was the hope? He prepared them with three promises that would sustain them through difficult days. They will sustain you as well.

I. The Promise of a Place with the Father

"Let not your hearts be troubled. Believe in God; believe also in me. In my Father's house are many rooms. If it were not so, would I have told you that I go to prepare a place for you? And if I go and prepare a place for you, I will come again and will take you to myself, that where I am you may be also. And you know the way to where I am going" (John 14:1–4). What a great promise.

As a kid, I remember singing a hymn based on this verse: "I've got a mansion just over the hilltop."[1] Great song, but that is not precisely the picture Jesus was painting. The Greek word translated "mansion" in the old King James Version simply means "a room" or "a place." Moreover, it is not a physical house where we live but a position of belonging in the family. Jesus is making a space for us with the Father.

He isn't building as an architect; he is preparing as a defense attorney. He is, in this very moment, pleading your case before the Father. His argument is his own nail-scarred hands. The verdict is "not guilty." His sacrifice makes a way for you with the Father. Notice that in verse 1 he said, "Believe in God; believe also in me." After that, he never used the term *God* again; rather, he said "Father," and he said it twenty-three times! Don't miss this. Because of Jesus's death, resurrection, and ascension, we now relate to God as our Father. We are no longer just his creation; we are also his children. That means he will never leave us or forsake us. We pray to him as Abba, we approach him with confidence, and he stands between us and our enemies. Come on! That's *way* better than a mansion!

Like most of us, Thomas missed it: "Lord, we do not know where you are going. How can we know the way?" (verse 5). He, too, was thinking about a place rather than a position. Jesus clarified: "I am the way, and the truth, and the life. No one comes to the Father except through me" (verse 6). Some will object to such an exclusive statement. It may not be politically correct, but is it true? Who else came back from the grave? Who else lived a sinless life? Who else so transformed ethics, leadership, politics, and social justice? There is no other who has shown us who God is and offered us a path to his presence (John 1:18; Acts 4:12; Hebrews 1:3).

Philip's request clarifies this point: "Lord, show us the Father, and it is enough for us" (John 14:8). Jesus's reply is his defense of his exclusive claim: "Have I been with you so long, and you still do not know me, Philip? Whoever has seen me has seen the Father" (verse 9). What does this mean? Simply this: if you can't believe Jesus's words alone, then look at his actions. Who else healed blind eyes, loved his enemies, cared for outcasts, calmed storms, died for our sins, and rose from the dead? No one!

2. The Promise of Success Through the Spirit

The disciples were devastated by the thought of Jesus leaving them. They could not imagine carrying out his mission without him. However, Jesus saw more clearly: "Truly, truly, I say to you, whoever believes in me will also do the works that I do; and greater works than these will he do, because I am going to the Father" (verse 12). How in the world is that possible? Can we do greater works than Jesus himself? Yes, he said we would. We may not do more fabulous miracles than turning water to wine or raising the dead. However, by every other metric, Jesus's followers have vastly expanded his ministry: the number of converts, breadth of geography, depth of social justice, height of political influence, and weight of cultural impact. How did all this happen? Jesus identified two resources driving our impact:

1. **Prayer.** Because we are God's children and not merely servants, our prayers have massive impact. As Jesus said, we could ask anything in his name and get a yes from God (verses 13–14). This promise is repeated in John 15:7, 16; 16:23–26; 1 John 3:22; 5:14–15. Obviously, this blank check is not for personal gain but for mission-critical tasks. If we ask the Father for what we need

to build Jesus's kingdom, we are going to get a yes. It may not come in our time frames, but it will come every time.

2. **The Spirit.** More importantly, Jesus will ask the Father to send us the Helper (John 14:16). This Greek word, *paraklētos,* means "called alongside." The Holy Spirit comes alongside us to ensure our effectiveness as Christ's ambassadors. He is our coach, mentor, and guide. He comforts, leads, helps, protects, encourages, and convicts. Jesus promised, "He dwells with you and will be in you" (verse 17). The Spirit was with the apostles while Jesus was alive but would be in them after Jesus ascended. You see, only those redeemed by Jesus are sealed by God's Spirit (2 Corinthians 1:22; Ephesians 1:13). None in the Old Testament had this divine gift (John 7:38–39). Right here, for the first time in history, the Spirit was presented as a person, distinct from the Father. The Trinity was finally fully revealed. Not only does the Spirit help us pray, but the indwelling Spirit also prays for us (Romans 8:26). Hence, the Spirit and prayer go hand in hand to ensure we carry to completion the commission of Jesus.

On earth, Jesus was limited to one place at a time. After his ascension, the Father sent the omnipresent Spirit to be with each of us all the time. Because the Spirit is in us, we have constant access to the Father. That's what Jesus meant when he said, "In that day you will know that I am in my Father, and you in me, and I in you" (John 14:20). This is merely the tip of the proverbial iceberg of how the Spirit supports Christians. For a full list, see the further resources for this chapter.

3. The Promise of Love in Jesus

"Whoever has my commandments and keeps them, he it is who *loves* me. And he who *loves* me will be *loved* by my Father, and I will *love* him and manifest myself to him" (verse 21). This sounds a bit mushy. However, as I think about my own dark night of the soul, what I needed most was someone who loved me enough to be with me in my pain. That is what is on offer here.

Judas (not Iscariot) was confused: "Lord, how is it that you will manifest yourself to us, and not to the world?" (verse 22). At first glance, Jesus's answer seems irrelevant: "If anyone loves me, he will keep my word, and my Father will love him, and we will come to him and make our home with him" (verse 23). How did that answer the question about why Jesus would reveal himself to insiders and not outsiders? Here is how: it is in obeying Jesus that we fully see Jesus. Only when we do what he says do we fully experience his presence and power. Every parent has replied, "Because I said so," to a child asking, "Why?" When the child obeys, the question is answered. That is why Jesus added, "The Helper, the Holy Spirit, whom the Father will send in my name, he will teach you all things and bring to your remembrance all that I have said to you" (verse 26).

This brings us full circle: "Peace I leave with you; my peace I give to you. Not as the world gives do I give to you. Let not your hearts be troubled, neither let them be afraid" (verse 27). Our peace in the midst of trouble comes from Jesus's presence. God became present in the person of Jesus. And when Jesus left, his presence remained with us through his Spirit living in us.

Key Points

- Jesus promised to prepare a place for us. That is, he is making a way for us to have an eternal relationship with the Father.

- The Holy Spirit is our advocate, coming alongside us so we can carry out Jesus's mission.

- When we obey Jesus's commands, the Holy Spirit empowers us to experience the love of the Father.

This Week

❏ **Day 1 (Eyes):** After reading the essay, consider this question: What hope do you need?

❏ **Day 2 (Ears):** What was promised through the coming of the Holy Spirit in Joel 2:28–32 and Ezekiel 36:22–36?

❏ **Day 3 (Heart):** Meditate on John 1:18; Acts 4:12; Hebrews 1:3. How is Jesus exclusively the way to the Father?

❏ **Day 4 (Voice):** Discussion:

- Share about a time when you felt alone or abandoned.
- What is it that makes Jesus uniquely qualified to introduce people to God?
- Have you ever experienced the power or presence of the Spirit? What was that like?
- How does the Spirit empower you to fulfill God's call on your life?

❏ **Day 5 (Hands):** Ask God for something you need in order to do your part in fulfilling his mission.

Further Resources: Quest52.org/44

45

How Can We Learn Grit from How Jesus Suffered?

Biblical Concept: Suffering
Read: Mark 14:32–52 with Matthew 26:36–56;
Luke 22:39–53; John 18:1–11

It all started in a garden. God placed his prized possession in a well-watered garden. There it all went wrong when Satan temped Adam and Eve. Their bite of betrayal launched a course of death and destruction. Here we are again in a garden. Jesus prayed in the face of death and destruction. His obedience would reverse the curse of a world that betrayed God. His suffering started here.

Gethsemane

Gethsemane is an olive grove on the Mount of Olives. It faces Jerusalem and is one of the only quiet places near the densely packed capital. Between Gethsemane and the temple lies the Kidron Valley. There is a first-century memorial to Absalom along the very path Jesus would have taken to Gethsemane. The memorial is a reminder of David's son who betrayed his father a thousand years earlier (2 Samuel 15). This is the path David took to flee from his son. Halfway up the hill, he turned around, looked at the city, and wept. The foreshadowing is thick. Jesus was the King of the Jews, betrayed by his own people. On the very spot where King David wept, Jesus knelt in agony before his Father.

Eight apostles were stationed at the gate. Jesus told them to pray so they wouldn't fall into temptation (Luke 22:40). He then took Peter, James, and John into the garden. He wanted his support group with him. He told them, "My soul is very sorrowful, even to death. Remain here and watch" (Mark 14:34). Mark used three words to describe Jesus's state of consternation. We might translate them as "distressed," "dismayed," and "grieving." He felt he could die right there from the weight of sorrow. This may be more literal than we think. Luke, the physician, noted that "his sweat became like great drops of blood falling down to the ground" (Luke 22:44). This may indicate a medical condition called hematidrosis where capillaries burst and a person sweats blood. Jesus was in real trouble.

Jesus withdrew about a stone's throw away. He was within sight but out of earshot of the three. He fell on his knees (Luke 22:41), then on his face (Matthew 26:39), and prayed, "Abba, Father, all things are possible for you. *Remove this cup from me*" (Mark 14:36). Was Jesus really asking to be released from the Cross? Would that not make him less valiant? *No!* We cannot compare Jesus to other brave martyrs who marched to their deaths stoically. Martyrs die for a cause; Jesus took on the sins of the world (1 Peter 2:24). The cup in the Old Testament is a symbol of God's wrath (Jeremiah 25:15–16)! Jesus was about to absorb *the wrath of God* and feel separation from his Father. We all know what that is like; Jesus had never experienced it—*ever*. He would become sin itself (2 Corinthians 5:21), and it was killing him. His bravery was not in how he felt in the moment but in his obedience to God's will.

In the depth of his suffering, he needed the support of his friends. He went to them and found them asleep. We could make excuses for them. After all, sorrow is exhausting (Luke 22:45). Yet Peter, who claimed he would die for Jesus, couldn't stay awake to pray with him? What Jesus told Peter he could say to most of us: "The spirit indeed is willing, but the flesh is weak" (Matthew 26:41). In Jesus's view, prayer is more important than sleep, especially when we're facing significant trials. Perhaps the reason we can't keep our promises to Jesus is that we don't stay awake with him in prayer.

While we're on the subject, allow me one more observation. Often we think there is something wrong with us when God says no to our requests. Yet according to the biblical record, God said no to David when he wanted to build the temple (1 Chronicles 22:7–8). He said no to Paul when he asked to have his thorn in the flesh removed (2 Corinthians 12:7–9). He said no to Jesus in the garden. If God says no to you, you are in pretty good company. You may, in fact, be exactly where God wants you.

Three times Jesus asked, "Remove this cup from me" (Mark 14:36). In other words, it wasn't a done deal after the first prayer. He kept asking. Each time he concluded his prayer with this: "Yet not what I will, but what you will" (verse 36). In that thin slice of time between Jesus's request and his submission, our eternal salvation hung in the balance. No one could force him to the cross. It was his submission to the Father that won our salvation. Likewise, it's our submission to God that will bring salvation to society. If we don't willingly carry our own cross, the world may never know the love of Christ, who died for their sins.

The Kiss of Death

After the third time of finding his friends asleep, Jesus said, "Rise, let us be going; see, my betrayer is at hand" (verse 42). With those words, they noticed the clamoring crowd wielding swords and clubs at the gate of the garden. The other eight apostles were now wide awake but unaware of what was happening. Jesus marched to meet the crowd. They had been sent from the Sanhedrin with a warrant for his arrest. "Judas came, one of the twelve, and with him a crowd with swords and clubs, from the chief priests and the scribes and the elders" (verse 43). John called it "a band of soldiers" (18:3), which is a military regiment of six hundred soldiers. That may seem like overkill until you remember his popularity with the crowds. A company like that might, in fact, have been borrowed from Pilate to keep peace during the feast. The fact that Pilate's wife had a dream about Jesus and that the trial took place just after dawn suggests that Pilate was aware of the arrest (Matthew 27:1–2, 19).

At the head of the entourage was Judas, one of their own. He likely led the soldiers first to Mary's house, where the Last Supper was held. When they weren't there, he took them to the garden where he knew Jesus frequently prayed. John Mark, the author of the gospel, was likely a teen at the time. He might have heard the bustle in the upper room of his home and the beating feet coming down the stairs as the group left. If our reconstruction is correct, he also would have heard the pounding on the door and the conversation of the men looking for Jesus. He was a smart kid; he figured out where Jesus had gone and set out on a dead run to warn him. But the company of soldiers took a long time to clear the street before he could exit. By the time he got to the garden, it was too late. More on this in a moment.

When the eight saw their associate Judas through the flickering light of the soldiers' torches, it suddenly sank in exactly what he was doing. No one said a word until Jesus broke the silence: "Whom do you seek?" (John 18:4). "Jesus of Nazareth," they replied. "I am he," Jesus confessed, making Judas's kiss unnecessary (verse 5). John tells us the soldiers literally fell to the ground (verse 6). Likely they were so stunned by Jesus's forthrightness that they stepped back and stumbled over one another's feet. As they stood back up and composed themselves, Judas stepped forward. "Rabbi!" he said as he kissed him (Mark 14:45). That is, of course, a normal greeting for men in the Middle East. The word Mark used (*kataphileō*), however, suggests an intense kiss. He feigned deep friendship, but he was not fooling anyone but himself.

The deed was done; the identification secured. Jesus was immediately arrested. Peter would have none of it. Wielding a sword, he took a quick slice at Malchus, the servant of the high priest (John 18:10). Malchus dodged the blow, but the sword still glanced off his skull, severing his ear. Jesus ordered Peter to sheath his sword with a sagacious rebuke: "All who take the sword will perish by the sword" (Matthew 26:52). Only Luke, the physician, described how Jesus miraculously healed Malchus, snapping his ear back on like a Lego block (22:51). If you were the soldier detaining Jesus, you would have just gotten really nervous. And Peter just got away with assault because there was no longer any evidence of his crime.

Jesus turned his rebuke to the chief priests: "Have you come out as against a robber, with swords and clubs to capture me? Day after day I was with you in the temple teaching, and you did not seize me. But let the Scriptures be fulfilled" (Mark 14:48–49). He accused them of false arrest and cowardice for coming at him at night rather than in the light of day in the temple they supposedly controlled. With that, the apostles fled, leaving Jesus alone in the dark.

Some young man was there wearing only his linen tunic. The soldiers grabbed ahold of his garment. He was agile and slipped out of it, then ran naked into the night. Who was this streaker? Who else would care about this peculiar eyewitness detail except John Mark, the author of the book? The point of this curious detail is that Jesus was desperately alone, abandoned by his closest friends; one even endured the shame of nakedness to get away.

Suffering is not the hard part. Suffering alone is. Because Jesus suffered alone in the Garden of Gethsemane, our curse from the Garden of Eden was reversed so that we will never suffer alienation from our God.

Key Points

- Jesus's suffering began in Gethsemane.
- Three times he prayed to be released from the Cross. God said no.
- Even Jesus's best friends fled, leaving him alone in the dark with his enemies.

This Week

❑ **Day 1 (Eyes):** As you read the essay, what did you learn about how to go through suffering?

❑ **Day 2 (Ears):** What are the similarities between Gethsemane and Absalom betraying David in 2 Samuel 15?

❑ **Day 3 (Heart):** Meditate on your own suffering: Romans 8:17; Colossians 1:24; 1 Peter 2:21–23.

❑ **Day 4 (Voice):** Discussion:
- What is the most difficult thing you've ever had to endure?
- How did you pray differently during that time?
- Based on Jesus's suffering, what advice would you give to others who are suffering?
- What would make you better able to endure times of trouble?

❑ **Day 5 (Hands):** Take time today to remind someone who is suffering that he is not alone.

Further Resources: Quest52.org/45

46

How Do You Stay in Control in a Crisis?

Biblical Concept: Opposition
Read: Mark 14:53–72 with Matthew 26:57–75;
Luke 22:54–65; John 18:12–27

Criminal Minds, Law & Order, and *The Blacklist.* There, I confessed it; I'm obsessed with crime dramas. I have a visceral desire for justice. When bad guys get what's coming to them, something in me rejoices. What makes these particular crime dramas so interesting is that it is not always clear who the bad guys are. Even the good guys have moral flaws, and the bad guys have some redeeming qualities. So it is in this biblical story of Caiaphas and Peter. Jesus alone seems to have had integrity amid crisis, and that gave him control when everyone else was spinning out of control. There is a lesson here that most of us desperately need to learn.

The Trial of Jesus

After his arrest, Jesus was taken to the high priest, the highest official in Israel. Under Roman occupation, high priests were the liaison to the emperor, even above the puppet kings like Herod. That put the high priest at the top of the political pyramid.

According to Jewish law, the high priest held his office for life. However, the Romans knew that the power of that position only grew over time. That's why they replaced the high priest frequently, often annually. Here's where it gets extra interesting. Annas held the office from AD 6 to 15. That was a *long* run. He was able to get one of his sons installed as high priest after him (AD 16–17), followed by his son-in-law, Caiaphas, who held the office from AD 18 to 36; then his four other sons became high priest after Caiaphas. He was a massively influential politician to hold power for that long. John's gospel (the most Jewish of the four) tells us that Jesus was first taken to Annas (the Jewish high priest for life) before being transferred to Caiaphas, the high priest installed by the Romans (18:12–14). Caiaphas called an emergency meeting of the Sanhedrin (their Supreme Court).

As an interesting aside, an ossuary was found in southeast Jerusalem in 1990 with *Caiaphas* inscribed on the lid. An ossuary is a stone box used to collect the bones of a deceased person about a year after the person died. This practice was common only from about AD 30 to 70. Since there is only one Caiaphas in the historical record of the time, since the box was found near the site of the high priest's palace,[1] *and* since it is from the right time, most scholars agree this box contains the bones of the biblical high priest who condemned Jesus to death. If you want to see it, you can go to the Israel Museum in Jerusalem, where it is on display. Incredible. We have the burial box of the man who put Jesus to death, while Jesus's grave is empty.

Caiaphas marshaled a string of "witnesses" against Jesus. They spouted all kinds of accusations about what he said or did. One that stood out was a statement Jesus made three years earlier: "I will destroy this temple that is made with hands, and in three days I will build another, not made with hands" (Mark 14:58). They misquoted Jesus. He did not say that *he* would destroy the temple but that if *they* did, he would raise it up. Furthermore, Jesus was talking about his own body, not a building. Even their incoherent accusation was fulfilling Jesus's prediction. Because the witnesses couldn't align their libel, Caiaphas was at risk of having to acquit Jesus.

So Caiaphas intervened: "Are you the Christ, the Son of the Blessed?" (verse 61). Well, that was a problem. You see, just as in our legal system, judges were prohibited from asking defendants to incriminate themselves. If you compare the biblical narrative with the Jewish rules of jurisprudence, there were actually ten distinct violations in this trial:

- Jesus was arrested through a bribe.

- He was arrested without a specific charge.

- The trial was held at night.

- There were false witnesses with conflicting stories.

- He was not allowed to cross-examine the witnesses.

- He was asked to incriminate himself.

- The high priest declared his sentence without first asking for a vote.

- He was struck in the face during the trial without just cause.

- The charges against him were changed when he was transferred to Pilate.

- He was convicted and sentenced on the same day.

Even though Caiaphas was out of line asking Jesus to incriminate himself, Jesus answered his question. Why would he respond to an illegal question when he had stonewalled the earlier interrogation? Because it was the first honest question he had been asked. The high priest asked, "Are you the Christ, the Son of the Blessed?" Jesus's answer was provocative. He said, "I am" (verse 62), which, in Hebrew, is the name of God: Yahweh. Oh boy. As if that weren't inflammatory enough, he added, "You will see the Son of Man seated at the right hand of Power, and coming with the clouds of heaven" (verse 62). No one missed it; Jesus was citing Psalm 110:1 and Daniel 7:13. If you dip into the context of each of these passages, you will hear a direct threat to the position the high priest held. The gloves were off.

Caiaphas tore his robe, which was a Jewish sign of extreme consternation (Genesis 37:29; 2 Kings 18:37). "That's blasphemy!" he roared. If Caiaphas was right, Jesus deserved death by stoning according to the law (Leviticus 24:10–23). If, however, he was wrong, he was about to make a galactic mistake! So the punishment began. The soldiers played a game something like blindman's buff. The Romans called it *kollabismos*.[2] This might have been based on a misreading of Isaiah 11:2–4, that the Messiah could discern by smell. They beat him with their fists and with a rod (at least that's what the word *rhapizō* seems to indicate) and spit on him. Then they asked him to reveal who did it (Matthew 26:67–68). According to Isaiah 52:14, he was beaten beyond recognition. Jesus's trial was going badly; Peter's was going worse.

The Trial of Peter

While Jesus was on trial inside the palace, Peter was on trial in the courtyard. These homes were constructed around a central courtyard with one entry gate that could be carefully watched. John knew the high priest's family and was therefore allowed to enter the courtyard. Peter had to wait outside until John could talk to the guard to get him admitted (John 18:15–16).

There he was, warming himself by the fire. The soldiers, undoubtedly, were recounting their heroic capture of this nefarious criminal. How Peter must have bitten his tongue. The girl monitoring the gate recognized him as a follower of Jesus. The little blabbermouth came right up to him and said, "You also were with the Nazarene, Jesus" (Mark 14:67). Teenage girls are easy to brush off. "I have no idea what you mean," he fibbed. Peter was on a secret mission, likely to somehow effect an escape for Jesus. Why else would he have been there?

He walked away from the fire and into the shadows by the gate. They were less likely to identify him there, and he could escape more quickly if they did. The pesky pubescent slave girl gathered a crowd and started pointing at him, telling the soldiers, "This man is one of them" (verse 69). Peter was more vociferous this time: "I swear to God I don't know the man." That bought him a bit of time, but in the crowd was a relative of Malchus (John 18:26). He identified Peter beyond a shadow of a doubt. Peter called down curses upon himself [*anathematizō*] (Matthew 26:74), swearing a third time he did not know Jesus (Matthew 26:74).

In that moment, two things happened. The rooster crowed (a second time, according to Mark), reminding Peter of Jesus's words. That shrill cry woke Peter, and he realized he had just denied Jesus, the very thing he had sworn he would never do. His motives were likely noble—to help Jesus escape. But because he took matters into his own hands rather than trusting God's plan, he was forced into a situation in which there were no good options.

The second thing that happened was even more difficult for Peter. When the cock crowed, Jesus turned and caught Peter's eye (Luke 22:61). He knew that Jesus knew exactly what he had done. Peter broke down and wept. Mark's odd phrase (*epibalōn eklaien*) expresses utter brokenness (14:72). He was undone by what he had done. In Jesus's worst moment, Peter had let him down in the worst way.

The contrast between Peter's trial and Jesus's trial is instructive. Jesus was in total control even when he was being railroaded. Peter lost control even when he was trying to take control. What was the difference between them? The answer to that question informs us how to stay in control in a crisis. Peter tried to manipulate the situation to his own desired outcome. Because he was asleep in the garden, he was confused in the courtyard. Jesus, on the other hand, prepared for the crisis in prayer. He wrestled in the garden. It was on his knees that he battled for control.

He prayed, "Not my will, but yours" (Luke 22:42). Once he submitted to God's will, he was in control of every situation he faced. Submission to God in prayer is the preparation we need for any crisis.

Key Points

- The trial of Jesus was unjust and illegal, yet Jesus submitted to it.
- Peter lost control in the courtyard because he tried to take control.
- Jesus was in control of the trial because he determined in the garden to submit to God's will.

This Week

❏ **Day 1 (Eyes):** After reading the essay, consider this question: How do you respond in crisis?

❏ **Day 2 (Ears):** There was a pit in Caiaphas's house where Jesus was likely held. Pilgrims who visit it today are encouraged to read Psalm 88. Read this psalm and imagine Jesus being there.

❏ **Day 3 (Heart):** Meditate on what these verses say about crisis: 2 Corinthians 4:16–18; Hebrews 2:18; James 1:2–4.

❏ **Day 4 (Voice):** Discussion:

- What advice would you give to a kid mistreated at school? Do you follow that advice when you are mistreated?
- Share about a time when you were mistreated. How did you handle it?
- What are you trying to control right now that you need to yield to God?
- Are there actions you need to take in this crisis that you are procrastinating on?

❏ **Day 5 (Hands):** Schedule a full hour to pray over a crisis in your life. Wrestle with what you need to respond to and what you need to yield control of.

Further Resources: Quest52.org/46

47

How Do You Endure Pain?

Biblical Concept: Endurance
Read: Matthew 27:11–26 with Mark 15:1–15;
Luke 23:1–25; John 18:28–19:6

The trial of Jesus is well known from passion plays, Hollywood renditions, and Bible reading. However, a lot was going on in the background that sheds light on the story. Let's take just a moment to peek behind the curtain of history.

Caiaphas, the high priest, sentenced Jesus to death for blasphemy, but he had no authority to execute capital punishment. That would have to come from Pilate, the Roman governor from AD 26 to 36. This explains why Jesus was crucified rather than stoned (the Jewish method of execution), thus fulfilling Psalm 22. Pilate was known to be anti-Semitic; he had no qualms about killing a Jew. However, he was also a Roman official who put a premium on legal justice, so he would have to be convinced a crime had been committed.

The locals had a bitter history with Pilate. He tried to install shields honoring the emperor in Herod's palace in Jerusalem. Jewish nationalists pitched a fit and forced him to take them down by appealing to the emperor. Pilate lost that round and never forgot it. We learn from Luke 13:1

that Pilate killed some Galileans while they were making a sacrifice in the temple—not cool. It might have been retaliation for the shields, or perhaps he thought they were rebels. He further agitated the Jews when he took funds from the temple treasury to build an aqueduct for the city. He thought he was doing them a favor; they thought he had robbed the temple. Pilate won round two. Jesus was the tiebreaker.

Pilate's personal history back in Rome was checkered. His patron was a politician named Sejanus, an adviser to Emperor Tiberius. When Tiberius went off the rails (he really was crazy), Sejanus plotted his assassination. He got caught and was executed on October 18, AD 31. As you can imagine, Pilate's connection to Sejanus put him under suspicion. Thus, Pilate was vulnerable if the Jewish leaders reported any misconduct. In fact, that was what eventually got him deposed in AD 36, when his slaughter of some Samaritans was reported to Rome.

Endure False Accusations with Faith

You can feel the tension from the moment the Jewish leaders took Jesus to Pilate. They "did not enter the governor's headquarters, so that they would not be defiled, but could eat the Passover" (John 18:28). That is not exactly how you win friends and influence people. Pilate went outside to hear their request: "What accusation do you bring against this man?" (verse 29). Answer: none! They asked Pilate to condemn Jesus without any stated charges (verse 30). Well, that was *not* happening.

Since Pilate couldn't care less about the Jewish charge of blasphemy, they had to come up with charges he *would* care about. They said, "We found this man misleading our nation and forbidding us to give tribute to Caesar, and saying that he himself is Christ, a king" (Luke 23:2). Charge 1: he misled the nation—sedition. Rome did, in fact, come down hard on agitators since it was the only way to protect their ever-expanding borders. However, the Jewish leaders were doing as much agitating as Jesus. Charge 2: he forbade Jews to pay taxes. False! Jesus told a crowd in the temple to give to Caesar what was Caesar's (Matthew 22:15–22). Charge 3: he claimed to be king. Absolutely true and 100 percent lethal if he was convicted. So that was the charge Pilate investigated.

Pilate asked, "Are you the King of the Jews?" Jesus replied cryptically, "You have said so" (Matthew 27:11), as if to say, "You're the one saying that, not me." John shared an additional detail that is instructive: Jesus asked, "Do you say this of your own accord, or did others say it to you about me?" (18:34). He was trying to discern what Pilate meant by *king*. Was he a king in opposition to the emperor? No. Was he King of the Jews, the promised Messiah? Yes. Pilate acted as if Jesus were being belligerent: "Do you not hear how many things they testify against you?" (Matthew 27:13). He wasn't being belligerent; he was simply trying to be clear. Answering irrelevant accusations would not solve the problem. Jesus did what few of us can manage in the face of opposition. He was silent (Isaiah 53:7). He didn't answer a single false accusation. Pilate was "greatly amazed" and should have been (Matthew 27:14). That is exactly the right approach to ultimately silence your foes. The more we defend ourselves, the more ammunition we offer to our enemies.

Jesus clarified, "My kingdom is not of this world. If my kingdom were of this world, my servants would have been fighting, that I might not be delivered over to the Jews. But my kingdom is not from the world. . . . For this purpose . . . I have come into the world—to bear witness to the truth" (John 18:36–37). This triggered Pilate: "What is truth?" (verse 38). Truth was standing right in front of him. Yet without waiting for a reply, Pilate went out to the Jews and declared, "I find no guilt in him" (verse 38). Seven more times Pilate tried to release Jesus:

1. "I did not find this man guilty of any of your charges." (Luke 23:14)
2. "Whom do you want me to release for you: Barabbas, or Jesus?" (Matthew 27:17)
3. "I have found in him no guilt deserving death." (Luke 23:22)
4. "I find no guilt in him." (John 19:4)

5. "Take him yourselves and crucify him, for I find no guilt in him." (John 19:6)
6. "From then on Pilate sought to release him." (John 19:12)
7. He washed his hands, saying, "I am innocent of this man's blood." (Matthew 27:24)

How can we endure false accusations? With faith. Throughout the Bible, the righteous were always vindicated, whether in this life or the next. Eventually your innocence will be seen and the evil of those who pretend to be righteous will be exposed. Our faith in God's goodness allows us to stand firm in the face of false accusations.

Endure Rejection with Hope

Pilate's wife interrupted the proceedings with an urgent message: "Have nothing to do with that righteous man, for I have suffered much because of him today in a dream" (Matthew 27:19). She might have had this dream because Pilate dispatched a cohort of soldiers to arrest Jesus the night before. In the ancient world, dreams were interpreted not as subconscious concerns but as communiqués from the gods. Pilate now had divine confirmation of his own intuition—Jesus was innocent. He knew the Jewish leaders had delivered Jesus up out of envy (verse 18).

Pilate attempted to release Jesus using something like a presidential pardon. By releasing a prisoner, he gained approval from the crowd. He pitted Jesus against an insurrectionist named Barabbas. Such rebels would use any means necessary to overthrow their own government, which was complicit with Rome. This included murder, extortion, intimidation, and terrorism. This year, he let them choose Jesus or Barabbas. Jesus preached peace; Barabbas fomented violence. Pilate surely had heard of Jesus's popularity with the people at the Triumphal Entry on Sunday, the cleansing of the temple on Monday, or the great discussions on Tuesday. Yet today the leaders held sway over the crowd in the courtyard (verse 20). The crowd's cry was clear: "Barabbas" (verse 21). Jesus would take his place on a cross between two "robbers" (*lēstēs*), likely companions of Barabbas, complicit in insurrection.

Jesus had now been rejected by Judas, Peter, Pilate, and the crowds who had hailed him as king just five days earlier. How do you endure that kind of rejection? You hope. Hope is the flip side of faith. While faith looks back on the faithfulness of God, hope looks forward, past your present pain, to trust that God will ultimately vindicate you and save your enemy.

Endure Pain with Love

Pilate then asked, "What shall I do with Jesus who is called Christ?" (verse 22). The crowd cried in unison, seemingly echoing a chorus from hell, "Crucify him!" In frustration Pilate thundered back, "Why? What evil has he done?" (verse 23). They simply shouted louder, "Crucify him!" Pilate saw this was going nowhere fast. His resolve for justice was weakening; it faltered fatally when the chief priests played their trump card: "If you release this man, you are not Caesar's friend. Everyone who makes himself a king opposes Caesar" (John 19:12). That was blackmail. They played to Pilate's weak relationship with the emperor. Dirty but effective.

Pilate washed his hands, renouncing any complicity in the execution. By the way, washing one's hands judicially was not a Roman practice. It was a Jewish ritual. He was mocking them, but what did they care? They got what they wanted. "I am innocent of this man's blood; see to it yourselves," said Pilate (Matthew 27:24). The people responded, "His blood be on us and on our children!" (verse 25). Be careful what you pray for; you might just get it.

We must remember, Jesus did not die because of the villainy of his enemies. He chose this in the garden. He suffered *for* us, not merely *because* of us. He loved Peter and Pilate, Judas and the Jews who killed him. His suffering brought salvation. Ours can too. We endure because we know that our suffering can bring hope, healing, and forgiveness. Grit and determination can take you only so far through pain. Love knows no bounds.

Key Points

- Righteousness is always ultimately vindicated. We can endure false accusations if we have faith in God's faithfulness.

- There is no pain worse than rejection. Hope takes faith and pushes it forward past the pain to trust that God will ultimately vindicate you and save your enemy.

- Loving your enemies has greater power than grit to enable you to endure pain.

This Week

❑ **Day 1 (Eyes):** After reading the essay, consider this question: How is your level of faith, hope, and love?

❑ **Day 2 (Ears):** What predictions from Isaiah 52:13–53:12 were fulfilled in Jesus's execution?

❑ **Day 3 (Heart):** Meditate on how God treats his enemies and how we should imitate him: Romans 5:10; 12:20; Hebrews 10:12–13.

❑ **Day 4 (Voice):** Discussion:

- Have you ever been rejected, betrayed, or hated? What was that like?
- What can you do to show love in action to a person who has rejected you?
- Are there any specific strategies that Jesus used at his trial that you could offer as counsel to a friend who has been fired, divorced, sued, or cheated in business?
- How can the pain we endure increase the faith, hope, and love of others?

❑ **Day 5 (Hands):** Write out a prayer that you would want your enemies to pray for you (three sentences). Now pray it for your enemies.

Further Resources: Quest52.org/47

48

Why Did Jesus Die?

Biblical Concept: Atonement
Read: Matthew 27:27–54 with Mark 15:16–39;
Luke 23:26–47; John 19:16–30

The entire message of the Bible can be seen in the shadow of three trees. The first is the tree of the knowledge of good and evil in the Garden of Eden. Sin entered our world and marred God's good creation. At the end of the Bible, we see the tree of life growing in the New Jerusalem. In the shadow of this tree, all is made right and God again dwells in our midst. The middle tree is a rugged beam of wood on which our Savior hung between heaven and earth. This tree, this cross, spans the great divide between the other two trees. In the long shadow of this tree, we find life in his death.

Before the Cross

It helps executioners if their victim is dehumanized. So the soldiers beat Jesus beyond human recognition (Isaiah 52:14). They used a flagellum. The technology is simple. Take a stick about eighteen inches long. Secure to it multiple leather strands, each embedded with sharp objects such as glass, metal, or knucklebones of sheep. The victim is stripped naked and tied to a pillar. A soldier on either side slaps the strands against the flesh, then pulls down sharply, raking the victim's back, buttocks, and legs. The strands also wrap around the victim, lacerating the quads, abs, and chest and often gouging out the eyes. Six out of ten men died from flogging alone, sometimes because of loss of blood, sometimes because of their bowels falling from the gaping wounds in their torsos.

Jesus's flogging was followed by a mock coronation. The soldiers dressed him in a scarlet robe (likely a faded cape from a military commander). After twisting together thorns, they embedded a crown in his skull. A reed was placed in his hand for a scepter. Using fists trained for battle, they pummeled his face, then spit on him in contempt, all the while mocking raucously: "Hail, King of the Jews!" (Matthew 27:29).

Afterward, they ripped the robe from the coagulated blood on his back, reopening the wounds, and replaced it with a *patibulum,* the crossbar of the cross. Typically it weighed about a hundred pounds, which seemed heavier against gaping wounds. Then they led Jesus through the narrow streets of the Via Dolorosa to a place called Golgotha, meaning "place of a skull" (*calvāria* in Latin). At one point, the weight of the cross overcame him. Simon from Cyrene, a Passover pilgrim, was forced to carry the cross. Simon's children, Alexander and Rufus, seem to have been well known to Mark's Roman audience (15:21; Romans 16:13).

Ahead of the procession walked a Roman soldier carrying the *titulus,* a placard that clearly spelled out the charges against the victim, attempting to deter other criminals from following suit. In Jesus's case the charges read, "Jesus of Nazareth, the King of the Jews," translated into Aramaic, Greek, and Latin (John 19:19–20). No one could miss it.

On the Cross

Once on site, they offered Jesus wine mixed with myrrh, a mild analgesic. Jesus refused it, fully absorbing the curse he was under:

- hanged on a tree (Deuteronomy 21:23; Galatians 3:13; 1 Peter 2:24)

- executed outside the city (Leviticus 24:14; Hebrews 13:12–13)

- hung between two criminals (Isaiah 53:12)

- bearing the sins of humanity (Isaiah 53:5; 1 Peter 2:24; 3:18)

Oddly, there are no details of the Crucifixion itself. This was not the kind of thing people talked about in polite company. Besides, once you had seen one, no one needed to describe it. But there is a more important reason for the scant details: Jesus's physical pain is not the point. His spiritual suffering was far greater than physical torture. Jesus took our place; he became our sin—hence, he was separated from God (Romans 3:21–26; 2 Corinthians 5:21; Hebrews 9:26–28).

Crucifixion was invented by the Persians. It began simply as impaling the victim on a spike placed under the sternum. "Unfortunately," the victim died too quickly. The Romans perfected the method to prolong the agony of the execution. By nailing the hands behind the complex of wrist bones, no essential arteries were severed, but the median nerves were, sending searing agony through the shoulder blades. Four- to five-inch spikes, likewise, were nailed through the calcanei (heel bones), sending similar pain through the pelvis. There were surely experimental variations, but the single heel bone recovered by archaeologists with the nail still in shows what I just described.

A *sedile* (wooden peg) was fixed to the *stipes* (upright beam of the cross) just under the tailbone. This supported the body and prolonged the pain. Victims crucified in this manner lasted several days. Birds of prey would peck at the helpless victims' eyes while wild dogs tore at their open wounds. The cause of death was not loss of blood, nor was it asphyxiation. After all, with his last breath, Jesus gave a loud cry, hardly possible if he couldn't breathe. Crucifixion victims died from stress to their bodies. In Jesus's case it was a myocardial rupture. How do we know? When the soldier pierced his side, blood and water flowed out. This indicates that his heart ruptured and the blood from the ventricles pumped into the fluid of the pericardial sac. Jesus literally died of a broken heart.

Around the Cross

Jesus's companions during the Crucifixion were two criminals. His executioners intended to shame him by flanking him with insurrectionists. They actually affirmed him by fulfilling Isaiah 53:9, showing God's hand in his death. Likewise, when the guards gambled for his garments, they followed God's script of the execution (Psalm 22:18).

Crucifixions were done near major arteries into the city. Those who passed by Jesus shook their heads and said, "You who would destroy the temple and rebuild it in three days, save yourself! If you are the Son of God, come down from the cross" (Matthew 27:40). The leaders joined in the mockery: "He saved others; he cannot save himself" (verse 42). That was true, but not how they intended. Jesus could not save others *and* save himself. Our salvation is predicated on his suffering.

The soldiers joined the crowds in taunting Jesus (Luke 23:36). Even those on the crosses next to him voiced their contempt. They suggested Jesus should save himself *and* them (Matthew 27:44; Luke 23:39)! The whole mob thought they were being clever; they were merely quoting *and fulfilling* Scripture (Psalm 22:7–8).

God responded with three miraculous signs:

1. **Darkness** fell over the land from noon to three o'clock in the afternoon as a sign of judgment (Amos 8:9–10). This was not an eclipse; it lasted too long. It was not a Sirocco (sandstorm); it was too dark. This was God's hand.
2. The **curtain** of the temple was torn from top to bottom. It was a veil between the holy place and the holy of holies, sixty feet by

thirty feet by four inches. There was no way a curtain that thick could be torn from the top, except by God. This was more than a miracle; it was an open door: "We have confidence to enter the holy places by the blood of Jesus, by the new and living way that he opened for us through the curtain, that is, through his flesh" (Hebrews 10:19–20).

3. An **earthquake:** "The earth shook, and the rocks were split. The tombs also were opened. And many bodies of the saints who had fallen asleep were raised, and coming out of the tombs after his resurrection they went into the holy city and appeared to many" (Matthew 27:51–53). Freaky, but a powerful preview of our own resurrection!

From the Cross

In the throes of agony, Jesus spoke seven times from the cross. Sayings 1, 4, and 7 were addressed to his Father. Sayings 2, 3, 5, and 6 were for the benefit of his disciples. Let's eavesdrop on his "deathbed" conversations:

> **Saying 1: "Father, forgive them, for they know not what they do"** (Luke 23:34). This was not exactly a king's pardon (Acts 3:17; 1 Corinthians 2:8) but an offer of redemption to all who would accept him by faith (John 3:16–17; Romans 6:23; 1 Peter 2:24).

> **Saying 2: "Today you will be with me in paradise"** (Luke 23:43). One of the bandits ridiculed Jesus with the rest of the crowd. His partner, pinned on the other side of Jesus, rebuked him: "Do you not fear God, since you are under the same sentence of condemnation?" (verse 40). Then he said to Jesus, "Remember me when you come into your kingdom" (verse 42). Jesus promised him salvation.

Saying 3: "Woman, behold, your son! . . . Behold, your mother!" (John 19:26–27). Among the crazed crowd were a few faithful followers. Jesus's mother was among them. He gave Mary into the care of John, his closest believing relative. History suggests John cared for her until her death.

Saying 4: "My God, my God, why have you forsaken me?" (Matthew 27:46; Mark 15:34). This was the only prayer Jesus ever prayed that didn't start with "Father." That's because he was quoting Psalm 22:1. Psalm 22 is the most detailed description of crucifixion in all ancient literature, *and* it was composed six hundred years before crucifixion was practiced! Many ask why God turned his back on Jesus. As 2 Corinthians 5:21 explains, "He made him to be sin who knew no sin, so that in him we might become the righteousness of God." This rejection was not permanent (Acts 2:27, 31), but it was necessary to overcome sin and death.

Saying 5: "I thirst" (John 19:28). This may seem like a frivolous detail. However, John clarified that it was a fulfilled prophecy from Psalm 69:21: "For my thirst they gave me sour wine to drink." The soldiers dipped a sponge into their vinegar wine and lifted it on a flimsy hyssop branch (Jesus was likely not more than two feet off the ground). Even this was symbolic since hyssop was what the high priests used to sprinkle blood on the Day of Atonement.

Saying 6: "It is finished" (John 19:30). The Greek word translated "finished" is interesting. It can describe a task accomplished, a dangerous feat performed, a promise fulfilled, orders executed, or an oath kept, but the most interesting meaning, I think, is a debt paid. "When Christ had offered for all time a single sacrifice for sins, he sat down at the right hand of God" (Hebrews 10:12).

Saying 7: "Father, into your hands I commit my spirit!" (Luke 23:46). This is a quote from Psalm 31:5, but the entire psalm is a commentary on his experience (verses 2, 4–5, 7, 11–14, 22, 24). With his final breath, he cried out to his Father, affirming his faith. He had finished his mission. He lived a perfect life and died as an atoning sacrifice.

Every detail and each word fulfilled the ancient prophecies and God's eternal plan. The Lamb of God paid the price for the sins of the world. Jesus's death redeemed us. At long last, the curse of Eden could be lifted.

Key Points

- The cross of Christ is the centerpiece of the entire Bible.
- Each detail of the Crucifixion fulfilled a prophecy.
- Jesus paid the price for our sins.

This Week

❏ **Day 1 (Eyes):** After reading the essay, how would you describe what Jesus did for you?

❏ **Day 2 (Ears):** Read Psalm 22. Underline every phrase that describes the crucifixion of Jesus.

❏ **Day 3 (Heart):** Meditate on what Jesus accomplished for us on the cross: Romans 3:21–26; 2 Corinthians 5:21; Hebrews 9:26–28.

❏ **Day 4 (Voice):** Discussion:

- What is the greatest sacrifice that anyone has made for you (other than Jesus)? What motivated that person to make that sacrifice?
- Of those surrounding the cross, whom do you relate to most? Can you feel what that person might have felt?
- The cross of Jesus should make us feel grateful, loyal, and free. Which of these three do you demonstrate the most?
- If his cross covers *all* our sins, what should we do, feel, and say about the cross?

❏ **Day 5 (Hands):** Google an image of Jesus on the cross. Sit with it in silence for at least fifteen minutes, meditating on what he has done for you. Break the silence with a prayer of gratitude for your full and final release from the guilt and shame of sin.

Further Resources: Quest52.org/48

49

Did Jesus Really Rise from the Dead?

Biblical Concept: Resurrection
Read: John 20 with Matthew 28; Mark 16; Luke 24

Just as the Cross is the center of the Bible, the Resurrection is the foundation of our faith. Paul put it succinctly: "If Christ has not been raised, then our preaching is in vain and your faith is in vain" (1 Corinthians 15:14). The death and resurrection of Jesus are two sides of the same coin. This is Christianity in a nutshell.

Through the Eyes of Insiders

It was Sunday morning. The horizon lightened before dawn. Mary Magdalene and the other women gathered their oils and headed to the edge of town. Though Joseph of Arimathea and Nicodemus had already slathered seventy-five pounds of ointment on Jesus's body, it wasn't *the women's* ointment or *their* expression of love. It was their turn.

They were just discussing the physics of four women rolling away a huge boulder when they noticed that would not be a problem. It was already rolled away. Now they had a bigger problem. The body they had intended to anoint was gone. Suddenly it got darker. Mary instinctively raced to inform the apostles that grave robbers had senselessly stolen their vanquished hero. Still breathless, she blurted out, "They have taken the Lord out of the tomb, and we do not know where they have laid him" (John 20:2).

Peter and John raced to the tomb to survey the situation. John, who appears to have been younger, outpaced his former fishing partner. Peering in, John discovered that the body was, in fact, missing. What thief would defile Jesus's corpse, not to mention himself? No one had motive or opportunity! Even worse, the linen wrappings were still on the stone where the body had been laid and the head covering neatly folded. It was as if his body had simply vanished. This was morbidly bizarre—who would take the time to strip Jesus's body naked before stealing it?

Peter arrived and pushed past John at the entrance. Staring at the spectacle, he saw the headcloth folded separately. The only other time this type of head covering is mentioned is John 11:44, connecting the raising of Lazarus to Jesus's own resurrection (that's an Easter egg for the reader). John stepped into the tomb tentatively. He began to believe even though he had not yet put the pieces of the scriptural puzzle together. This was the prophetic promise of resurrection *right here, right now* (Psalm 16:10; Isaiah 53:10–11; Hosea 6:1–2).

Through the Eyes of an Outsider

Peter and John returned to their hideout, pondering what all this could mean. Mary stood there wailing. Then two angels, dressed in white, sat at the head and feet of where Jesus had been laid. From their perspective, weeping was the last thing she should have been doing. They didn't understand her emotion, and she didn't comprehend their identity. "Why are you weeping?" they asked. It seemed obvious to Mary: "They have taken away my Lord, and I do not know where they have laid him" (John 20:13). Before the angels answered, she turned away, only to encounter a "gardener." Jesus repeated the question, "Woman, why are you weeping?

Whom are you seeking?" She replied, "Sir, if you have carried him away, tell me where you have laid him, and I will take him away" (verse 15).

Jesus's one-word reply opened her eyes: "Mary." There must have been something in the way he said her name. So many men had called her name, but none with the love and dignity Jesus gave her. She recognized him immediately and cried out in her native Aramaic, "Rabboni!" ("teacher"). Mary latched on (verse 16). Jesus responded, "Do not cling to me, for I have not yet ascended to the Father; but go to my brothers and say to them, 'I am ascending to my Father and your Father, to my God and your God'" (verse 17).

There was no time to hang on to the moment. She had work to do—important work. She was the very first witness to the Resurrection. Think about that. This was the single greatest announcement in human history, and all four Gospels agree that the honor was given to Mary, a woman. At that time, women were property, not witnesses. And this particular woman had a past that was far from noble. Let this truth sink into your soul: Jesus has a role for you, an honorable role, regardless of your past or position. Mary ran to the upper room and announced, "I have seen the Lord" (verse 18). They thought she had lost her mind (Luke 24:11).

The Resurrection was on no one's radar even though Jesus had predicted it several times (Matthew 16:21; 17:23; 20:19). Belief in resurrection was not common. The Greeks and Romans did not believe in resurrection, nor did they want one. Their worldview valued shedding the mortal shell with its frailty and suffering. Only some sects of Jews believed in resurrection. However, they believed only in a corporate (national) and eschatological (at the end of the age) resurrection. No one believed that an individual in this space and time would rise from the dead. No one.

Through the Eyes of a Skeptic

The apostles were fugitives, for all intents and purposes. They were hunkered down in the upper room with the door locked. It was Sunday evening, and their hearts stopped when they heard beating on the door. Terrified that it was soldiers coming to arrest them, they instead heard familiar friends. Two disciples had run seven miles from Emmaus, their hometown. They sounded as crazy as the women (Luke 24:33, 35). "The Lord has risen indeed," they cried breathlessly. Ten apostles, minus Judas Iscariot and Thomas, discussed wildly what this could mean.

They were cut short by a foreign but familiar voice: "Peace be with you" (Shalom in Hebrew). They turned in shock and awe at what they saw (John 20:19). Luke described how fearful they were, using three Greek words that mean "terrified," "alarmed," and "troubled" (24:37–38). They thought they were seeing a ghost (verse 37). After all, he had just passed through a locked door (John 20:19). Jesus extended his hands to reveal the scars and lifted his tunic to show where the spear had punctured his side. They were incredulous. Jesus asked whether they had anything to eat. Someone handed him a piece of fish. He ate it as evidence; apparently ghosts don't do that.

They were speechless, so Jesus began again: "Peace be with you. As the Father has sent me, even so I am sending you" (verse 21). It was no longer a greeting; it was a commission—and not just a commission but empowerment as well. He breathed on them, saying, "Receive the Holy Spirit. If you forgive the sins of any, they are forgiven them; if you withhold forgiveness from any, it is withheld" (verses 22–23). Since "breath," "wind," and "spirit" are the same word in Greek, this action was an obvious prelude to Pentecost. This was what Jesus had promised (John 7:39; 16:7). The Holy Spirit would empower them to preach the gospel message for the first time in just fifty days. Jesus's resurrection results in our mission—always!

Thomas missed the whole thing. I don't know whether he was out shopping or arranging more secure lodging, but he was MIA. You can imagine the excitement when he skulked through the door: "We have seen the Lord" (John 20:25). That was a thunderbolt he had to experience for himself. He protested, "Unless I see in his hands the mark of the nails, and place my finger into the mark of the nails, and place my hand into his side, I will never believe" (verse 25). Make no mistake: Thomas was loyal and brave; he had proved that (John 11:16; 14:5). He just couldn't believe without seeing for himself. Truth be told, no one else did either, except possibly John. So let's not be too tough on Thomas. After all, we are him.

The next eight days had to be maddening for Thomas. Everyone else was giddy; he was grumpy, unwilling to let his heart go where his eyes had not. Then it happened. Just as before, Jesus appeared behind a locked door. Same MO. Same greeting: "Shalom." Jesus even used the exact verbiage of Thomas from a week before: "Put your finger here, and see my hands; and put out your hand, and place it in my side. Do not disbelieve, but believe" (John 20:27). He believed. Boy, did he believe. His confession trumped every previous one. In fact, in the history of Israel, no Jew had ever said this to another human being: "My Lord and my God!" (verse 28).

Jesus spoke to Thomas but also to us. Listen in: "Have you believed because you have seen me? Blessed are those who have not seen and yet have believed" (verse 29). All the evidence we need to believe is already given in John's gospel: "Jesus did many other signs in the presence of the disciples, which are not written in this book; but these are written so that you may believe that Jesus is the Christ, the Son of God, and that by believing you may have life in his name" (verses 30–31). John wrote his gospel so we would have all the reason we need to believe. And if we believe, we will have life in Jesus's name.

You Decide

Volumes have been written on the evidence for the Resurrection. Let me offer here the barest summary. To those who say that one cannot rise from the dead, let me humbly suggest that you already believe this. You believe that life sprang forth from nonlife, whether it was an evolutionary process or the action of a Creator. So the real question is whether the evidence suggests that it happened again with Jesus. Any fair historical quest must reasonably answer four questions (see *Core 52*, chapter 44):

1. Why did the early Christians never venerate the tomb of Jesus as Mary did the first morning? After all, Jews were known for honoring the graves of loved ones.

2. How do we account for the radical change in Peter (coward to courageous), Thomas (doubter to shouter), Paul (persecutor to preacher), James (opposing to leading), and John (hothead to humble)? And why did ten of the eleven apostles die as martyrs for their proclamation of the Resurrection if it never happened?

3. Why did the Resurrection become the centerpiece of Christian faith when Jews believed only in a corporate resurrection at the end of the age and Greeks and Romans neither believed in nor desired a resurrection?

4. What accounts for a Jewish church moving worship from Sabbath to Sunday and including two vital sacraments (baptism and the Lord's Supper), both of which proclaim the Resurrection?

There is ample evidence if you want to believe and an eternal reward if you do.

Key Points

- Jesus's followers never venerated his tomb because it was empty.

- The accounts of the resurrection are neither fiction nor fabricated.

- Every key leader of the church was radically transformed by the Resurrection.

- The church itself requires a resurrection for Sunday worship, communion, baptism, and the core of its original preaching.

This Week

❏ **Day 1 (Eyes):** After reading the essay, consider this question: Have you considered the Resurrection the epicenter of your faith?

❏ **Day 2 (Ears):** Read Psalm 16. Research where verses 8–11 are quoted in the New Testament.

❏ **Day 3 (Heart):** Meditate on 1 Corinthians 15:3–8; 1 Thessalonians 4:14; 1 John 1:1–2.

❏ **Day 4 (Voice):** Discussion:
- Share something that you believe only because you saw it.
- What person in this story do you relate to most? Why?
- What evidence for the resurrection of Jesus is most compelling to you?
- Share a doubt that you have or have had about your faith. Now share why you might doubt that doubt.

❏ **Day 5 (Hands):** Make a short list of why you believe in the resurrection of Jesus. Share it with a pastor who can help sharpen it; then share it with a friend.

Further Resources: Quest52.org/49

50

What Does Jesus Expect Us to Do Now?

Biblical Concept: Commission

Read: Matthew 28:16–20 with Mark 16:15–18;
Luke 24:47–49; John 20:21–23; Acts 1:8

If I were honest, I would tell you that, after decades of ministry, I'm still intimidated when sharing my faith, especially with my family. It is no small thing to risk your relationship with someone who doesn't share your commitment to Christ. But Jesus is worth the risk. If he could lay his life down for us, we can lay our reputations on the line for him. This was Jesus's final command before leaving this earth. His last command must become our first priority. After all, it is predicated on one simple fact: "All authority in heaven and on earth has been given to me" (Matthew 28:18). Clearly, his commands are not suggestions. He is the universal Lord. His lordship actually takes a lot of pressure off because this is his mission and merely our co-mission. Our job is not to "win the world," as if it depended on our ability. No, our job is simply to make Jesus famous in our circles of influence. To brag about him in a winsome way so others will be attracted to our Savior. With that in mind, what precisely is he asking us to do?

Make Disciples

In our English Bibles, the commission looks like it includes four verbs: *go, make, baptize,* and *teach.* In the original, however, there is only one verb: *mathēteuō* ("make disciples"). The other words are participles supporting that action. We might translate it like this: "As you go, make disciples of the people groups you meet. How? By baptizing them into Christ and training them to mature in Christ by practicing his commands." (Note 1: *Nations* refers not to governmental affiliations but to ethnic groups. Note 2: Rather than cognitive learning, *teaching* implies practical application like an apprenticeship.)

So, what does it mean to make disciples? Simply put, a disciple is a learner. Not a student who thinks thoughts after you but an apprentice who imitates what you do. How, then, do we make apprentices for Jesus? First, it happens "as you go." Discipleship begins by inviting someone into your life. To be a spiritual apprentice, she needs to be with you when you eat, when you discipline your kids, and when you work, worship, and play. Many think of discipleship as a face-to-face Bible study. That's part of it, but discipleship is shoulder-to-shoulder modeling of Jesus's life.

He commissioned us to teach others how to obey his commands. Notice, this is not merely teaching the commands. It is modeling the disciplines involved in carrying out the commands—specifically, to love God and love people. It is that simple, but it is not that easy. Loving God covers a range of disciplines, beginning with baptism and continuing through prayer, Bible reading, confession, fasting, meditation, and service. Loving others includes forgiveness, fellowship, generosity, confrontation, and restitution, among other disciplines.

Obviously, we can't do everything at once. It is a process. I got curious about the process of making disciples, so I looked up every time the word *disciple* is used in the New Testament. There are 269 uses in 253 verses. In each passage I simply asked what it took to be a disciple. I specifically focused on what body parts are required to do what Jesus asked. This revealed three stages of discipleship:

1. **Investigation: eyes and feet.** In John 1, when John the Baptist
   saw Jesus, he cried out, "Behold, the Lamb of God!" Because of
   that, two of John's disciples followed Jesus. When Jesus noticed
   them, he asked, "What are you seeking?" Honestly, they didn't
   really know. They just knew Jesus was a big deal. All they could
   think to say was "Rabbi, where are you staying?" Jesus's response
   was simple and clear: "Come and you will see" (verses 36–39).
   The initial stage of discipleship really is that simple. Hang out
   long enough to see whether this is something you want to commit to. Fifty-nine times, discipleship is described as following
   Jesus—being where he was. Another ten times, it required seeing
   what he was doing.

2. **Instruction: ears and mouth.** Second, we are to listen to what
   Jesus says and ask questions for clarification. Ultimately, we will
   use our mouths to declare the kingdom, but that's a later level of
   discipleship. Forty-three times, the Gospels describe the disciples
   listening to Jesus. Thirty-seven times, they asked questions or
   made a statement (which Jesus usually had to correct). We listen
   to develop our worldviews, not increase our biblical knowledge.
   It is not enough to know the Bible intellectually. Our goal is to
   know Jesus personally.

3. **Application: hands.** A disciple does what Jesus does. Fifty-eight
   times, the disciples had to use their hands to carry out the tasks
   Jesus assigned. Here is where it gets really interesting. If you look
   for the five body parts in the four Gospels, they are pretty evenly
   distributed. Not so in the book of Acts. Of the thirty times the
   word *disciple* is used, nineteen of them imply using our hands
   and ten imply using our feet, but not to come *to* Jesus but to go
   out *from* him. Only once in Acts did discipleship require listening or learning something new. What can we make of this? In
   the context of the church, being a disciple is primarily about
   going and doing. As we mature as Christians, learning gives way

to practicing what we have trained for as apprentices. It is also interesting that, after the book of Acts, the word *disciple* is never used again in the New Testament. The apprentices had become practitioners.

Practical Guide to Making Jesus Famous

When Jesus arrived on our planet, his name was Immanuel, "God with us" (Matthew 1:23). When he left the earth, he promised to be with us to the end of the age (28:20). He has accomplished that by sending his Holy Spirit to guide us. The Spirit in us is every bit as present, instructive, convicting, and inspiring as Jesus was to his disciples. What that means is that we are still apprentices of the Spirit as we lead novices to begin their own journey of discipleship. If you want to make someone a disciple of Jesus, the Spirit will be a present and practical guide, providing everything you need to accomplish this task. Having said that, here are some things you can do today to mentor an apprentice of Jesus:

- **Start with family.** Most people who make a disciple start with a family member. Parents, of course, have enormous influence on their children. But siblings (particularly older ones) can naturally lead their brothers and sisters to walk the path of Jesus. It is also not uncommon for children to lead their parents to Christ. Because your family sees your behavior more than anyone else, radical loyalty to Jesus and sacrificial love for others can be compelling within your home. From your family, you can move out through the concentric circles of teammates, colleagues at work or school, and immediate neighbors. Challenge: Make a list of five people you have influence over, and begin to pray daily for them to come to Jesus. Ask God to give you insight and opportunities to share your faith with them.

- **Share a meal.** Meals are spiritual. If you want to lead someone to Christ, invite that person to dinner. Your home is the
best place (if possible) because he gets to see how you live. This
is not a bait and switch to corner him for evangelism. You
really are just trying to get to know him. Come up with three
questions you want to ask to get to know more about him personally. These questions may even give you an opportunity to
share your own story. Challenge: If you feel comfortable, tell
him you typically give God thanks for your meals and ask
whether that would make him uncomfortable. If he says no,
you can let him know you pray for him daily and ask, "Is
there anything specific you would like me to pray about?"

- **Invite to church.** After you have had someone over for a meal
or gone to some social events with her, invite her to another
meal, after church. Your invite can sound something like this:
"There's a group of us going out to eat after church. Would
you like to join us?" Remember, however, she doesn't know
where your church is, when it meets, or how long it will last.
So an invite to church should also include some details: "Typically the service lasts for an hour, and we wear business casual
or jeans. We can pick you up, or if you want to meet us in the
parking lot, we can walk you in so it's not weird." Another
thing to think about is that most people will say no the first
time. Statistically, one in three will say yes, but it may take
three invites before a person's schedule is clear. Challenge:
Plan on inviting three people three times. Usually one will say
yes. Most people who come to Christ do so at a local church.

One final observation. People convert (to anything) when the weight
of influence shifts from outside the group to inside. In other words, your
friend will convert when the opinions of those inside the church outweigh
the opinions of those outside the church. Therefore, evangelism should

always be a team sport. The more people your friend knows and respects who follow Christ, the easier it will be for him to make Jesus Lord. When enough of us do this, the commission will be completed.

Key Points

- We all have insecurity about sharing our faith.
- Don't overcomplicate making disciples. You are simply walking with people in the direction of Jesus.
- Start by inviting someone to a meal and then to church.

This Week

❑ **Day 1 (Eyes):** After reading the essay, consider this question: Are you leading anyone to follow Jesus?

❑ **Day 2 (Ears):** Read Isaiah 19:16–25; 25:1–12. What do these predict about God's desire for the nation?

❑ **Day 3 (Heart):** Meditate on what Jesus expects us to do now: Romans 10:14–15; 2 Corinthians 5:20; Colossians 1:28.

❑ **Day 4 (Voice):** Discussion:

- Who was most influential in leading you to Jesus? What did that person do?
- What is keeping you from sharing your faith? How will you overcome those barriers?
- After reading this essay, what would you say is your greatest strength in leading someone to Christ?
- Who are the five people on your daily prayer list that you hope will come to Christ?

❑ **Day 5 (Hands):** Choose one of the three challenges above, and complete it this week.

Further Resources: Quest52.org/50

51

How Can We Make Jesus Famous?

Biblical Concept: Ascension
Read: Acts 1:9–11

I took my New Testament class to a progressive synagogue for a cultural field trip. The rabbi said she believed that the Messiah was not an individual but an age of enlightenment. After the service, during a time of refreshments, an older gentleman in the congregation sidled up to me and said in a low tone, "Some of us are looking for the Messiah." I was interested. "What would the Messiah look like?" I asked.

His answer was a point-by-point description of Jesus. He was a history professor at the local university, so we began to talk as colleagues. I said, "You have just described Jesus of Nazareth, so why don't you follow him?" He replied, "One reason: he did not regather the twelve tribes of Israel as the prophets promised." I was speechless. He had a point; I had no reply. I spent the next year looking into it. What I discovered was earthshaking. Jesus did not, in fact, regather the twelve tribes of the Jews inside the borders of Israel. Rather, he expanded the borders of Israel to include every tongue and tribe and nation. The book of Acts describes just how that happened.

What Does Jesus Intend to Accomplish?

For forty days after the Resurrection, Jesus appeared periodically to the disciples. He coached them how to reach the world. At one point, they asked excitedly, "Lord, will you at this time restore the kingdom to Israel?" He replied, "It is not for you to know times or seasons that the Father has fixed by his own authority" (Acts 1:6–7). Like my friend in the synagogue, the apostles expected Jesus to be the king of their nation. Jesus has his sights set higher. He intends to be the king of all the earth.

The problem was not that they misread the Scriptures. The prophets had indeed predicted that the heir of David would rule as king. The problem was that they underinterpreted the promises, beginning with God's promise to Abraham: "In you all the families of the earth shall be blessed" (Genesis 12:3). Isaiah added more clarity:

> It shall come to pass in the latter days
> 	that the mountain of the house of the LORD
> shall be established as the highest of the mountains,
> 	and shall be lifted up above the hills;
> and *all the nations shall flow to it.* (2:2)

The disciples back then undervalued Jesus's spiritual reign over all the earth. Today we tend to undervalue Jesus's earthly reign. Jesus called for a kingdom, not merely a church. What's the difference? For starters, a church is led by a preacher; a kingdom is ruled by a king. A church has members; a kingdom has citizens. A church has rules like "don't run in church"; a kingdom has laws, and you can run all you want.

If the church is to fulfill the mission of Jesus, we must think bigger about what we're up to. Our goal isn't merely to take people to heaven. Our goal is to bring heaven to earth. You see, the ascension of Jesus (which we will look at in a moment) was not his exodus from earth. It was his enthronement in heaven. He is now seated in heaven as ruler over all the earth. Our commission is to extend his reign in heaven to every corner of the globe.

How Are We to Expand His Kingdom?

If you are intimidated by this prospect, *you should be.* Think of how these provincial fishermen felt. Peter, Andrew, James, and John had no training in international politics, theology, language, or organizational leadership. They were in way over their heads. That's why Acts 1:8 is so important to them—and to us: "You will receive power when the Holy Spirit has come upon you, and you will be my witnesses in Jerusalem and in all Judea and Samaria, and to the end of the earth."

This verse says two things we must not miss. First, the commission will not be accomplished through our ingenious efforts. It will be accomplished through the power of the Holy Spirit. He was active through Acts. The Spirit empowered the apostles to preach. He gave visions and dreams. He moved people like pawns on a chessboard. He cast out demons and broke down racial barriers. He hindered, encouraged, guided, provided, led, and rebuked.

Second, Acts 1:8 provides a map of the geographic expansion of the kingdom. It began in Jerusalem (Acts 1–7), then went to Judea and Samaria (Acts 8–12), and ultimately reached the ends of the earth (Acts 13–28). It was not as if the apostles decided to go reach their neighbors. Whenever anyone in Acts crossed a geographic boundary to preach, it was through the prompting of the Holy Spirit or the pressure of persecution. Clearly, the mission we participate in is God's mission more than ours. This applies to you reading this right now. If you look in the rearview mirror, you will see God's track record of putting you in the right place at the right time for his glory.

The more we are in sync with the Spirit, the more fully we can partner with him. This is, obviously, an oversimplification, but there are two key elements to what the Spirit did that made the church so effective in evangelism. First, the Spirit broke down barriers of race. Aside from faith in Jesus, there is nothing more talked about in the book of Acts than ethnic inclusion. In fact, chapters 6–11 is a tour de force of expanding ethnic evangelism: Hellenistic widows, Samaritans, the Ethiopian eunuch, Paul (the apostle to the Gentiles), and finally the first Gentile convert named Cornelius. God moved mountains to make that happen, and he is no less determined to reach all tongues and tribes and nations today.

Second, the Spirit was strategic in taking evangelists to centers of influence. Acts 17–28 shows Paul reaching the educational capital of the empire in Athens, the economic capital in Corinth, the pagan religious capital in Ephesus, and the political capital in Rome, as well as returning to Jerusalem, the capital of worship of the one true God. What that tells us is that the Holy Spirit targets centers of influence. If you are to reach full effectiveness in evangelism, you should pay attention to how the Spirit might empower you to leverage your own influence to target influencers. Oh sure, God wants all people to hear the gospel. But they will listen with more open hearts when it comes from influential people and places. Let's be smart about making Jesus famous.

When Will Jesus Return?

"When he had said these things, as they were looking on, he was lifted up, and a cloud took him out of their sight. And while they were gazing into heaven as he went, behold, two men stood by them in white robes, and said, 'Men of Galilee, why do you stand looking into heaven? This Jesus, who was taken up from you into heaven, will come in the same way as you saw him go into heaven'" (Acts 1:9–11).

This scene describes what has been called the Ascension. Jesus rose to heaven. The two men dressed in white were angels. How do we know? White clothes in the Bible signify God's messengers (Mark 16:5; Luke 24:4; John 20:12). The cloud represents God's presence (Exodus 24:15–18; Luke 9:34–35; 21:27; Revelation 11:12). So, the angels, who had been in God's presence, came to instruct the apostles after Jesus returned to God's presence.

The Ascension has not gotten a lot of attention in sermons. However, it is a big deal in the rest of the New Testament (Luke 9:51; John 3:13; Acts 2:32–33; 5:30–31; 7:55; Romans 8:34; Ephesians 1:20–21; 4:8–10;

Philippians 2:9–11; Colossians 3:1; 1 Timothy 3:16; Hebrews 1:3; 8:1; 10:12; 1 Peter 3:21–22). So, what is Jesus doing? He is sitting down at the right hand of the Father as our advocate. Paul described the scene in Romans 8:34: "Who is to condemn? Christ Jesus is the one who died—more than that, who was raised—who is at the right hand of God, who indeed is interceding for us." That makes his ascension as important for our salvation as his death and resurrection.

The disciples were so focused on Jesus leaving that they paid no attention to the angels' arrival. That had to be frustrating for the angels. With the verb Luke used to describe the scene, the verse could be read, "The angels were in the present state of having stood there." And the boys took no notice. Finally, the angels broke the silence: "Men of Galilee, why do you stand looking into heaven?" (Acts 1:11). That was an important question.

When they were with Jesus, they fixated on the past: "Lord, will you at this time restore the kingdom to Israel?" (verse 6). When Jesus left, they focused on the future. But today is the only thing we can control, and we have work to do. There are still entire people groups who have not been included in the kingdom of Christ. Some are in distant lands, and reaching them will require the strategic effort of the church. Others are already within your circle of influence, and reaching them will require your obedience to the Spirit's promptings. Rather than fixating on the past or focusing on the future, let's get down to the business of preparing people for Jesus's return.

Key Points

- The church of Jesus Christ is a kingdom with citizens, laws, and boundaries.

- The Holy Spirit empowers us to expand the boundaries of Jesus's kingdom to the ends of the earth.

- Jesus will return in the same way he ascended from the earth.

This Week

❏ **Day 1 (Eyes):** After reading the essay, consider this question: What are you doing to prepare others for Jesus's return?

❏ **Day 2 (Ears):** How is Micah 4:1–8 fulfilled through the church?

❏ **Day 3 (Heart):** Meditate on the nature of Jesus's current reign: Philippians 2:9–11; Colossians 1:20; Revelation 19:16.

❏ **Day 4 (Voice):** Discussion:

- How would you think or act differently if you saw your local church as part of a global kingdom?
- Describe a time when you felt the Spirit empowering you to share your faith.
- What circle of influence do you have? It could be with family, with friends, at work, or in the community.
- How could members leverage each person's circle of influence to make an impact for Jesus far greater than you could individually?

❏ **Day 5 (Hands):** Plan a project in your community, leveraging various Christians' gifts and influence to make Jesus famous.

Further Resources: Quest52.org/51

52

Who Is Jesus?

Biblical Concept: Return
Read: Revelation 1:13–17; 5:5–6; 19:11–16

Our quest for Jesus ends with Revelation. Many find this book confusing because we keep asking it a question it was never designed to answer: "When is Jesus returning?" If we ask the right questions, however, Revelation is crystal clear. Here is the best question: "Who is Jesus?" Revelation gives us three detailed portraits of the ascended Christ. If we fix our eyes on these images of Jesus, we can survive any season of suffering.

Son of Man

"In the midst of the lampstands one like a son of man, clothed with a long robe and with a golden sash around his chest. The hairs of his head were white, like white wool, like snow. His eyes were like a flame of fire, his feet were like burnished bronze, refined in a furnace, and his voice was like the roar of many waters. In his right hand he held seven stars, from his mouth came a sharp two-edged sword, and his face was like the sun shining in full strength. When I saw him, I fell at his feet as though dead.

But he laid his right hand on me, saying, 'Fear not, I am the first and the last'" (Revelation 1:13–17).

This first portrait of Jesus is a mind bender. He is the Son of Man. That's what he called himself. It's a term used in the Old Testament, not as an insult but rather as a reminder that we are merely humans. God is God; we are "sons of men." The only exception is Daniel 7:13–14, where "a son of man" was exalted with "the Ancient of Days," who gave him "dominion and glory and a kingdom, that all peoples, nations, and languages should serve him." Daniel wondered at the vision. How on earth could a human figure share the glory of the God of heaven?

If you put Daniel 7:9–10 beside the descriptions of Jesus in Revelation, you see the parallels:

Ancient of Days in Daniel 7	Son of Man in Revelation
Hair of his head was white like wool.	**Hairs** of his head were white like wool.
His throne was **fiery flames**.	His eyes were like a **flame of fire**.
Books of judgment were opened.	A **scroll** of judgment was opened.

In Daniel we wonder how a son of man got way up there. In Revelation we wonder how God ever came down here as a son of man. Jesus is the answer. We finally see him in his heavenly garb, and he looks just like God.

We may not know when he's returning, but we are crystal clear on what he's doing right now in preparation for his return.

Lamb of God

"One of the elders said to me, 'Weep no more; behold, the Lion of the tribe of Judah, the Root of David, has conquered, so that he can open the scroll and its seven seals.' And between the throne and the four living creatures and among the elders I saw a Lamb standing, as though it had been slain, with seven horns and with seven eyes, which are the seven spirits of God sent out into all the earth" (Revelation 5:5–6)

Revelation 5 opens in heaven. God is seated on the throne with a scroll in his right hand. It reveals the judgments on the earth and is full of writing on both sides of the scroll. John is curious—like *really* curious. He is dying to know what is written on the scroll and breaks down in tears because no one has the authority to open the scroll. No one in heaven or on earth, except one. The One. The Lion of the tribe of Judah. The Messiah has conquered, earning him the right to reveal what is in the scroll.

John is heartened and wide eyed, waiting for the Lion to strut across the stage. Some stagehand, however, switched the figures. Instead of the Lion, out comes a Lamb. He is bloodied and beleaguered. He has seven eyes and seven horns. To us he looks like a mutant from Chernobyl, but these are biblical codes. Seven is three (the number of God) plus four (the number of humanity). So the number seven represents the work of God among humans. His seven eyes mean he sees all that is going on in the world. Jesus is fully aware of our human experience. Seven horns represent God's complete power to protect us in this world.

More importantly, the Lamb has been slain. He has seen suffering, just like you. He knows the pain of rejection, betrayal, beating, and abandonment. Whenever we pour out our pain in prayer, Jesus responds, "I know." Moreover, his sacrifice was not just for the sins of the world. It was for *your* sins. He knows your pain and sits in it with you. He knows your sin and took the punishment for you. In the Resurrection, the Lamb that was slain rose as a Lion that conquered.

We may not know when he's returning, but we are crystal clear on what he's already done in preparation for his return.

Conquering King

"I saw heaven opened, and behold, a white horse! The one sitting on it is called Faithful and True, and in righteousness he judges and makes war. His eyes are like a flame of fire, and on his head are many diadems, and he has a name written that no one knows but himself. He is clothed in a robe dipped in blood, and the name by which he is called is The Word of God. And the armies of heaven, arrayed in fine linen, white and pure, were following him on white horses. From his mouth comes a sharp sword with which to strike down the nations, and he will rule them with a rod of iron. He will tread the winepress of the fury of the wrath of God the Almighty. On his robe and on his thigh he has a name written, King of kings and Lord of lords" (Revelation 19:11–16).

Because Jesus has been so long in coming, we sometimes feel like his return is still a long way off. Middle school students act the same way. When the teacher runs to the principal's office, they sit at their desks working away, at least at first. However, the longer the teacher is away, the more prone the students are to play. Before long, there is pandemonium. The problem is, the longer the teacher is away, the more imminent is her return. Likewise, with Jesus's return, each passing day draws human history closer to completion. Now more than ever, we should be vigilant, watching and waiting for his return.

When Jesus came to earth the first time, he came to shepherd his people. When he returns, he will be an equestrian warrior against his enemies. When he came the first time, it was with eyes of compassion. When he returns, it will be with eyes of fire. His initial crown was made of thorns; when he comes again, he will be laden with diadems. As the Son of Man, he wore a peasant's garb; as a warrior, he will don a robe dipped in blood. During the Incarnation, he was called Jesus of Nazareth. During his return, his name will be tattooed on his thigh: King of kings and Lord of lords. On earth he was beaten and did not retaliate. From heaven he will return with a sword—not in his hand but protruding from his mouth. His words are his weapon with which he will judge the nations.

Some have called this the Battle of Armageddon, but there is no battle. Oh sure, the armies of earth align against his majesty. They gather for battle with their weapons and strategy. But according to the Bible, not a single shot is fired. Jesus simply speaks. With a single declaration, he obliterates his enemies and establishes his eternal reign.

We may not know when he's returning, but we are crystal clear on what he will do when we next lay eyes on him in the clouds.

The Purpose of the Portraits

Three times John painted a picture of what Jesus looks like now. If you read the remainder of Revelation, you will realize that each portrait precedes a particularly difficult problem Christians face. Chapter 1 comes right before Jesus's letters to the seven churches. He rebuked, encouraged, and critiqued the churches, which had the same issues we struggle with today. But every problem the church faces can be solved by a clear view of Jesus, the Son of Man. Keep your eyes on him.

Chapter 5 comes right before the tribulation described in Revelation 6–18. The world is full of evil, disasters, and pain. None of us are exempt from suffering. But Revelation offers us a portrait of hope. Jesus, the Lamb that was slain, is the Lion that conquers. Every struggle you have with sin and suffering is conquerable through the blood of the Lamb and the power of the Lion. Keep your eyes on him.

Chapter 19 comes right before the final judgment. No doubt, we face uncertain days and perilous battles. Nonetheless, Jesus, with a mere word, will overcome our enemies and usher us safely into eternity (verses 17–21). In the darkest night of the soul, one glimpse of the conquering King, whose coming is sure, will relieve our weary hearts. Keep your eyes on him.

He is the ultimate end of our quest.

Key Points

- Looking to Jesus, the Son of Man, solves every problem the church faces.
- Looking to Jesus, the slain Lamb, comforts us in all the pain we experience.
- Looking to Jesus, the conquering King, overcomes all our worries about an uncertain future.

This Week

❑ **Day 1 (Eyes):** After reading the essay, consider this question: How do you see Jesus?

❑ **Day 2 (Ears):** Read Daniel 7:9–14. What did Jesus look like before the Incarnation?

❑ **Day 3 (Heart):** Meditate on how you should respond to Jesus: Revelation 1:17; 5:12–13; 19:6–8.

❑ **Day 4 (Voice):** Discussion:

- Do you have a picture of Jesus in your home? What does it look like?
- As you reflect on this past year's quest, what has surprised you about Jesus?
- Which concerns you most right now: (1) the state of your church, (2) the trials you currently face, or (3) the uncertainty of the future? Which portrait of Jesus speaks to that?
- If Jesus returned right now, what would you wish you had done last month to prepare for his coming?

❑ **Day 5 (Hands):** What do you need to do to continue your quest, chasing after the heart of Jesus? Identify your next steps.

Further Resources: Quest52.org/52

Overview

#	Section/ Series	Question	Concept	Day 2	Day 3
	Person: Beginning				
1	John 1:1–18	Is God Jesus?	Incarnation	Pss. 2; 110	Rom. 9:5; Titus 2:13; Heb. 1:8
2	Matt. 1:1–17	Is life random?	Genealogy	Josh. 2; 6	Gal. 4:4; Heb. 11:31; James 2:25
3	Luke 1:26–45	Can God use me for big things?	Annunciation	Isa. 9:1–7	Col. 1:15–17; Heb. 1:3; Rev. 1:8
4	Luke 2:1–20	Does God play favorites?	Nativity	Ps. 23; John 10:1–18	Matt. 23:12; James 4:10; 1 Pet. 5:5–6
	Person: Purpose				
5	Luke 2:41–52	Did Jesus know he was God when he was a boy?	Maturity	1 Sam. 24	Rom. 13:3–7; Eph. 6:2–3; 1 Tim. 5:17
6	Mark 1:1–13	If Jesus was perfect, why was he baptized?	Baptism	Num. 13–14	Rom. 6:1–7; 1 Cor. 10:1–5

#	Section/ Series	Question	Concept	Day 2	Day 3
7	Luke 19:1–10	Did Jesus have a life purpose?	Life purpose	Eccles. 5:8–6:12	Rom. 1:16; 2 Tim. 1:7–8; 1 Pet. 3:15–16
8	Mark 10:32–45	Did Jesus have a life purpose?	Life purpose	Josh. 1	1 Cor. 9:19; 2 Cor. 4:5; 1 Pet. 5:2–3
	Person: Relation- ships				
9	Luke 5:1–11	How do I rec- ognize God's call on my life?	Calling	1 Sam. 3	2 Cor. 5:20; 1 Pet. 2:9–10; 4:10–11
10	Mark 3:31–35	How do you get into Je- sus's inner circle?	Family	Isa. 49	1 Cor. 12:13; Eph. 2:14; Col. 3:11
11	Luke 7:36–50	Does my past determine my future?	Shame	Exod. 2:11–4:17	Rom. 8:1; 1 Tim. 1:15; 1 John 1:9
12	John 3:1–21	Who are so- cial influenc- ers for Jesus?	Influence	1 Sam. 10:9–27; 13:1–15	Acts 10:34; Rom. 2:11; James 2:1–7
13	John 4:4–42	Who are so- cial influenc- ers for Jesus?	Influence	2 Kings 6:24–7:20	Rom. 1:16; 1 Cor. 1:20; 3:18–19
	Power: Wonders				
14	John 2:1–12	Is Christianity boring?	Celebration	Song of Sol. 5	2 Cor. 11:2; Eph. 5:23; Rev. 21:9

#	Section/ Series	Question	Concept	Day 2	Day 3
15	Mark 4:35–5:20	Can Jesus turn my storm into a story?	Chaos	Ps. 2	Eph. 1:20–21; Col. 2:9; Rev. 1:17–18
16	Mark 6:31–52	Can Jesus provide for my needs?	Provision	Exod. 16	Acts 20:28; 1 Pet. 2:25; Rev. 7:17
17	Mark 9:2–13	Is Jesus really divine?	Divinity	Mal. 3–4	2 Cor. 3:7; Phil. 2:8–11; 2 Pet. 1:16–18
	Power: Signs				
18	Mark 1:29–39	Does Jesus care about my pain?	Pain	Lev. 26:1–26	Heb. 12:12–13; James 5:16; 1 Pet. 2:24
19	Mark 1:40–45	Can Jesus make me clean?	Purity	2 Kings 5	2 Cor. 7:1; Eph. 5:26; 2 Tim. 2:21
20	Luke 7:1–10	Is Jesus impressed with me?	Inclusion	Gen. 12:1–9; 14:1–24	Acts 10:1–8, 22–23, 28–29, 34–35
21	Mark 5:21–43	Can Jesus restore my relationships?	Restoration	Ruth	Luke 8:2–3; Phil. 4:2–3; James 2:25
22	John 11:17–44	Can Jesus give me life?	Life	1 Kings 17:8–24; 2 Kings 4:18–37	1 Cor. 6:14; 15:20–28; 2 Cor. 4:14

#	Section/Series	Question	Concept	Day 2	Day 3
	Power: Claims				
23	Mark 2:1–17	Can Jesus forgive me?	Forgiveness	Ps. 32	Rom. 4:7; Eph. 1:7; Heb. 9:22
24	John 5:1–18	What do we need from Jesus?	Loyalty	1 Sam. 18:1–4; 19:1–7; 20:1–42	Rom. 4:5; Col. 1:23; 1 Thess. 1:3
25	John 9:1–41	Can Jesus help me see clearly?	Clarity	2 Sam. 22	2 Cor. 4:6; Eph. 1:18; Rev. 3:17
26	Matt. 12:22–45	Can Jesus accept me?	Liberation	Jonah	Heb. 6:4–6; 10:26; 1 John 5:16
	Preaching: Teaching				
27	Luke 4:16–30	What did Jesus say about social justice?	Justice	1 Kings 17:8–24; 2 Kings 5:1–14	Acts 13:46; Rom. 1:16; 2:9–10
28	Matt. 5:3–48	What did Jesus say about morality?	Ethics	Exod. 20:1–17	Rom. 13:9; Gal. 5:13; 1 John 3:16–18
29	Matt. 6:1–18	What did Jesus say about religious duties?	Piety	1 Sam. 13; 17	Gal. 1:10; Col. 3:23; 1 Thess. 2:4
30	Matt. 6:19–34	Why does Jesus care so much about my money?	Wealth	Prov. (selections)	Eph. 5:5; 1 Tim. 6:17–19; Heb. 13:5

#	Section/ Series	Question	Concept	Day 2	Day 3
	Preaching: Stories				
31	Luke 15:11–32	How does Jesus feel about prodigals?	Prodigals	2 Chron. 7:11–22	Acts 3:19; 2 Cor. 7:9–10; 1 Pet. 2:25
32	Matt. 13:1–23	How do I hear God's voice?	Parables	Isa. 6	Acts 28:26–27; Rom. 11:8; 2 Cor. 3:14
33	Luke 10:25–37	How can I be sure I'm saved?	Bias	Lev. 19:9–18; Deut. 6	1 John 3:15–16; 4:16–21; 5:13
34	John 10:1–21	How did Jesus lead?	Leadership	Ezek. 34	Heb. 13:20; 1 Pet. 2:25; 5:4
	Preaching: Training				
35	Matt. 10:1–42	How can we share our faith effectively?	Evangelism	Exod. 3–4	Rom. 10:9–10; Heb. 13:15; 1 Pet. 3:15
36	Matt. 11:2–11	Do you ever doubt your doubts?	Resilience	Isa. 42:1–4; 49:1–6; 50:4–9; 52:13–53:12	Rom. 8:14–17; 2 Cor. 3:17–18; Eph. 1:13
37	Mark 7:1–23	What makes you a good person?	Morality	Isa. 58	Acts 15:20; Rom. 14:14; 1 Cor. 8:7
38	Matt. 16:13–28	Who do you say Jesus is?	Declaration	1 Kings 12	2 Cor. 4:10–12; Gal. 2:20; Phil. 3:10–11

#	Section/ Series	Question	Concept	Day 2	Day 3
39	Luke 10:38–42	What's worth worrying about?	Anxiety	Ps. 37	Phil. 4:6
	Passion: Preparation				
40	Luke 19:29–44	Was Jesus political?	Politics	Ps. 118	Acts 17:7; 1 Cor. 15:24–25; Rev. 11:15
41	Mark 11:12–25	Was Jesus political?	Authority	Isa. 56:1–8; Jer. 7:1–11	1 Cor. 6:16–19; 2 Cor. 6:16; Eph. 2:19–22
42	John 13:1–20	Was Jesus full of himself?	Humility	Dan. 4	Rom. 7:6; 2 Cor. 4:5; Gal. 5:13
43	Mark 14:1–25	What did Jesus think about himself?	Sacrament	Exod. 12	1 Cor. 5:7; 1 Pet. 1:19; Rev. 5:12
	Passion: Suffering				
44	John 14:1–31	How can I survive difficult days?	Hope	Ezek. 36:22–36; Joel 2:28–32	John 1:18; Acts 4:12; Heb. 1:3
45	Mark 14:32–52	How can we learn grit from how Jesus suffered?	Suffering	2 Sam. 15	Rom. 8:17; Col. 1:24; 1 Pet. 2:21–23
46	Mark 14:53–72	How do you stay in control in a crisis?	Opposition	Ps. 88	2 Cor. 4:16–18; Heb. 2:18; James 1:2–4

#	Section/ Series	Question	Concept	Day 2	Day 3
47	Matt. 27:11–26	How do you endure pain?	Endurance	Isa. 52:13–53:12	Rom. 5:10; 12:20; Heb. 10:12–13
48	Matt. 27:27–54	Why did Jesus die?	Atonement	Ps. 22	Rom. 3:21–26; 2 Cor. 5:21; Heb. 9:26–28
	Passion: Victory				
49	John 20	Did Jesus really rise from the dead?	Resurrection	Ps. 16	1 Cor. 15:3–8; 1 Thess. 4:14; 1 John 1:1–2
50	Matt. 28:16–20	What does Jesus expect us to do now?	Commission	Isa. 19:16–25; 25:1–12	Rom. 10:14–15; 2 Cor. 5:20; Col. 1:28
51	Acts 1:9–11	How can we make Jesus famous?	Ascension	Mic. 4:1–8	Phil. 2:9–11; Col. 1:20; Rev. 19:16
52	Rev. 1:13–17; 5:5–6; 19:11–16	Who is Jesus?	Return	Dan. 7:9–14	Rev. 1:17; 5:12–13; 19:6–8

Notes

Chapter 2: Is Life Random?

1. For those of you who actually did fact-check me, congratulations, you get a digital gold star. Just for clarity, we count Jeconiah in the third section, after the Exile, since that is where Matthew puts him in verse 12.

Chapter 6: If Jesus Was Perfect, Why Was He Baptized?

1. Flavius Josephus, *The Wars of the Jews*, in *The Works of Josephus: Complete and Unabridged*, trans. William Whiston, rev. ed. (Peabody, MA: Hendrickson, 1987), 707.

Chapter 11: Does My Past Determine My Future?

1. Pliny the Elder, *The Natural History of Pliny*, trans. and ed. John Bostock and H. T. Riley (London: Henry G. Bohn, 1855), 3:167.

Chapter 12: Who Are Social Influencers for Jesus? Part 1

1. William Barclay, *The New Daily Study Bible: The Letter to the Hebrews* (Louisville, KY: Westminster John Knox, 2002), 145.

Chapter 19: Can Jesus Make Me Clean?

1. Jacob Neusner, *The Mishnah: A New Translation* (New Haven, CT: Yale University Press, 1988), 984.
2. Alfred Edersheim, *The Life and Times of Jesus the Messiah*, 8th ed. (New York: Longmans, Green, 1899), 1:495; "Leprosy," Jewish Virtual Library, www.jewishvirtuallibrary.org/leprosy.

Chapter 23: Can Jesus Forgive Me?

1. Alfred Edersheim, *The Life and Times of Jesus the Messiah,* 8th ed. (New York: Longmans, Green, 1899), 1:516.

Chapter 25: Can Jesus Help Me See Clearly?

1. John Newton, "Amazing Grace," *The Broadman Hymnal* (Nashville: Broadman, 1940), public domain.

Chapter 30: Why Does Jesus Care So Much About My Money?

1. Bob Dylan, "Gotta Serve Somebody," *Slow Train Coming,* Sony Music Entertainment, 1979.
2. "Facts & Statistics," Anxiety & Depression Association of America, https://adaa.org/about-adaa/press-room/facts-statistics.
3. Alison Escalante, MD, "U.S. Leads in the Worldwide Anxiety Epidemic," *Psychology Today* (April 26, 2019), www.psychologytoday.com/us/blog/shouldstorm/201904/us-leads-in-the-worldwide-anxiety-epidemic.
4. Alexander Konnopka and Hannah Konig, "Economic Burden of Anxiety Disorders: A Systematic Review and Meta-Analysis," Pharmacoeconomics, January 2020, https://pubmed.ncbi.nlm.nih.gov/31646432.

Chapter 33: How Can I Be Sure I'm Saved?

1. John M. Darley and C. Daniel Batson, " 'From Jerusalem to Jericho': A Study of Situational and Dispositional Variables in Helping Behavior," *Journal of Personality and Social Psychology* 27, no. 1 (1973): 100–108.

Chapter 36: Do You Ever Doubt Your Doubts?

1. Flavius Josephus, *The Antiquities of the Jews,* in *The Works of Josephus: Complete and Unabridged,* trans. William Whiston, rev. ed. (Peabody, MA: Hendrickson, 1980), 484.

Chapter 39: What's Worth Worrying About?

1. Sharon Begley, "In the Age of Anxiety, Are We All Mentally Ill?," Reuters, July 13, 2012, www.reuters.com/article/us-usa-health-anxiety/in-the-age-of-anxiety-are-we-all-mentally-ill-idUSBRE86C07820120713.

2. "Facts & Statistics," Anxiety & Depression Association of America, https://adaa.org/about-adaa/press-room/facts-statistics.

3. "Facts & Statistics."

4. You can also view this video by googling "Core52 lesson 48." Mark Moore, "Core 52, Lesson 48: Worry (Philippians 4:6)," August 31, 2019, YouTube video, 6:20, www.youtube.com/watch?v=5RBPGuryFkQ.

Chapter 41: Was Jesus Political? Part 2

1. T. W. Manson, "The Cleansing of the Temple," *Bulletin of the John Rylands Library* 33, no. 2 (1951): 279.

Chapter 44: How Can I Survive Difficult Days?

1. Ira Stanphill, "Mansion over the Hilltop," Singspiration Music, 1949.

Chapter 46: How Do You Stay in Control in a Crisis?

1. See "The Caisphas Ossuary," Great Archaeology: History of Archaeology, www.greatarchaeology.com/Caiaphas_ossuary.php and "Inside BAR," Biblical Archaeology Society Online Archive, www.baslibrary.org/biblical-archaeology-review/18/5/7.

2. D. L. Miller, "Empaizein: Playing the Mock Game (Luke 22:63–64)," *JBL 90* (1971): 309–13.

Mark E. Moore, bestselling author of *Core 52*, is a teaching pastor at Christ's Church of the Valley in Phoenix, Arizona, one of the fastest-growing and most dynamic churches in America. He previously spent two decades as a New Testament professor at Ozark Christian College. His goal is to make Scripture accessible and relevant to people trying to make sense of Christianity. Mark and his wife, Barbara, live in Phoenix.

About the Type

This book was set in Garamond, a typeface originally designed by the Parisian type cutter Claude Garamond (c. 1500–61). This version of Garamond was modeled on a 1592 specimen sheet from the Egenolff-Berner foundry, which was produced from types assumed to have been brought to Frankfurt by the punch cutter Jacques Sabon (c. 1520–80).

Claude Garamond's distinguished romans and italics first appeared in *Opera Ciceronis* in 1543–44. The Garamond types are clear, open, and elegant.

Did *Quest 52* move you?
Challenge you?
Motivate you?

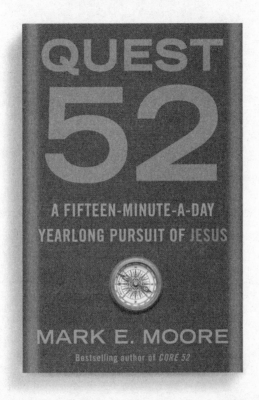

Share your thoughts with Pastor Mark about how
Quest 52 inspired you at **Quest52.org/Quest52Stories**

Check out *Quest 52 Student Edition*! Go deeper into
God's Word with your kids or students.

Keep Going in Your Study of God's Word with *Core 52*!

ECPA BESTSELLER & FINALIST FOR THE CHRISTIAN BOOK AWARD

Build your Bible IQ and Christian worldview in just fifteen minutes a day!
Over the course of a year, *Core 52* will help you master
the 52 most important passages in the Bible.

WATERBROOK

Free church resources, video curriculum, discussion questions,
Bible memory tools, and more at **Core52.org!**